THE MODERN
AMERICAN NOVEL

Essays in Criticism

*Studies in Language
and Literature*

The
MODERN
AMERICAN
NOVEL

Essays in Criticism

EDITED WITH AN INTRODUCTION BY

MAX WESTBROOK

University of Texas

RANDOM HOUSE • NEW YORK

Preface

In selecting the following essays on the modern American
novel, I have tried to follow those editors whose collections
show respect both for the integrity of the literature and for
the condition of the student and the lay reader. Each essay
selected is, in my judgment, criticism of high merit. Some
are extremely demanding. All deserve re-reading. But each
one concentrates on the novel at hand. Studies which assume that the reader is familiar with the complete works of
a given author have not been included.

Novels selected for study are those which might be
assigned in a typical college course in the American novel
since 1914. There are of course many other valid choices,
but my effort has been to represent the most standard
selections. Similar thinking has guided the omissions.
Three Lives and *U.S.A.*, for example, are certainly important; but both, for various pedagogical reasons, are usually
handled in lectures, or suggested as outside reading.

The post World War II novel is too recent for firm
judgments, and here my editorial reasoning has been less
sure. But *The Catcher in the Rye*, despite recent objections
to the Salinger "cult," seemed an obvious choice; and *Henderson the Rain King* was selected because Saul Bellow has
come to look like the most substantial of contemporary
novelists.

No effort has been made to represent the major types
of criticism, although, as it worked out, there is consider-
able variety of critical approach. Essays designed to attack

rather than to explain are not included. Some of my decisions necessarily included certain practical considerations. The length of the essay selected, for example, is not intended as a reflection of my estimate of the importance of the novel. I thought it more sensible to look for a good essay than to look for an essay of a prescribed number of pages.

Basically, I have tried to select studies which open up the novel, studies which take a position and see it through, but which do so in a way that leads to further questions, to further thought. A good critic, it seems to me, shows us something fundamental about how the novel is put together, and, in the process, returns us to the novel itself, to a second and more incisive reading.

My own introductory essay is theoretical, but it is intended as practical pedagogy. Classroom experience has led me to believe that students who do not like to contemplate the nature of fiction may find it difficult to improve their ability to read. They may repeat the same mistakes. If told that an understanding of certain principles of literary theory is a prerequisite to intelligent reading, the student is inclined to object. I can fall in love, he may say, without studying someone's theory of love.

Granted, but the point is that anyone who reads a novel, even if he has never read or heard of literary theory, brings with him some notion of what a good novel is, some attitudes toward heroes and values and experiences. An assumed theory, however informal or partial, is deceptive, troublesome. It can shape our response to a novel without our being aware of the process. The responsible reader needs to be conscious of at least some of the most elementary principles of literary theory.

Headnotes for each author include biographical comments and brief critical discussions designed to stimulate further thought. There are also a selected, descriptive bibliography and a list of nineteen study questions.

Critics, magazine editors, and publishers have been generous in granting permissions to reprint, and I want to express my sincere appreciation to them, and to Valerie M. Raeder of Random House, whose assistance in the editing of the manuscript has been knowledgeable, efficient, and courteous. Professors W. J. Handy and R. W. Lewis, Jr. have made suggestions which I have gratefully followed. A very special thanks is due to my wife, Frankie Lea.

Contents

THE MODERN
AMERICAN NOVEL

Essays in Criticism

———

Introduction

THE POSSIBILITY
OF FICTION

We do not perceive a sentence of fiction in the mechanical way that a camera photographs a sentence. What we perceive depends, in part, on our concepts. What is to one reader an example of "escapism" may be to another reader an example of "sensitivity." One man's "villain," at times, is another man's "hero."

That such differing perceptions occur is common knowledge, but to be content with this observation as an adequate description of the process of reading is to deny that fiction is possible. If fiction has no meaning except that assigned by the individual reader, then it cannot be said to *mean* at all, or to have any coherent status. In order to see that successful novels reach a discipline of meaning that embarrasses our differing perceptions, it is necessary to examine the popular worship of the terms *objective* and *subjective*, a worship which stunts our growth as readers and makes it difficult for us to see that language and story can become a distinct kind of knowledge.

The words *objective* and *subjective* are perhaps the most overrated discriminations in intellectual history. In the minds of many people, they describe the two possible modes of thought, thus providing a neat category for each of man's serious activities: mathematics and the natural sciences are objective, religion and the fine arts are subjective, and the social sciences are—with apologies—not yet altogether objective. To label forms of knowledge in this simple fashion, however, is to deny both the achievements and the possibilities of the human mind. Fundamentally, it is to blur a necessary distinction between the observed and the observer.

Religion, for example, is not objective in the sense that its principles can be proved or disproved according to logical or scientific standards, nor is it subjective in the sense that God's shape is the product of individual whim. And yet religion *is* objective in the historical sense, in its existence as event and document in the lives of human beings; and it is subjective in that religion can mean to me only what it means to me. I cannot be another man's sensibility and have his intimate knowledge and experience of religion, nor can anyone else have mine or be me.

Such discriminations, though needed for the development of one's understanding, represent only an initial step, for they do not distinguish one kind of knowledge from another. What I have just said of religion may also be said of mathematics and the natural sciences. The proposition that two plus eight equals ten is one that I, for example, willingly accept. But to me that's all there is to it. I do the sum by rote. To a mathematician, by contrast, even a simple proposition in arithmetic will have more complicated meaning; and thus, from one point of view, mathematics is subjective.

Underlying a dependence on the terms *objective* and *subjective* is the assumption that legitimate knowledge must be subject to proof according to logical or scientific standards, but the assumption is erroneous. No man can prove his interpretation of the Constitution of the United States, not even in its application to a given year in our history, but this does not mean that the principles of freedom and equality must be denied all claim to objective reality and reduced to the status of the personal, the subjective. Not even our most intimate decisions—a man's choice of a sweetheart for example—can be denied all claim to the objective. It is true that love is content to get along without proofs and logic, and yet a man normally believes in his private self that his lady possesses some qualities which function in the objective world, some qualities which are judged admirable according to standards that exist apart from the merely personal preferences of the private self.

The purely subjective, as a matter of fact, does not express or represent one's own individuality, for that which is true for one man alone and not even potentially true for anyone else is a vagary and cannot be called *true* in any meaningful sense of the term. The corollary is that the purely objective—though it may describe something which does exist, something which does affect lives —cannot allow the presence of individual sensibility or account for human values. What we might call objective truths—that sodium and chloride can be combined to make salt, that two plus two equals four, or even that body chemistry has an effect on personality—cannot be used as modes of apprehension, cannot be thought through for the purposes of selecting a wife, a religion, an ethic, a political belief. The modern allegiance to the terms *objective* and *subjective* is misguided.

The student must be disabused of this allegiance before he can read literature sucessfully. If he thinks that disagreements among critics prove that literature is merely a matter of taste or bias or environmental influence, if he believes that the eighteenth century's disaffinity for Shakespeare is proof of critical relativism, if he reads of "shockingly" different ethical practices among island natives and thinks he has discovered a refutation of universalist ethics, if he believes that the fact of chemical participation in human personality disproves Plato, then he is handicapped by the mistaken notion that knowledge must be objective or subjective. The eighteenth century attitude toward

Shakespeare is evidence of cultural relativism only if you assume that literature must be objective (that is, true regardless of local conditions) or subjective (that is, true only for certain people in a certain time and place). Ethical practices which are aberrant from the viewpoint of Western civilization likewise argue for relativism only if you assume that knowledge, to be legitimate knowledge, must lend itself to that type of agreement men are able to achieve in the fundamentals of mathematics and the natural sciences.

It is necessary, I think, for the student of literature to learn that art—like religion and politics and the humanities in general—cannot be neatly labeled objective or subjective. Art is neither absolute (in the sense that personality, character, and experience are irrelevant to judgment) nor relative (in the sense that meaning is simply a matter of personal taste or group indoctrination). A work of art may mean to each reader whatever it means to each reader and yet make an honorable claim to integrity of meaning, and what is more all men know this, though many deny it for reasons of their own. To see with clarity one image, one scene, is to know for always that it is possible for the artist to break through bias and environment—his and yours—and to reach what has been called the subjective universal; and the possibility also holds for the ethical world. The anthropologist who has lectured on cultural relativity does not come home to his wife, embrace her, and feel that he is merely a product of society embracing a product of society. The student who argues boldly for a belief in determinism knows when he has cheated or been cheated, and when an act of honesty or dishonesty has occurred in his life no amount of abstract argument about determinism or relativism will wipe out his sense of having been touched by universal meaning.

But that sense, however deep its origins, is not enough for those who want to learn. Some understanding is desired. In the field of modern American fiction, the effort to understand better can be aided by a study of three elementary distinctions: the sensibility of the author, those values which inhere in the work of art, and the sensibilities of the individual reader. My intention in this brief essay—let me quickly add—is not to cover any of the three. My hope is merely that I can illustrate, in pedagogical fashion, the possibility of art.

Fortunately—since it could not be done anyway—it is not necessary to list the variations in sensibility that occur among authors, ages, and readers. It is necessary for anyone who would read literature well to learn that language and story can be a way of thinking and that an individual can learn to understand a sensibility that is alien to his own.

Those reactions to art which a reader sanctions by such comments as "That's the way it seems to me" are usually the result of accidental experience and thus may express more of his culture than of his best and individual potential. But the way you feel is no more final than the way you reason, unless, because of character or circumstance, you stop learning. The artist, in order to be an artist, has had to discipline his emotions, to learn of meanings that go beyond the simple-minded tags *objective* and *subjective* and involve the most intimate self in experiences of universal integrity. The student, to become a reader, must do the same.

The modern American novelist plays many roles, but he is seldom a propagandist. More often, he is a gadfly, one who testifies by outrage and exposé, by dramatizing man's failures rather than by praising his success. Overt and partisan testimony to a belief in church or government or custom is testimony that most American novelists associate with shallowness, sentimentality, immaturity, or hypocrisy. Belief, it is felt, should be tougher, more broad-minded, more restrained or modest, and thus a story about cowardice may be a representation of the reality of courage, a story about perverts and thieves may have a meaning that is offensive only to those who would prefer to leave the den closed and to walk in oblivious respectability on the other side of the street.

Such stories, furthermore, cannot accurately be called negative or perverse or one-sided. The artist of outrage may have an integrity that agitates, and is not like your own, and yet is legitimate. For behind such stories lies the belief that modern American society pays high respect to commercial and conformist values, that we are too often abject before cultural monopolies and personal fears, that too many of our traditional institutions are at bottom destructive to the very values they claim to uphold. Thus one typical hero in twentieth century fiction is the misfit, the man whose virtue is distorted because society's values are distorted. For the same reason, one typical villain is the man who has enough insensitivity or greed or cowardice to permit him to accept the distorted values of society, to cater to them, and to profit from them. Some of our traditional signs of merit—business ability, a capacity for action, adjustment to one's fellow man—come to be the most reliable indications of villainy.

It is as dangerous to generalize about the modern American novel as it is to generalize about a generation of undergraduates, but it is nonetheless true that many students live amidst influences which are antithetical to that sensibility which sees the hero as a misfit. The current emphasis on "relating to the group," to take the most obvious example, can cause students to misread a novel so fundamentally that they take the hero for the villain or, perhaps more typically, dismiss the novelist as a sick or diabolical personality. Among the best of numerous books on this current emphasis is David Riesman's *The Lonely Crowd*. Most young people today, according to Riesman, are "other-directed." Moral judgments are not based on traditional principles or on the conscience of the individual, but on the current values of the group to which the individual belongs. Adjusting to group values thus becomes a virtue, and the person who refuses to adjust is thought to be sick or perverse or he may be considered an egoist who places his own opinions above those of the democratic group.

Other-direction, as Riesman makes clear, is a characteristic, not an absolute. All people are somewhat other-directed, and no one is controlled entirely by others. But other-direction, the qualification granted, is antithetical to the thinking of most modern American novelists. Hemingway and Faulkner, for example, though fully aware of the power of environment and the dangers of egoism, believed in certain universal values and in the reality, the affirmation of the individual's dedication to those values. Faulkner, in his Nobel Prize speech, called them "the old verities," listing "love and honor and pity and pride and compassion and sacrifice." In his definition of *pundonor* (chapter nine of *Death in the Afternoon*), Hemingway suggests a comparable set of values. Students reaching maturity in a time that emphasizes other-direction—even if they are reluctant to follow the times—may find themselves subconsciously resentful of heroes who fight and suffer and sometimes die for beliefs which are the opposite of those represented by group adjustment. Faulkner's Ike McCaslin may seem merely a social deviate, one who refuses the reclamation that lies in acceptance of group values. Hemingway's Frederic Henry may seem merely an escapist, an egoist, a traitor.

Quite different contemporary influences can also lead to a misreading of the alien hero. I have had intelligent students react unsympathetically to *The Sun Also Rises* on the grounds that the novel advocates excessive drinking, sexual promiscuity, and escapist patterns of living. This student judgment—the result of moral instruction most Americans would like to see more of—is critically naïve, but it raises in a fundamental way the legitimate question of the relation of belief outside the novel to belief within the novel. Another version of much the same problem may be traced to the politically conservative home, which tends to develop in students an emotional affinity for minor novelists like Herman Wouk and Ayn Rand and an emotional antipathy for better novelists like Nathanael West and Saul Bellow.

Since the purpose of this introductory essay is to argue for the possibility of fiction, the disparity in sensibilities which I have described provides an appropriate test case. The artist who feels that society's values are distorted and that the modern hero is an exile in his own land must be able to think with his sensibility, must be able to create through language and story a meaning that has integrity. If he cannot, then his stories are merely private or partisan and can make no claim upon the attention of serious men. It must be possible, also, for students of another generation to read with integrity, to see beyond extra-literary differences to a meaning that is valid for all men who care. If this is not possible, if one must be liberal in order to read *The Grapes of Wrath* or conservative to read *By Love Possessed* or southern to read Faulkner or Jewish to read Bernard Malamud, then fiction is at best a warped and emotional treatment of matters which should be left to research and reason, or religion and ethics, or to the individual's whim.

The question thus proposed cannot be given a definitive answer even in a book-length study. Certainly no rigorous or final answer can be provided here. My intent is to illustrate the possibility of writing and reading through conflicting sensibilities to an integrity of meaning that is beyond partisanship. It is therefore legitimate, I trust, for me to work with examples rather than with the more formal principles of aesthetics. The central aim of either approach is to show that literature does *mean* (as opposed to evoke) but that it means in its own peculiar way. It is always selective and, consequently, always in a sense injudicious. *A Farewell to Arms* is not designed to show, according to the principles of history, what went on in Italy in World War I; nor is *The Catcher in the Rye* obligated to the principle of balance and coverage which guides the sociologist. The selective insight of Hemingway and of Salinger is nonetheless relevant to our lives and relevant in profound ways. Thus the first step is for the student to begin contemplating the difficult question of *how* literature means, for its methods are essentially non-logical.

The proposition is difficult, perhaps, but it is not exotic. Each of us has experienced in his own life that general type of non-logical meaning which is characteristic of fiction. To experience love, for example, is to touch a reality which is non-logical, which is both relevant and irrelevant to the more tangible and practical aspects of reality. Those who have any luck with human relations know that love cannot be measured by a discursive standard, counting gifts or measuring smiles, keeping a scorecard of deeds. And yet we cannot say that love, if it is genuine, will find no reflection in the actual world of gifts and smiles and deeds. Here, it seems to me, is a rough analogy to the relation between literature and life.

The Catcher in the Rye does not stand in literal or practical relation to actuality. The novel does not mean that all or most teen-agers are like Holden Caulfield or should be like Holden, or that Salinger advocates the selling of luggage for the purpose of financing New York excursions, or that Salinger agrees with those value judgments of Holden's which are clearly immature. And yet, at the same time, the world of actuality is not irrelevant to *The Catcher in the Rye.* Holden Caulfield's experiences and judgments are meaningful insights into that world in which we live. What almost everyone knows in actual experiences like love but what so many of us fail to transliterate into the reading of a novel is that the meaning of human experience is only partly literal. Meaning works through the tangible things of life, but tangible things are seldom an adequate way of describing the significance of what we do and what we want. If you ask a young lady why she has fallen in love with George, she may answer by using abstractions (he is kind, strong, wonderful) or by using concretions (he is six feet two, makes good grades, has a sports car, and dances well). The young lady, however, knows that abstractions do not distinguish George from Harry or Bill, and she knows that height and grades and possessions and dancing ability do not make a literal standard by which she measures the value of a suitor. What she will mean by her specific comments is that she sees—senses—in the way George works and plays and lives a person, a being she admires and has come to love. George, like all of us, must express himself through things and actions, but things and actions are not merely literal.

A scene in Hemingway's *A Farewell to Arms* may be used to illustrate this distinction in fiction. Frederic Henry, the hero, has been seriously wounded in combat. In the hospital, three doctors consult in committee fashion and decide they must wait six months before operating. Frederic Henry offers them a drink, which they refuse, and then insists on seeing a higher ranking surgeon, a major. His request is reluctantly granted and the major arrives within two hours. He proves to be the opposite of the first three doctors. He accepts a drink from Frederic Henry, promises to bring a better cognac for his patient, flirts with the nurse, and says that he positively cannot operate before tomorrow morning.

To the literal-minded, this means that Hemingway is saying all good men drink, but even the most elementary use of one's sensibility will suggest an altogether different meaning. Hemingway is not attacking teetotalers; he is attacking a committee brand of cowardice, an enfeebled human spirit which reflects itself in the way a drink is refused, in the reason for refusing a drink, in the inability to make a decision without consulting someone else who can be used to share a responsibility that cowardice fears. Hemingway's meaning, then, is relevant to the actual lives of actual men, and he has expressed that meaning through the representation of concrete experience; but his materials do not provide a literal standard of values.

The illustration I have used is a simple one, but the distinction applies to more complex literary techniques. The point is that when we fail to move from the literal to the symbolic level of apprehension, we fail to see what is in front of us. We merely reveal information about ourselves. The person who judges others by their religion, politics, or social category is simply testifying to his own affiliations and to the poverty of his own insight, his own inability to think except through formulas. He is not seeing the individuals in front of him. By the same token, the person who dismisses Hemingway because of "all that drinking" or James Gould Cozzens because of "all those snobs" or Faulkner because "life isn't really that bad" is merely revealing information about himself. He is not reading the novel.

Once this distinction is seen, my rough analogy between reading people and reading fiction should be dropped, for literature is ordered in a way which makes it quite different from that actual world to which it is nonetheless relevant. The distinction, furthermore, describes a potential of art, not a guarantee. The artist, after all, is fallible, and he may fall from representation into the literal, into the "message example." The critical reader, for instance, may want to question Cozzens' portrait of the liberal in *Guard of Honor* or Herman Wouk's portrait of the intellectual in *The Caine Mutiny* or Nelson Algren's brutal fight scene at the end of A *Walk on the Wild Side*. There is a discipline of the sensibility, and it is at least as obligatory for the artist as it is for the reader.

Certainly, the student will want to go beyond my advice to a study of the more formal principles of literary criticism, never forgetting that the best way to learn to read fiction is to read fiction, slowly and with full attention. My purpose in this section has simply been to argue that we cannot begin to read intelligently until we learn that language and story in the successful novel is a way of seeing beyond the formulas of partisan belief into the more permanent meanings of human experience.

In this section I want to discuss one of the principles by which a novelist can make of language and story a way of thinking. As is so often the case when contemplating the principles of art, the best way to say what you do mean is to say what you do not mean.

The narrative form centers around a problem which the author, by the way he writes, defines as a certain kind of problem existing in a context of more or less certain restrictions. To keep to the conditions he has set is for the author to write with integrity; to change those conditions merely for convenience, prejudice, or effect is for the author to violate a fundamental principle of structure. Most students have encountered this principle in discussions of the *deus ex machina* of Greek comedy. All of us are familiar with Hollywood and TV Westerns which use the cavalry to violate the simple conditions that characterize the typical horse opera. If the scenarist is at all competent, there will have been what is called a "plant," an earlier mention of the cavalry in an effort to create some semblance of motivation. But a "plant" is a feeble prop for a structural flaw that remains uncorrected.

If the narrative has some merit but falls short of art,

then its structural flaw tends to be a shift in the grounds of the problem. Our interest is captured by the dramatization of a significant problem, perhaps a psychological problem or an ethical conflict in which the hero faces the necessity of betraying one of two values, both of which he wants to uphold. In the end, however, the hero is rescued from his dilemma when the significant problem is allowed a prudential solution. The sub-literary narrative ends, in short, by saying that problems in being are not *really* problems in being but merely situations that call for understanding, good intentions, faith in the status quo, for a "new" idea the author knows his audience has long since accepted. Within this strategy there lies a psychological trap. When a man is under pressure, the inner self makes a defensive plea. It prefers to call a problem-in-being a problem-in-management or prudence. All of us who are less than saints seek in our daily lives our own personal *deus ex machina*.

And thus it is that dishonest fiction has an insidious appeal. Because we wish—sometimes—for the magic rescue, because we are tempted to dishonor our sins with the word *mistake*, novels about problems that turn out to be prudential accord with our most intimate hopes and take on the air of reality. Yet novels which pretend to explore boldly a controversial or profound question only to shift grounds to achieve a solution that does not come out of what has gone before, novels which merely confirm a partisan belief or console a preconceived audience are dishonest. By contrast, our best fiction—the comic as well as the tragic—accepts the commitment to structure. It rejects the lie of sentimentality.

Integrity in structure, as a principle rather than a rule, always requires the use of the faculty of aesthetic judgment. It does not release the author from the necessity of creating, nor does it release the reader from the necessity of reading with sensitivity. Provided this limitation is kept in mind, the principle can profitably be stated: since the narrative form asks the reader to care on the basis of certain assumed conditions, it should maintain or develop those conditions in a way which honors the initial caring. Changes or additions must not be retroactive. The author must develop out of the final conditions a caring that is inherent in the beginning conditions.

Since this principle applies to all known narratives (including that comedy which mocks structure, and including basic world views such as the religious, the humanistic, and the naturalistic, and including techniques that vary from the most personal to the most impersonal), it can reasonably be called a universal; and since it applies in life as well as in literature, it can reasonably be called a form of knowledge. Thus fiction has the capacity to be objective, in the sense that what it says is real, and yet remain subjective, in the sense that it is a presentation to the individual sensibility and its meaning cannot be proved.

Motion pictures, unfortunately, are not always available for the convenience of the instructor and the student, but one of the best ways to learn this basic principle of structure is to compare a novel with its filmed version when the film is an excellent transliteration except for the ending. The examples that occur to me are *From Here to Eternity* and *Tea and Sympathy*. Both films are excellent, but both are undercut by the "Hollywood ending." The tardy general in *From Here to Eternity* and the moralizing letter in *Tea and Sympathy* make a mockery of reactions the narratives have asked—and almost certainly received —from their audience. In actual experience, the same type of dishonesty appears in any situation in which we ask for sympathy or a decision but withhold information or ignore explanations which would make the desired response untenable.

It should be remembered, of course, that the principle

of integrity is but one of many. It is a major but not the sole principle of judgment. The validity of this single principle, however, is adequate to demonstrate the possibility of art, for it applies to diverse cultures, writers, readers, and systems of ethics. By means of such principles, the artist can make of language and story a way of thinking. He can appeal to our better selves.

THEODORE DREISER

(1871 – 1945)

In some ways Theodore Dreiser belongs to the generation of American novelists preceding the modern one. His
concern for socio-economic problems and his labored style
are not in the current mode and may seem dated. His
handling of sex—to readers familiar with novels like *Lady
Chatterley's Lover* and *One Hundred Dollar Misunderstanding*—may seem innocuous or even prudish. But a
look at Dreiser in the context of his own times reveals
a boldness and a modernity which mark him as a seminal
figure in the development of the modern American novel.

In Dreiser's time many readers felt that fiction should
provide entertainment and, in the process, testify to the certainty of Victorian morals. The feeling is graphically represented by a line from Oscar Wilde's satire *The Importance
of Being Earnest*. Miss Prism, whose name fits her character, comments on a novel she had once written: "The
good ended happily, and the bad unhappily. That is
what Fiction means." Sophisticated readers know that
literature attends to morals in much more subtle and realistic ways, but the average reader of Dreiser's day approved
of Miss Prism's statement. One of the all-time best sellers
in America, for example, is Horatio Alger, whose novels
show that virtue is rewarded (financially, here on this
earth) and that evil is punished (literally, here on this
earth). Dreiser's first novel, *Sister Carrie* (1900), was taken
by the Miss Prisms who read it to be a book which
advocated evil. Carrie, Dreiser's heroine, becomes the mistress of one man, later becomes the mistress of another
man, and yet, at the end of the novel, she is well on her

way to a successful career on the stage. Carrie is vaguely unhappy with her success, but this was not enough for readers who felt that fiction should preach a moral. Carrie, they thought, should be punished, unmistakably punished.

Even more important than Dreiser's fight against message-hunting censors was his commitment to a theme and technique called naturalism. According to standard sources, naturalism is the belief that man is shaped by hereditary and environmental forces beyond his control. More specifically, naturalism is the belief that man's inner sense of willing toward a good or toward an evil is an illusion merely. Thus, for the naturalist, it makes no sense to blame the wicked, for they are merely doing what they have been made to do. Likewise, it makes no sense to praise the virtuous, for they too are merely doing what they have been made to do. The naturalistic novelist, then, cannot judge his characters, but must adopt a style which, at least in its tone, is that of the scientist, the unbiased reporter of what is.

Our traditional concept of naturalism, however, is not satisfactorily confirmed by a close reading of the novels called naturalistic. We may have allowed our understanding to become confused by the role of Dreiser—and others —as a *cause célèbre*. Dreiser's awkward syntax, for example, has been defended in the name of democracy and in protest against writers who fear or ignore the harsh side of life, a defense which implies, illogically, that there is something undemocratic about good sentence structure. Furthermore, certain standard themes of naturalism (nature's indifference to man, accidents which control or destroy) may not be written as testimony to negativism, but rather as protest to the Horatio Alger belief that weather, luck, and events generally serve the needs of the good at heart, of the good little poor boy who knows with unrealistic clarity the moral rules of proper people who live on the other side of town.

And in *Sister Carrie* itself—supposedly a pat example of naturalism—Dreiser writes of the possibility of approaching the ideal. In *Jennie Gerhardt* (1911), Dreiser describes a heroine capable of real—as opposed to determined and therefore meaningless—love and sympathy. Dreiser's trilogy (*The Financier*, 1912; *The Titan*, 1914; *The Stoic*, 1947) is perhaps more negativistic, but here, as in naturalistic novels generally, the hero is a victim of his own consciousness more than of heredity and environment. This is true, for example, of Clyde Griffith in *An American Tragedy* (1925), Dreiser's finest novel. Unlike Carrie's friend Ames, whose intellectual capacities raise him above the blind struggle for survival, Clyde Griffith cannot think well.

Many critics have turned, quite understandably, to Dreiser's life, for there we find the same paradox which characterizes the fiction: a genuine sympathy for man and yet a strong urge to become top dog in that animalistic struggle which is life. Raised in extreme poverty, harassed by the fanatic religion of his family, Dreiser throughout his life was both sympathetic and selfish. As a young man he washed dishes, shoveled coal, worked as a newspaper reporter, rejected college as being unrealistic; and yet, after writing *Sister Carrie*, his protest for a better understanding of the common man, he began working for pulp and slick magazines of a most unrealistic sort and made a good deal of money doing it. Late in his life, long after he had won his fight against narrowly moralistic censorship, he flirted pathetically with spiritualism and communism, revealing yet another side of his complex nature.

Whatever the best resolution of the Dreiser problem may be, it is certain that recent corrective criticism, which concentrates on the novels as novels, is a great improvement over earlier studies which tend to reduce the novels to anecdotal illustrations of ideas. The essay that follows is an excellent example of this new and more rewarding approach.

DREISER'S
*AN AMERICAN TRAGEDY**

A Critical Study

by RICHARD LEHAN

In our "age of criticism," it is surprising to find that there is only one detailed critical study of Dreiser's *An American Tragedy*.[1] The feeling has been that because Dreiser's novel is ponderous, his themes explicit, his characters representative, a critical study is a contradiction in terms. Scholarly interest in Dreiser has, therefore, been almost totally limited to examining him as a naturalist and social critic—or to evaluating him as a thinker. Such bias cuts off critical focus at the outset; and (with the exception of

---

* From Richard Lehan, "Dreiser's *An American Tragedy*: A Critical Study," *College English*, XXV, 3 (December, 1963), 187–193. Reprinted with the permission of the National Council of Teachers of English and Richard Lehan.

Passages from *An American Tragedy* reprinted by permission of The World Publishing Co. and Dell Publishing Co.

[1] F. O. Matthiessen, "Of Crime and Punishment," published in *Theodore Dreiser* (New York, 1951), pp. 187–211. There have, of course, been studies of critical aspects of *An American Tragedy*. For an excellent study of the relationship between setting and violence see Frederick J. Hoffman's "The Scene of Violence: Dostoevsky and Dreiser," *Modern Fiction Studies* (Summer 1960). For two very good studies of the relationship between Dreiser's philosophical ideas and his literary method see Eliseo Vivas' "Dreiser, an Inconsistent Mechanist," *Ethics* (July 1938); also Alexander Kern's "Dreiser's Difficult Beauty," *Western Review* (Winter 1952). For an interesting discussion of Dreiser's development as a naturalist see Charles C. Walcutt's "The Three Stages of Theodore Dreiser's Naturalism," *PMLA* (March 1940).

Alexander Kern and Eliseo Vivas) commentators insist that Dreiser is a careless novelist at the same time as they acknowledge a certain "power" and "emotional effect" in his novels. If one examines *An American Tragedy* in terms of the novels of Henry James, then Dreiser will be found wanting. Even if one examines Dreiser's fiction within terms of his own logic, Dreiser's faults are many. And yet there is a logic to his novels; and if the logic is not its own justification, it can help explain the source of "power" in *An American Tragedy*, a power which has too long seemed gratuitous. In this paper, I try to suggest in what ways there is a relationship between (1) the setting of the novel and a character's psychological state of mind, (2) the meaning of one scene and another which it foreshadows, (3) the meaning of one character and the meaning of his "ratio" equivalent, (4) the key symbols and themes, (5) the use of irony and the meaning of the novel, and (6) the style and the meaning of action and of character in *An American Tragedy*.

A number of things about the novel are obvious and do not need extensive attention: Dreiser is using the word "tragedy" in the modern and not the Aristotelian sense of the word. He believes that man is determined by forces beyond his control, primarily environmental and hereditary. Clyde, born in the slums, of weak parents, romanticizes the idea of wealth, associates it with beautiful women, and longs for the life of riches and pleasure—which will always be beyond his grasp. Clyde's world gets more luxurious as he moves through the novel. The scenes in the novel whet his appetite; and the more Clyde sees, the more he wants. The typically innocent and passive character of naturalistic fiction, Clyde lives in a world he does not understand, reacts impulsively to a particular scene, and exists in a one-to-one relationship with the world that contains him.[2] When Clyde first sees the Green-

---

[2] The differences between the documentary novel of Dreiser and the symbolic novel of Albert Camus are so great that simi-

Davidson Hotel, he is overwhelmed by what in reality is ostentatious and gaudy wealth, and finds the hotel "more arresting, quite than anything he had seen before."[3] When Clyde first sees Sondra Finchley, he again reacts in a mechanistic way, and "her effect on him was electric—thrilling—arousing in him a curiously stinging sense of what it was to want and not to have" (p. 241). What is not so obvious is that this same kind of one-to-one relationship exists between Big Bittern and Clyde's mind. There is a definite similarity between the language Dreiser uses to describe Big Bittern and Grass Lake and the language he uses to describe Clyde's thoughts. The "green slime" at Big Bittern that lies beneath piles of rotten wood (p. 489) equates with that region in the "depths" of Clyde's mind where a "darker or primordial" self speaks (p. 496). The Giant Efrit—which emerges from Clyde's troubled mind, like a genii appearing "as smoke from the mystic jar in the net of the fisherman" (p. 496, cf. also pp. 503–504)—parallels the giant, ogre-like dark pines which surround Grass Lake:

> It was black or dark like tar, and sentineled to the east and north by tall, dark pines—the serried spears of armed and watchful giants, as they now appeared to him—ogres almost—so gloomy, suspicious and fantastically erratic was his own mood in regard to this. (p. 513)

The dark, gloomy, ominous woods with its bogs "festooned with funeral or viperous vines" and its pockets of

---

larities of detail go unnoticed. Like Meursault, Clyde lives in a world of chance, is a passive character, commits an "accidental" murder, is brought to "justice" by a self-righteous society, and is finally executed. The events in *An American Tragedy* have become a kind of formula, used for different thematic ends by both existential and naturalistic novelists. Cf. James M. Cain's *The Postman Always Rings Twice*, Richard Wright's *Native Son*, and Willard Motley's *Knock On Any Door*.

[3] Theodore Dreiser, *An American Tragedy* (New York: Dell, 1959), p. 45. All further quotations will be taken from this edition, page references indicated in parentheses after the quote.

"green slime" create in Clyde a psychological condition
that allows him to contemplate and then later almost
commit murder. Not only is there a metaphorical equivalent between Clyde's mind and the setting of the novel, but
the scene supplies Clyde with the motives and psychological mood for action.

The emphasis in *An American Tragedy* is, of course,
on Clyde, but the only real difference among the characters
from the lower class is that some have more contact with
wealth and luxury than others. All are motivated by a
desire for a better life, and this leads to a kind of "ratio"
relationship. For example, Roberta *is* to Clyde as Clyde *is*
to Sondra; and Roberta *is* to Clyde as Clyde *was* to
Hortense Briggs (see p. 388). Dreiser completes the ratio
by making Hortense a lower-class Sondra Finchley (see p.
347). And Dreiser reinforces the ratio by describing
Clyde's meeting Roberta in a way that identically parallels
Sondra's meeting Clyde. While canoeing one Sunday,
Clyde sees Roberta and asks her to accompany him:
" 'Oh, please don't say no. Just get in, won't you?' " (p.
283). Later on, Sondra, waiting in her chauffeur-driven
car, meets Clyde and eventually asks him to accompany
her, just as Clyde had asked Roberta: " 'Won't you get in,
please, and let me take you where you are going. Oh, I
wish you would' " (p. 331). The similarity of scenes, far
from being accidental, reduces character to mechanistic
relationships and suggests that physical attraction is the
only motive that can ameliorate social differences.

Not only does *An American Tragedy* establish "character ratio," but one incident in the novel anticipates another. The fate of Esta, Clyde's sister, foreshadows the fate
of Roberta Alden. Clyde—forced to choose between helping Esta, or buying Hortense a new coat—buys the coat.
The lack of will Clyde reveals here anticipates the way he
will act after the Kansas City car accident and after Roberta tells him that she is pregnant. Narrative progression

in *An American Tragedy* suggests that characters will react
in one situation as they did in a previous situation, providing the situations are consistently similar.

The situation thus becomes all important, and each
situation repeats the meaning of character. To this extent,
An American Tragedy is primarily a study of social motives. As everyone knows, Dreiser intended to call his
novel *Mirage*,[4] but such a title made Clyde's faulty vision
too personal. Dreiser changed the title because Clyde
Griffith's story is a kind of representative anecdote, a documentary case that illustrates a typical kind of person.
Clyde is not the only character who is motivated by the
lure of success. The word "dream" is used over a hundred
times in the novel and suggests the motives behind a number of lives. Roberta Alden leaves Blitz in the hope of
realizing her "dream" in Lycurgus (see p. 269); Mason,
the prosecuting attorney, comes from a background as
poor as Clyde's and aspires to a judgeship (see p. 591);
even Swenk, the arresting officer, blazes "with a desire to
arrest and handcuff someone," and is lured on by "great
dreams of being the one to capture the murderer" (p.
585). Clyde's character is indeed typical, and at the end of
the novel Dreiser turns the screw once more when he
suggests that Russell, Clyde's nephew, is to repeat Clyde's
story.

A number of key symbols reinforce Dreiser's ideas.
An examination of the beginning and the ending of *An
American Tragedy* reveals not only a similarity of lan-
guage but also of imagery:

> Dusk—of a summer night.
> And the tall walls of the commercial heart of an
> American city of perhaps 400,000 inhabitants—such
> walls as in time may linger as mere fable. (p. 19)

and

---

[4] See Matthiessen, p. 189.

> Dusk of a summer night.
> And the tall walls of the commercial heart of
> the city of San Francisco—tall and gray in the eve-
> ning shade. (p. 860)

Clyde's story takes place between "walls." In Lycurgus,
Clyde walks in the shadow of enormous factory walls and,
ironically, "the high red walls of the building suggested
energy and very material success, a type of success that
was almost without flaw, as he saw it" (p. 199). The walls
of society fold in on Clyde, centripetally, and it is most
significant that to get from Three Mile Bay to Big Bittern
one has to go "between towering walls of pines" (p. 489).

The bird that cries so ominously before and after the
death of Roberta Alden also seems symbolic. Interestingly
enough, bird references connect the incident at Big Bittern
with the incident of the fatal auto trip in Kansas City.
Before Sparser runs over the girl, the car speeds by a dark
woods and "a flock of crows rose and winged direct
toward a distant wood lightly pencilled against a foreground of snow" (p. 141). In this context, it is most
significant that Dreiser later refers to Sondra Finchley as a
"bright-colored bird" (p. 581), and that Clyde, hesitating
to run away from Sondra just before he is arrested, pauses
"while vesper sparrows and woodfinches sang" (p. 588).
Finchley and woodfinch, Sondra, the brightly colored bird;
the crows which fly toward a distant wood (Big Bittern?);
the bird of fate (Dreiser puns on the word "weird": "the
weirdness of it," "the weird . . . cry," "that devilish bird . . .
the weir-weir") which cries so ominously in the black
forest—they all become one in a world where the dream
leads to self-destruction, the lures of success lead to dis-
aster.[5]

---

[5] Even the most sympathetic and perceptive readers of Dreiser
have failed to see the extent to which Dreiser employs and sus-
tains symbolism. Alexander Kern, for example, believes that
"though he occasionally uses symbol, they are rarely maintained.

This is the world of the hunter and the hunted, of the victim and prey. When Clyde first arrives at Lycurgus, he notices on his uncle's lawn "one lone cast iron stag pursued by some cast iron dogs" (p. 208). Eventually Clyde becomes the stag, pursued by the sheriff and his deputies. The description of Clyde's arrest and trial is full of animal and pursuit imagery. Clyde is described as a "hunted animal," as a "prey," and as a "desperate animal." Swenk comes after him like a "seeking animal." Mason goes after Clyde in the courtroom "like a wild bull." And Jephson tries to defend him with the shrewdness "of a lynx or a ferret." Although this language is heavily cliché, it reveals Dreiser's ultimate definition of man.

Dreiser's heroes have a perspective that is no more inclusive than the animals in a Darwinian jungle. There is a continued irony in *An American Tragedy* stemming from the fact that while the novel is told from the omniscient point of view, Clyde never understands the meaning of events which befall him. Clyde lacks conscience because he lacks consciousness which, in *An American Tragedy*, exists only on the authorial level. Whereas the reader can anticipate Clyde's fate, Clyde himself is always insensitive to what is about to happen. It is most ironic, for example, that Clyde, who will plot the murder of Roberta, becomes indignant when Esta's consort deserts her (see p. 115). It is again ironic that just before Clyde meets Roberta in his uncle's factory, "the large number of women upstairs seemed very remote and of no consequence" (p. 255). It is ironic that Roberta should be reading a seed catalogue just before she discovers that she is pregnant (see p. 320).

Not all of the irony in *An American Tragedy* stems from the use of point of view. In a world where forces

---

The combat of the lobster and the squid in *The Financier* and the song of the weir-weir bird in *An American Tragedy* are typical and obtrusive," Kern, *op. cit.*, p. 134.

frustrate the ambitions of men, irony becomes a manifest quality of action. It is ironic in this sense that Mason and later the townspeople take an immediate dislike to Clyde because they think that he is rich. It is ironic when Clyde's desire for money gets him into trouble and his lack of money prevents him from getting out of it. It is ironic that Clyde is condemned by a society that believes in absolute justice, but he lives in a society in which money has created a double standard of justice—where Belknap, unlike Clyde, is saved by his father's money from the unpleasant consequences of a premarital affair (see p. 630), and where the doctor to whom Roberta first goes has performed abortions for the girls from wealthy families (see p. 430). It is ironic that Clyde plans to murder Roberta and is prosecuted by Mason—people with whom he shares the same background and the same drive to succeed, and people who are really very much like him. It is ironic that Clyde, first driven by the desire to live in an elegant world, and then abandoned by everyone but his mother, should be given two books in death-row—the *Arabian Nights* and *Robinson Crusoe* (p. 823). It is ironic that Clyde believes in an Aladdin world of magic but lives in a world of causality—that he should think of himself as a "pagan" (see pp. 85, 223, 260) and be prosecuted and put to death by a strictly religious community. It is ironic that the American dream should be associated with the westward movement, for as the Griffiths family moves westward— from Grand Rapids, to Detroit, to Milwaukee, to Chicago, to Kansas City, to Denver, to San Francisco—they get poorer and poorer.

The cruelest irony of all is that Clyde is really innocent of murdering Roberta. As Dreiser carefully tells us, Clyde does not have the strength of will to murder her, and he strikes Roberta unintentionally with the camera (see pp. 525–526). Clyde makes this perfectly clear to Reverend McMillan; but because Clyde was angry at the time of Roberta's death, and because he was glad that Roberta drowned, Reverend McMillan tells Clyde that he is guilty of murder in his "heart" (p. 843). Although Clyde is legally innocent, McMillan believes that he is guilty before God and, as a result, fails to give the governor the facts that could save Clyde's life (see p. 851).[6] Thus, Clyde, who struggles all his life to outdistance the slums and to move beyond his fanatically religious parents, is condemned by both society and the church for a crime he never legally committed. Certainly this kind of irony, in part, is responsible for the emotional impact— and the effect of *An American Tragedy* stems from more than just a rough accumulation of detail and incident.

Perhaps the reason that *An American Tragedy* seems like such a careless piece of work is that the style leaves much to be desired. Yet action in fiction exists in and not apart from the language, and Dreiser's style cannot be divorced from his method. Much of Dreiser's language is forced and contrived ("chemisms," "nerve plasm palpitation," "atavistic spur and fillip"). While this language does offend our literary sensibility, it is consistent with Dreiser's attempt to create a documentary effect and with his attempt to study in a "clinical" way poverty and its effects— Book I treating the causes of poverty, Book II the effect, and Book III (the trial) analyzing cause and effect. Movement from cause to effect is further revealed by transitional phrases—"in consequence," "and then," etc. (cf. pp. 405-414)—which best reflect the actual quality of

6 The function of Rev. McMillan has been misread by several commentators. Van Wyck Brooks, e.g., maintains that "it was left for the supposedly godless Dreiser to portray in his Duncan McMillan the Protestant minister as he ought to be." See "Theodore Dreiser," *University of Kansas City Review,* 16 (Spring 1950), p. 197. Lionel Trilling, about to refer to Rev. McMillan, says "this is not the first occasion on which Dreiser has shown tenderness toward religion and a responsiveness to mysticism." See "Reality in America," *The Liberal Imagination* (New York, 1953), p. 29.

Dreiser's thought and create an overwhelming sense of inevitability. There are a number of other similarities between the style and the structure and meaning of the novel. *An American Tragedy* employs the familiar block method with a great mass of accumulated material being arranged into blocks or units, each scene repeating and then anticipating another. Each individual scene parallels the structure of the novel as a whole, Dreiser grouping the details of the scene—in contrast to the style of (say) Henry James, where the details usually come piecemeal and where each detail is an expression of a character's sensibility and reveals an impression of mind.[7] Dreiser orders his detail so as to reveal a character responding to a fixed situation; scene thus becomes a part of motives, the descriptive passages coming first, the main characters reacting to a situation in a predictable way.

As for the quality of Dreiser's language in general, the following passage is fairly representative:

> Yet Clyde, because of that same fear that had guided him at Bear Lake, maintaining a profound silence. For why should he say that he had struck her, when he had not—intentionally at least? Or with what, since no thought of the camera had come up as yet.

---

[7] Compare Book I, chapter 17, of *An American Tragedy*, the scene describing the start of the auto trip. We have first a description of Kansas City, the environs described as walls enclosing Clyde. Then we have a description of the people in the car with special reference to Clyde who is moving outside the circumference of his previous existence. Then Dreiser moves into dialogue. We spiral down on Clyde, and movement of each scene, as of the novel, is from the general to the particular. Contrast this with Book XI, chapter 4 (the New York Edition) of *The Ambassadors*, the scene in which Strether sees Chad with Mme. de Vionnet. Here we have a continued and unrelenting relationship between the perceiver and the perceived, between the consciousness of a character and the object of his consciousness. James's technique allows an added dimension of character—a moral sense and conscience.

At the lake, after definite measurements by the county surveyor as to the distance from the spot where Roberta drowned to the spot where Clyde had landed, Earl Newcomb suddenly returning to Mason with an important discovery. For under a log not so far from the spot at which Clyde had stood to remove his wet clothes, the tripod he had hidden, a little rusty and damp, but of sufficient weight, as Mason and all these others were now ready to believe, to have delivered the blow upon Roberta's skull which had felled her and so make it possible for him to carry her to the boat and later drown her. Yet, confronted with this and turning paler than before, Clyde denying that he had a camera or a tripod with him, although Mason was instantly deciding that he would re-question all witnesses to find out whether any recalled seeing a tripod or camera in Clyde's possession.

And before the close of this same day learning from the guide who had driven Clyde and Roberta over, as well as the boatman . . . that all now recalled a "yellow bundle of sticks." . . .

And then Burton Raleigh declaring that it might not have really been a tripod, after all with which he had struck her. . . . And because of this conclusion, without any knowledge on the part of Clyde, however, Mason securing divers from among the woodsmen of the region and setting them to diving in the immediate vicinity of the spot where Roberta's body had been found. . . . (p. 611)

This passage is top-heavy with adjectives and participles (maintaining, returning, delivered, confronted, turning, denying, deciding, seeing, etc.). Dreiser generally uses far more adjectives than verbs and often (because he uses a participle instead of a verb) writes in sentence fragments. Is the grammar intentional? Probably not. The question needs, however, to be put differently: what is the effect of this style? The answer is that the style destroys what might be called "existential action," an event that has meaning in and of itself. Action in *An American Tragedy* is reflective and demonstrative. Each situation describes the nature of life in a deterministic world. Dreiser is thus primarily interested in specifying the quality of an act or behavior. And since adjectives are the part of speech which modify and qualify, it is not surprising that *An American Tragedy* labors under adjectival weight.

While the naturalistic elements in Dreiser's fiction have received intensive attention, little has been said about Dreiser's style and technique. Dreiser was not as careless a technician as most people believe. The problem has been that while critics will allow Milton his Ptolemaic astronomy, some refuse to allow Dreiser his mechanistic philosophy. As a result, Dreiser is summarily dismissed by many critics as ideologically unconvincing.[8] Yet not all of us have to be in philosophical agreement with an author to appreciate him; and once we suspend belief and prejudice we find that Dreiser's dramatic method is consistent with his world view. This is not to whitewash Dreiser: he is at times contrived, often overwrites, is sometimes tendentious, and resorts to bathos and to sentimentalizing character. These are serious faults—and stem from a zealous didacticism and lack of restraint. Dreiser, to be sure, has misused his method; but as I have tried to suggest, a great deal more needs to be said about the method itself.

---

[8] Cf. Lionel Trilling's "Reality in America." Also the essays by Stuart P. Sherman and Robert Shafer reprinted in *The Stature of Theodore Dreiser* (Bloomington, 1955), pp. 71–80 and 113–126 respectively.

SHERWOOD ANDERSON
(1876–1941)

Between the close of the Civil War and the beginning
of World War I, there occurred some fundamental
changes in the socio-economic patterns of American life.
Historians have used various terms to describe these
changes: the industrial revolution, the rise of science, the
age of technocracy, the birth of mass production. People,
like business and industry, seemed to change too or, at
least, they now faced a new and terrible challenge. Many
observers of the American scene felt that before technocracy, in the days of the individual craftsman, it was
possible for a man to express his soul in the work of the
day. But modern man, caught in the awesome backlash of
a machine age he himself had made, was suddenly op-
pressed by forces of dehumanization. Work, before mass
production techniques were developed, could be a thing of
pride; a man could express his individuality, his character,
by making a harness that was true, a shoe that would
stand up to wear. But work for the man on the assembly
line was different. He could feel little personal relationship
between himself and bolt number seventeen.

Sherwood Anderson is one of the most original of
those American novelists who were profoundly disturbed
by this sense of loss in the age of big business, mass
production, and social conformity. A troubled person
himself, Anderson spent his youth wandering from job to

job, unable to establish roots. Eventually, he became the manager of a paint factory, but he still longed for something else, something he could not find. For a time, the manager brooded. Business, to Sherwood Anderson, was without moral or aesthetic relevance. It was not life.

With an abruptness more legendary than factual, Anderson left his family, the paint business, and his practice of putting off or giving last place to a desire to express himself and his insight into his fellow man. He went to Chicago to become a writer. *Windy McPherson's Son,* his first novel, was published when he was forty. He wrote for the rest of his life, and several of his books are well worth the reading (*The Triumph of the Egg,* 1921; *Dark Laughter,* 1925); but the majority opinion today is that only one of his books is eminently successful. Yet that one book, *Winesburg, Ohio* (1919), is adequate to secure his place in modern American fiction.

A group of related short stories rather than a novel, *Winesburg, Ohio* is a study of the wounds and distortions of isolation. Its unity comes in part from certain devices (Winesburg as the basic setting, the use of a central viewpoint character, recurrent themes), but mainly from atmosphere, from a representation of that loss and loneliness and frustration which comes to those who live in a profane time. Anderson's characters may feel, within themselves, a genuine love; but any expression of love is distorted, as if by social necromancy, and the simple desire to love leads to misunderstanding, hurt, sickness, or is taken to be perversion. In the end there is loneliness and fear. What those who are contented with the status quo call wisdom or maturity or common sense or adjustment offers no solution. Anderson's lost people have not chosen isolation. Isolation is simply there, by virtue of what man is, by virtue of what Winesburg is. Adjustment to society, for the most part, is merely another name for loss, merely another kind of loneliness.

The style Anderson developed to express the inner experience of modern man is also basic in the history of American fiction. Anderson's indebtedness to Gertrude Stein, his influence on Hemingway, and his relationship with the then young William Faulkner are rich topics for investigation. Perhaps more than anything else, Anderson's style is a symbolic mode in which the symbol is enlarged to an event or series of events. Thus Anderson's stories lack plot in the traditional sense. The story, of course, is there, but it is there as an image in time, as a study of internal realities which are not revealed by the masks we wear in public.

THE BOOK OF
THE GROTESQUE*
by IRVING HOWE

The history of *Winesburg* is a curious instance of the way criticism, with its passion for "placing," can reduce a writer to harmless irrelevance. At various times the book has been banished to such categories as the revolt against the village, the rejection of middle-class morality, the proclamation of sexual freedom, and the rise of cultural primitivism. Whatever the justification for such tags may once have been, it is now quite obvious that Anderson's revolt was directed against something far more fundamental than the restrictions of the American village and was, for that

---

* From *Sherwood Anderson* by Irving Howe, copyright 1951 by William Sloane Associates, Inc., by permission of William Sloane Associates. "The Book of the Grotesque" first appeared in *Partisan Review*, January–February, 1951.

matter, equally relevant to the American city; that *Winesburg* is not primarily concerned with morality, middle-class or otherwise, if only because most of its characters are not in a position to engage in moral choice; that while its subject is frequently tangential to sex it expresses no opinions about and offers no proposals for sexual conduct, free or restricted; and that its style is only dimly related to anything that might be called primitive. If read as social fiction *Winesburg* is somewhat absurd, for no such town could possibly exist. If read as a venture into abnormal psychology the book seems almost lurid, for within its total structure the behavior of its hysterics and paranoids is quite purposeless and, in the absence of any norms to which their deviations might be compared, even incomprehensible. In fact, if read according to the usual expectations of 20th-century naturalistic or conventionally realistic fiction, *Winesburg* seems incoherent and the charge of emotion it can still raise inexplicable.

In its fundamental quality *Winesburg* is nonrealistic; it does not seek to gratify the eye with a verisimilitude to social forms in the way a Dreiser or a Lewis novel does. In rather shy lyrical outbursts the book conveys a vision of American life as a depressed landscape cluttered with dead stumps, twisted oddities, grotesque and pitiful wrecks; a landscape in which ghosts fumble erratically and romance is reduced to mere fugitive brushings at night; a landscape eerie with the cracked echoes of village queers rambling in their lonely eccentricity. Again and again *Winesburg* suggests that beneath the exteriors of our life the deformed exert dominion, that the seeming health of our state derives from a deep malignancy. And *Winesburg* echoes with American loneliness, that loneliness which could once evoke Nigger Jim's chant of praise to the Mississippi pastoral but which has here become fearful and sour.

Winesburg is a book largely set in twilight and darkness, its backgrounds heavily shaded with gloomy blacks and marshy grays—as is proper for a world of withered men who, sheltered by night, reach out for that sentient life they dimly recall as the racial inheritance that has been squandered away. Like most fiction, Winesburg is a variation on the theme of reality and appearance, in which the deformations caused by day (public life) are intensified at night and, in their very extremity, become an entry to reality. From Anderson's instinctively right placement of the book's central actions at twilight and night comes some of its frequently noticed aura of "lostness"—as if the most sustaining and fruitful human activities can no longer be performed in public communion but must be grasped in secret.

The two dozen central figures in Winesburg are hardly characters in the usual novelistic sense. They are not shown in depth or breadth, complexity or ambiguity; they are allowed no variations of action or opinion; they do not, with the exception of George Willard, the book's "hero," grow or decline. For Anderson is not trying to represent through sensuous images the immediate surface of human experience; he is rather drawing the abstract and deliberately distorted paradigm of an extreme situation, and for that purpose fully rounded characterizations could only be a complicating blemish.

The figures of Winesburg usually personify to fantastic excess a condition of psychic deformity which is the consequence of some crucial failure in their lives, some aborted effort to extend their personalities or proffer their love. Misogyny, inarticulateness, frigidity, God-infatuation, homosexuality, drunkenness—these are symptoms of their recoil from the regularities of human intercourse and sometimes of their substitute gratifications in inanimate objects, as with the unloved Alice Hindman who "because it was her own, could not bear to have anyone touch the furniture of her room." In their compulsive traits these figures find a kind of dulling peace, but as a consequence they are subject to rigid monomanias and are deprived of one of the great blessings of human health: the capacity for a variety of experience. That is why, in a sense, "nothing happens" in *Winesburg*. For most of its figures it is too late for anything to happen, they can only muse over the traumas which have so harshly limited their spontaneity. Stripped of their animate wholeness and twisted into frozen postures of defense, they are indeed what Anderson has called them: grotesques.

The world of *Winesburg*, populated largely by these back-street grotesques, soon begins to seem like a buried ruin of a once vigorous society, an atrophied remnant of the egalitarian moment of 19th-century America. Though many of the book's sketches are placed in the out-of-doors, its atmosphere is as stifling as a tomb. And the reiteration of the term "grotesque" is felicitous in a way Anderson could hardly have been aware of; for it was first used by Renaissance artists to describe arabesques painted in the underground ruins, *grotte*, of Nero's "Golden House."

The conception of the grotesque, as actually developed in the stories, is not merely that it is an unwilled affliction but also that it is a mark of a once sentient striving. In his introductory fantasy, "The Book of the Grotesque," Anderson writes: "It was the truths that made the people grotesques . . . the moment one of the people took one of the truths to himself, called it his truth, and tried to live his life by it, he became a grotesque and the truth he embraced a falsehood." There is a sense, as will be seen later, in which these sentences are at variance with the book's meaning, but they do suggest the significant notion that the grotesques are those who *have* sought "the truths" that disfigure them. By contrast the banal creatures who dominate the town's official life, such as Will Henderson, publisher of the paper for which George Willard works, are not even grotesques: they are simply clods.

The grotesques are those whose humanity has been outraged and who to survive in Winesburg have had to suppress their wish to love. Wash Williams becomes a misogynist because his mother-in-law, hoping to reconcile him to his faithless wife, thrusts her into his presence naked; Wing Biddlebaum becomes a recluse because his wish to blend learning with affection is fatally misunderstood. Grotesqueness, then, is not merely the shield of deformity; it is also a remnant of misshapen feeling, what Dr. Reefy in "Paper Pills" calls "the sweetness of the twisted apples."

Winesburg may thus be read as a fable of American estrangement, its theme the loss of love. The book's major characters are alienated from the basic sources of emotional sustenance—from the nature in which they live but to which they can no longer have an active relationship; from the fertility of the farms that flank them but no longer fulfill their need for creativity; from the community which, at least by the claim of the American mythos, once bound men together in fraternity but is now merely an institution external to their lives; from the work which once evoked and fulfilled their sense of craft but is now a mere burden; and, most catastrophic of all, from each other, the very extremity of their need for love having itself become a barrier to its realization.

The grotesques rot because they are unused, their energies deprived of outlet, and their instincts curdled in isolation. As Waldo Frank has noticed in his fine study of Winesburg, the first three stories in the book suggest this view in a complete theme-statement. The story "Hands," through several symbolic referents, depicts the loss of creativity in the use of the human body. The second story, "Paper Pills," directly pictures the progressive ineffectuality of human thought, pocketed in paper pellets that no one reads. And the third story, "Mother," relates these two themes to a larger variant: the inability of Elizabeth Willard, *Winesburg*'s mother-figure, to communicate her love to her son. "The form of the mother, frustrated, lonely, at last desperate," Frank writes, "pervades the variations that make the rest of the book: a continuity of variation swelling, swirling into the corners and crannies of the village life; and at last closing in the mother's death, in the loss forever of the $800 which Elizabeth Willard had kept for twenty years to give her son his start away from Winesburg, and in the son's wistful departure." In the rupture of family love and the consequent loss of George Willard's heritage, the theme-statement of the book is completed.

The book's central strand of action, discernible in about half the stories, is the effort of the grotesques to establish intimate relations with George Willard, the young reporter. At night, when they need not fear the mockery of public detection, they hesitantly approach him, almost in supplication, to tell him of their afflictions and perhaps find health in his voice. Instinctively, they sense his moral freshness, finding hope in the fact that he has not yet been calloused by knowledge and time. To some of the grotesques, such as Dr. Reefy and Dr. Parcival, George Willard is the lost son returned, the Daedalus whose apparent innocence and capacity for feeling will redeem Winesburg. To others among the grotesques, such as Tom Foster and Elmer Cowley, he is a reporter-messenger, a small-town Hermes, bringing news of a dispensation which will allow them to re-enter the world of men. But perhaps most fundamentally, and subsuming these two visions, he seems to the grotesques a young priest who will renew the forgotten communal rites by which they may again be bound together. To Louise Trunnion he will bring a love that is more than a filching of flesh; to Dr. Parcival the promise to "write the book that I may never get written" in which he will tell all men that "everyone in the world is Christ and they are all crucified"; to the Reverend Curtis Hartman the willingness to understand a vision of God as revealed in the flesh of a naked woman; to Wash Williams the peace that will ease his sense of violation; and to Enoch Robinson the "youthful sadness, young man's sadness, the sadness of a growing boy in a village at the year's end [which can open] the lips of the old man."

As they approach George Willard, the grotesques seek not merely the individual release of a sudden expressive outburst, but also a relation with each other that may restore them to collective harmony. They are distraught communicants in search of a ceremony, a social value, a manner of living, a lost ritual that may, by some means, reestablish a flow and exchange of emotion. Their estrangement is so extreme that they cannot turn to each other though it is each other they really need and secretly want; they turn instead to George Willard who will soon be out of the orbit of their life. The miracle that the Reverend Curtis Hartman sees and the message over which Kate Swift broods could bind one to the other, yet they both turn to George Willard who, receptive though he may wish to be, cannot understand them.

In only one story, "Death," do the grotesques seem to meet. Elizabeth Willard and Dr. Reefy embrace in a moment of confession, but their approach to love is interrupted by a stray noise. Elizabeth leaves: "The thing that had come to life in her as she talked to her one friend died suddenly." A few months later, at her deathbed, Dr. Reefy meets George Willard and puts out "his hand as though to greet the young man and then awkwardly [draws] it back again." Bloom does not find his Daedalus; the hoped-for epiphany comes at the verge of death and, as in all the stories, is aborted; the ritual of communal love remains unrealized.

The burden which the grotesques would impose on George Willard is beyond his strength. He is not yet himself a grotesque mainly because he has not yet experienced very deeply, but for the role to which they would assign him he is too absorbed in his own ambition and restlessness. The grotesques see in his difference from them the possibility of saving themselves, but actually it is the barrier to an ultimate companionship. George Willard's adolescent receptivity to the grotesques can only give him the momentary emotional illumination described in that lovely story, "Sophistication." On the eve of his departure from Winesburg, George Willard reaches the point "when he for the first time takes the backward view of life. . . . With a little gasp he sees himself as merely a leaf blown by the wind through the streets of his village. He knows that in spite of all the stout talk of his fellows he must live and die in uncertainty, a thing blown by the winds, a thing destined like corn to wilt in the sun. . . . Already he hears death calling. With all his heart he wants to come close to some other human, touch someone with all his hands. . . ." For George this illumination is enough, but it is not for the grotesques. They are a moment in his education, he a confirmation of their doom. "I have missed something. I have missed something Kate Swift was trying to tell me," he says to himself one night as he falls asleep. He has missed the meaning of Kate Swift's life: it is not his fault: her salvation, like the salvation of the other grotesques, is beyond his capacities.

In the story "Queer" these meanings receive their most generalized expression, for its grotesque, Elmer Cowley, has no specific deformity: he is the grotesque as such. "He was, he felt, one condemned to go through life without friends and he hated the thought." Wishing to talk to George Willard, he loses courage and instead rants to a half-wit: "I had to tell some one and you were the only one I could tell. I hunted out another queer one, you see. I ran away, that's what I did." When Elmer Cowley does call George Willard out of the newspaper office, he again becomes tongue-tied in his presence. Despairing over "his failure to declare his determination not to be queer," Elmer Cowley decides to leave Winesburg, but in a last effort at communication he asks George Willard to meet him at the midnight local. Again he cannot speak. "Elmer Cowley danced with fury beside the groaning train in the darkness on the station platform. . . . Like one struggling for release from hands that held him he struck, hitting George Willard blow after blow on the breast, the neck, the mouth." Unable to give Elmer Cowley the love that might dissolve his queerness, George Willard suffers the fate of the rejected priest.

From the story "Queer," it is possible to abstract the choreography of *Winesburg*. Its typical action is a series of dance maneuvers by figures whose sole distinctive characteristic is an extreme deformity of movement or posture. Each of these grotesques dances, with angular indirection and muted pathos, toward a central figure who seems to them young, fresh, and radiant. For a moment they seem to draw close to him and thereby to abandon their stoops and limps, but this moment quickly dissolves in the play of the dance and perhaps it never even existed: the central figure cannot be reached. Slowly and painfully, the grotesques withdraw while the young man leaves the stage entirely. None of the grotesques is seen full-face for more than a moment, and none of them is individually important to the scheme of the dance. For this is a dance primarily of spatial relationships rather than solo virtuosity; the distances established between the dancers, rather than their personalities, form the essence of the dance. And in the end, its meaning is revealed in the fact that all but the one untouched youth return to precisely their original places and postures.

When Anderson first sent his *Winesburg* stories to the *Masses*, *Seven Arts*, and the *Little Review*, he intended each of them to be a self-contained unit, as in fact they may still be regarded. But there was clearly a unifying conception behind all the stories: they were set in the same locale, many of the characters appeared in several stories, and there was a remarkable consistency of mood that carried over from story to story. Consequently, when Anderson prepared them for book publication in 1919, he had only to make a few minor changes, mostly insertions of place and character names as connectives, in order to have a unified book.

Particularly if approached along the lines that have been suggested here, *Winesburg* seems remarkably of a piece. The only stories that do not fit into its pattern are the four-part narrative of Jesse Bentley, a failure in any case, and possibly "The Untold Lie," a beautiful story measuring the distance between middle-age and youth. Of the others only "Tandy" is so bad that its omission would help the book. On the other hand, few of the stories read as well in isolation as in the book's context. Except for "Hands," "The Strength of God," "Paper Pills," and "The Untold Lie," they individually lack the dramatic power which the book has as a whole.

Winesburg is an excellently formed piece of fiction, each of its stories following a parabola of movement which abstractly graphs the book's meaning. From a state of feeling rather than a dramatic conflict there develops in one of the grotesques a rising lyrical excitement, usually stimulated to intensity by the presence of George Willard. At the moment before reaching a climax, this excitement is frustrated by a fatal inability at communication and then it rapidly dissolves into its original diffuse base. This structural pattern is sometimes varied by an ironic turn, as in "Nobody Knows" and "A Man of Ideas," but in only one story, "Sophistication," is the emotional ascent allowed to move forward without interruption.

But the unity of the book depends on more than the congruous design of its parts. The first three stories of

Winesburg develop its major theme, which, after several variations, reaches its most abstract version in "Queer." The stories following "Queer" seem somewhat of a thematic afterthought, though they are necessary for a full disposal of the characters. The one conspicuous disharmony in the book is that the introductory "Book of the Grotesque" suggests that the grotesques are victims of their wilful fanaticism, while in the stories themselves grotesqueness is the result of an essentially valid resistance to forces external to its victims.

Through a few simple but extremely effective symbols, the stories are both related to the book's larger meaning and defined in their uniqueness. For the former of these purposes, the most important symbol is that of the room, frequently used to suggest isolation and confinement. Kate Swift is alone in her bedroom, Dr. Reefy in his office, the Reverend Curtis Hartman in his church tower, Enoch Robinson in his fantasy-crowded room. Enoch Robinson's story "is in fact the story of a room almost more than it is the story of a man." The tactful use of this symbol lends *Winesburg* a claustrophobic aura appropriate to its theme.

Most of the stories are further defined by symbols related to their particular meanings. The story of the misogynist Wash Williams begins by rapidly thrusting before the reader an image of "a huge, grotesque kind of monkey, a creature with ugly, sagging, hairless skin," which dominates its subsequent action. And more valid than any abstract statement of theme is the symbolic power of that moment in "The Strength of God" when the Reverend Curtis Hartman, in order to peek into Kate Swift's bedroom, breaks his church window at precisely the place where the figure of a boy stands "motionless and looking with rapt eyes into the face of Christ."

Though *Winesburg* is written in the bland accents of the American story teller, it has an economy impossible to oral narration because Anderson varies the beat of its accents by occasionally whipping them into quite formal rhetorical patterns. In the book's best stretches there is a tension between its underlying loose oral cadences and the stiffened superimposed beat of a prose almost Biblical in its regularity. Anderson's prose is neither "natural" nor primitive; it is rather a hushed bardic chant, low-toned and elegiacally awkward, deeply related to native speech rhythms yet very much the result of literary cultivation.

But the final effectiveness of this prose is in its prevalent tone of tender inclusiveness. Between writer and materials there is an admirable equity of relationship. None of the characters is violated, none of the stories, even the failures, leaves the reader with the bitter sense of having been tricked by cleverness or cheapness or toughness. The ultimate unity of the book is a unity of feeling, a sureness of warmth, and a readiness to accept Winesburg's lost grotesques with the embrace of humility. Many American writers have taken as their theme the loss of love in the modern world, but few, if any at all, have so thoroughly realized it in the accents of love.

SINCLAIR LEWIS

(1885 – 1951)

Sinclair Lewis agreed with Theodore Dreiser that environment is a powerful force in men's lives, and he agreed with Sherwood Anderson that men—especially those with sensitive souls—are hard put to express an honest emotion in an age of conformity. And yet Sinclair Lewis is profoundly different from either Dreiser or Anderson. He is, at bottom, a writer of social satire, and his sense of alienation is that of the lover.

There is an old belief that satire cannot be written from the outside, that a liberal, for example, might write genuine satire on liberalism, yet produce only unfair invective when he turns to conservatism. The career of Lewis supports this belief. Born in Sauk Center, Minnesota, he graduated from Yale, wrote commercially for a time, traveled, and then began writing innocuous novels, the first of which is *Our Mr. Wrenn* (1914). In 1920, with the publication of *Main Street*, Lewis emerged as a social critic of major stature. Much of the power of *Main Street* is due to the author's empathy with his characters. Dreiser's empathy, by contrast, was with man's instinct for survival, with the problem of adapting to environment; Anderson's feelings went with the sensitive outcast; but Lewis felt at one with the middle class.

The hero of *Babbitt* (1922) is neither, in Dreiser's terms, a lobster nor a squid, and he is certainly no sensitive soul. His sins are venial—a frustrated attempt to cheat on a dull wife he genuinely loves and cannot betray. His trials, with significant exceptions, are mundane: a pathetic attempt to cut down on cigars, his efforts to be a social climber. The final portrait of Babbitt—with his devotion to mechanical conveniences, middle-class snobbishness, civic boosting, a phony business ethic—seems to be a dullness unto death. But such is not the complete picture. In the end it is also the dull middle class which shows heart and comes to the rescue of an errant member. And it is Lewis's genuine sympathy with the Babbitts of the world that gives his story its final pathos. This is social protest from the inside.

In addition to *Main Street* and *Babbitt*, Lewis wrote three novels of unmistakable merit: *Arrowsmith* (1925), *Elmer Gantry* (1927), and *Dodsworth* (1929). None of the five is difficult to read, and yet all five are effective in a way that embarrasses the current critical emphasis on sophisticated techniques. The chief source of that effectiveness may lie in Lewis's ear for middle-class speech and in his ability to catch the combination of goodness and evil which suggests to us somebody we know, and which suggests more of ourselves, perhaps, than we want to admit.

SINCLAIR LEWIS
The Cosmic Bourjoyce*

by MAXWELL GEISMAR

The opening pages of *Babbitt* are ripe with the promise of sleek, noiseless limousines, concrete bridges, dicta-

---

* From Maxwell Geismar, "Sinclair Lewis: The Cosmic Bourjoyce," *The Last of the Provincials*, Boston, Houghton Mifflin Company, 1947. Reprinted by permission of the publisher.

phones, gleaming railway tracks, immense new factories, and "the song of labor in a city built—it seemed—for giants." Babbitt's house is trim, glossy, laudable, and endowed with outlets for all types of electrical devices. The mattresses in Babbitt's bedroom are "triumphant modern mattresses" while the radiators have just the proper area for scientific radiation. This is a masterpiece among bedrooms, right out of Modern Houses for Medium Incomes, and every second house in Floral Heights has a bedroom precisely like it.

Such is George F. Babbitt's inviolable castle in Zenith, U.S.A., the new capital of the rising Middle-Class Empire. "In fact there was but one thing wrong with the Babbitt house: it was not a home." There is probably only one thing wrong, too, with Babbitt's wife: the loyal, industrious Myra who has passed from a feeble disgust for their closer marital relations to a bored acquiescence. Then there are Babbitt's two children, male and female, of course, who are respectively motor-mad and movie-mad, who are always escaping from their home directly after dinner, and whom Babbitt is no more conscious of than he is "of the buttons on his coatsleeves." As the novel moves outward from Babbitt's private to his public world, one realizes how admirably also Lewis has caught other salient characteristics of a whole middle portion of our society. And as Babbitt himself, the Equalitarian Emperor, flourishes and expands in the novel, one sees the increasingly narrow and rigid character of this society: the spiritual restrictions that accompany all this accumulating material grandeur.

For material possessions are the symbol of power to Babbitt. "In the city of Zenith, in the barbarous twentieth century, a family's motor indicated its social rank as precisely as the grades of the peerage determined the rank of an English family—indeed, more precisely, considering the opinion of old country families upon newly created brewery barons and woolen-mill viscounts." These possessions mark the difference between a real-estate salesman and a realtor—between the Athletic Club and the Union Club—between the state university and the eastern colleges—between Babbitt's less successful friends, the Overbrooks, whom he snubs, and the socially prominent McKelveys, who snub him. For the sake of these possessions Babbitt sacrifices both his physical vigor ("Ought to take more exercise; keep in shape . . .") and his peace of mind ("Like to go off some place and be able to hear myself think . . ."). In the course of acquiring possessions he is forced to alienate himself from the human beings who work with him. And, having acquired them, he is forced to mold his own personality into the pattern of the social institutions which dispense or safeguard these possessions—

> Just as he was an Elk, a Booster, and a member of the Chamber of Commerce, just as the priests of the Presbyterian Church determined his every religious belief and the senators who controlled the Republican Party decided in little smoky rooms in Washington what he should think about disarmament, tariff, and Germany, so did the large national advertisers fix the surface of his life, fix what he believed to be his individuality. These standard advertised wares—toothpastes, socks, tires, cameras, instantaneous hot-water-heaters—were his symbols and proofs of excellence; at first the signs, then the substitutes, for joy and passion and wisdom.

And yet, just as the eight thousand dollars that Babbitt finally works up to is a princely sum as compared with the twenty-five hundred a year that marked the economic royalty of Gopher Prairie, so, too, the increasing social pressure to own and display his possessions destroys whatever financial security Babbitt gains—and from Babbitt himself, the first portrait of this new economic citizen, to the Gideon Planish who will represent, in 1943, the last citizen of the boom period, it is difficult to think of a Lewis figure who is not frantically seeking a larger income in order to keep abreast of his debts.

Uneasy lies the head that wears the middle-class crown. Babbitt's greatest act of self-expression is the "gorgeous abandon" of tearing up a frayed collar. Similarly, his happiest memory is of his youthful relationship with "Paulibus"—Paul Riesling, the "bohemian" of Zenith—while his deepest spiritual fulfillment is centered around the Fairy Child of his dreams—

> He was somewhere among unknown people who laughed at him. He slipped away, ran down the paths of a midnight garden, and at the gate the fairy child was waiting. . . . He was gallant and wise and well-beloved; warm ivory were her arms; and beyond perilous moors the brave sea glittered.

It is interesting to notice, though, that even in these subliminal meditations Babbitt's sexual urges are sublimated. And what is remarkable about the novel's whole view of life is the "muted tone," as it were, to which everything in the novel must conform: there can be no full release, or the promise of release, for the characters' aspirations as well as their inhibitions. Thus "Chum" Frink, the High Poet of Zenith, out on a drunken spree, expresses his own sense of failure: "Know what I could've been? I could've been a Gene Field or a James Whitcomb Riley." And when Paulibus himself, the outcast of this society who is quite as imperfect as the society itself, does finally shoot his wife in desperation, the bullet lands in her shoulder. No wonder—uneasy as Babbitt is in his own domain, restricted on the one hand by these rigid emotional taboos, surrounded on the other hand by these mysterious Economic Presences whose whims actually determine his every move: no wonder that the prevailing mood of this new Middle-Class Mogul should be one of increasing irritation.

—If not of actual fear, or dread. Over the last half of *Babbitt*, indeed, as these psychological and economic pressures are more fully exerted on the novel's hero, there is an increasingly curious tone to Lewis's celebrated realistic study of the average American man, a tone that is suggested by the architecture of the Zenith Athletic Club itself—

> The entrance lobby of the Athletic Club was Gothic, the washroom Roman Imperial, the lounge Spanish Mission, and the reading-room in Chinese Chippendale, but the gem of the club was the dining-room, the masterpiece of Ferdinand Reitman, Zenith's busiest architect. It was lofty and half-timbered, with Tudor leaded casements, an oriel, a somewhat musicianless musicians'-gallery, and tapestries believed to illustrate the granting of Magna Charta. The open beams had been hand-adzed at Jake Offutt's car-body works, the hinges were of hand-wrought iron, the wainscot studded with hand-made wooden pegs, and at one end of the room was a heraldic and hooded stone fireplace which the club's advertising-pamphlet asserted to be not only larger than any of the fireplaces in European castles but of a draught incomparably more scientific. It was also much cleaner, as no fire had ever been built in it.

This is certainly the rape of the ages to house the dupes of the great American fortunes—or even, in the realm of the Middle-Class Empire, a sort of gatehouse to the regions of the damned.[1] And so it is.

For aren't the furnishings of the Zenith A.C. more than matched by its activities? Within these walls Vergil Gunch, president of the Boosters, Professor Pumphrey of the Riteway Business College, and T. Cholmondeley— "Chum"—Frink himself, these august personages and their associates, form the new Apostles of Commerce whom "They" have especially commissioned to preach the Gospel of Profits and to preserve only the financially fit. "They," of course, are represented in turn by the Chamber

---

[1] T. K. Whipple, in a discerning essay in *Spokesmen*, has caught this undertone in Lewis's work, and Robert Cantwell has amplified it in his excellent study of Lewis that appears in *After the Genteel Tradition*.

of Commerce, the State Association of Real Estate Boards (the SAREB), the Good Citizens' League, and the other organizations whose conferences and conventions fill the pages of *Babbitt* with that series of incredible and ghastly scenes of good fellowship and good business. Such an episode as that where Chum Frink pleads for the cause of Music in Zenith—"Some of you may feel that it's out of place here to talk on a strictly highbrow and artistic subject, but I want to come out flat-footed and ask you boys to O.K. the proposition of a Symphony Orchestra for Zenith. . . . Now, I want to confess that, though I'm a literary guy by profession, I don't care a rap for all this long-haired music. I'd rather listen to a good jazz band any time than to some piece by Beethoven that hasn't any more tune to it than a bunch of fighting cats, and you couldn't whistle it to save your life! But that isn't the point. Culture has become as necessary an adornment and advertisement for a city today as pavements and bank-clearances. . . . The thing to do, then, as a live bunch of go-getters, is to *capitalize Culture*; to go right out and grab it."—Or where the various delegations from Zenith, the Zip City; Shelby County, the Garden Spot of God's Own Country, Monarch, the Mighty Motor Mart; Hamburg, the Big Little City with the Logical Location; or Galop dé Vache, the Town for Homey Folks—present their credentials to the State Association of Real Estate Boards.[2]—Or where "Mike Monday," who has turned the minds of workmen "from wages and hours to higher things, and thus averted strikes" in every city he appears in, opens his spiritual exhortations. ("There's a lot of smart college pro-

---

[2] It is interesting, incidentally, to compare the main emphasis of Willa Cather or of Sherwood Anderson on the western countryside—the land itself—with Lewis's emphasis on real-estate developments. Miss Cather's heroes, for example, are those who own the land "for a little while," as she says, because they love it —but Lewis's heroes would probably be in a bad spot if they were forced to own the land for more than a little while.

fessors and tea-guzzling slobs in this burg that say I'm a roughneck and a never-wuzzer and my knowledge of history is not-yet. Oh, there's a gang of woolly-whiskered booklice that think they know more than Almighty God, and prefer a lot of Hun science and smutty German criticism to the straight and simple Word of God. . . .")—Or where Babbitt himself, as he approaches his office, the core of his life, the central source of all that material power and splendor that is spreading and flourishing as Zenith itself spreads and flourishes, finds himself walking faster and faster and muttering, "Guess better hustle," since—

> All about him the city was hustling, for hustling's sake. Men in motors were hustling to pass one another in the hustling traffic. Men were hustling to catch trolleys, with another trolley a minute behind, and to leap from the trolleys, to gallop across the sidewalk, to hurl themselves into buildings, into hustling express elevators. Men in dairy lunches were hustling to gulp down the food which cooks had hustled to fry. Men in barber shops were snapping, "Jus' shave me once over. Gotta hustle." Men were feverishly getting rid of visitors in offices adorned with the signs, "This Is My Busy Day" and "The Lord Created the World in Six Days—You Can Spiel All You Got to Say in Six Minutes." Men who had made five thousand, year before last, and ten thousand last year, were urging on nerve-yelping bodies and parched brains so that they might make twenty thousand this year; and the men who had broken down immediately after their twenty thousand dollars were hustling to catch trains, to hustle through the vacations which the hustling doctors had ordered.

—Such episodes as these—steadily accumulating in the course of the novel, growing more and more macabre in tone and more and more dense and oppressive in their atmospheric pressure, as it were, until they are finally almost overwhelming in their effect—form the milieu of Babbitt's public life. Notice, too, the series of nightmarish impressions he begins to have about his private life: the "incessant hiss of whispering" that he hears as he walks the streets in his moments of rebellion or of dissipation; the fits of primitive terror that he endures at night as he lies awake shivering at the prospect of "anything so unknown and so embarrassing as freedom"; the relapse into the "close hot tomb" of his Pullman berth after another jovial business session. Even the Fairy Child of Babbitt's dreams who has come to life in the Tanis Judique, who is his mistress, takes on, in a curious turn of the narrative, a dreamlike quality that is not altogether pleasant. And Myra Babbitt herself, as Babbitt sees her lying on the operating table, becomes in turn "a swathed thing . . . . a mound of white in the midst of which was a square of sallow flesh with a gash a little bloody at the edges; protruding from the gash a cluster of forceps like clinging parasites. . . ."

But Lewis has set his stage very early in one of the most violent and effective episodes in the novel—the first big "party" on Floral Heights at which Babbitt, the glad host, is practically overcome by the food and drink, the gossip, the boasting, the "jokes." "Everything about him was dim except his stomach, and that was a bright scarlet disturbance. He felt as though he had been stuffed with clay; his body was bursting . . . his brain was hot mud; and only with agony did he continue to smile and shout as became a host on Floral Heights." It is in this state that there appears before him the apparition of "the Wop poet" who has been called from the shadows by Zenith's amateur spiritualists.

"O, Laughing Eyes, emerge forth into the, uh, ultimates," cries Chum Frink. "You forgot to give um the address," chuckles Vergil Gunch—"1658 Brimstone Avenue, Fiery Heights, Hell." And Fiery Heights is absolutely the proper address, and the mangled specter of Dante is the true presiding genius of Zenith. . . . The central scenes of *Babbitt* can hardly be explained by the ordinary categories of "satire"—and this almost classical example of photographic American "realism" is realistic only in terms of its introductory setting—and there, also, only to a degree. In the central concept of the novel, in its final and dominant mood, and in the craft technics which first suggest and then fully project its true theme, *Babbitt* is, on the contrary, an imaginative work of a high order. It is, if anything, close to poetry. Or at least, from its inception in Babbitt's bedroom, "as neat and as negative as a block of artificial ice," to the conclusion of its latest and biggest real-estate deal, it is almost a perfectly conceived poetic vision of a perfectly standardized money society; it is our native *Inferno* of the mechanized hinterland. Even the "Great Strike" that grips Zenith toward the close of the novel is a middle-class nightmare of a workers' revolt in which the workers are as vague as they are ominous.

In this connection the familiar objection to the novel —the fact that even George F. Babbitt himself could never possibly be so *complete* a Babbitt—becomes, of course, the novel's main virtue; while the familiar criticism of the novelist's "ear" must also be set aside, temporarily anyhow. The language of Lewis's people is certainly not the language of the small-town and city people who have hitherto existed in the United States, nor even that of our present day Rotarians. It is not Mencken's and Lardner's language of the American people, either. But it can serve very well—tricky, synthetic, and prefabricated as it is—as the medium for some future Utopia of Rotary. It is the verbiage of a super-public-relations counsel in an absolute hysteria of brotherhood; it is the vocabulary of International Big Business designed and tooled for a race of synthetic and prefabricated common men; it is the new global lingo of the machine and the cartel.

F. SCOTT FITZGERALD

(1896–1940)

During the "roaring twenties," Americans bought cars and prohibition liquor and went on a mad party. The "war to end war," the "war to make the world safe for democracy," was over, and in its wake lurked the uneasy feeling that death had been defied, and the life that remained was a bonus, to be spent lavishly, or the feeling that death waited ahead in a world not really safe for anything, and one should live while he could. This, the "roaring" aspect of the twenties, is well known, but what is not generally given its due is another, an opposite though equally strong aspect of that decade.

Too many forget that prohibition itself was, from the viewpoint of the electorate, a conservative act. The three presidents elected during the twenties, for example, were Harding, Coolidge, and Hoover—all conservatives. The twenties did "roar," but they were also years in which the majority cry was "back to normalcy."

F. Scott Fitzgerald, the voice of the twenties, spoke for the wildness of his period, both in his art and in his life; but his fiction and at least one part of his life represent also a conservatism, and thus we must be judicious if we are to recognize fully the precarious combination that was the paradoxical author of The Great Gatsby.

Fitzgerald belonged to the upper middle class (Francis Scott Key was an ancestor), and he fell in love with the fabulous Zelda, a wealthy and beautiful party girl who told him quite frankly that she liked him but that he could not afford her. Industriously, Fitzgerald set to work and *This Side of Paradise* (1920) brought him fame and money. He and Zelda were married, and the party began. From America to Europe, the Fitzgeralds were the chief attraction for parties that have become a legend. Zelda, for example, is said to have danced wildly on tables, once climaxing her performance by removing her black lace panties and tossing them to Alexander Woollcott. Overcome by the gesture, Woollcott hurled himself from a high parapet, into the ocean below, as an appropriate response.

Even while racing toward an obvious destruction, however, Fitzgerald was a craftsman, an artist. His bursts of discipline—while turning out slick stories at high prices to finance the parties—are as incredible as they are pathetic. And his letters to his daughter (reprinted in *The Crack-Up*) reveal an artistic integrity which is confirmed by his best work, most notably *The Great Gatsby* (1925), *Tender Is the Night* (1934), and a dozen or so short stories.

A comparable paradox characterizes Jay Gatsby, the hero of Fitzgerald's finest work. Gatsby is a romantic who believes you can go back, who believes absolutely that the perfect moment of youth and love can be recaptured. Fitzgerald, who was inclined himself to dream of times of glory and romance, knew both the charm and the fate of Gatsby's dreams. In his formative years, Gatsby followed an idealized program of self-improvement, a program that suggests figures so unlike Gatsby as Ben Franklin and Abraham Lincoln, a program that sparked his success while it prepared him for his doom. There was enough fact in Gatsby's rise to mislead him into believing that he could win, and enough reality in the dream itself to lure him into compromises and poses that would be his undoing.

Gatsby's curious manner, his gaudy and hauntingly unreal parties, and his vague claims on respectability all contain this very American paradox. True, Gatsby's manner is a bit awkward. At times it seems patently false. Yet Gatsby's manner has about it a stubborn dignity. It is more honest, in the final analysis, than the smooth polish of a Jordan Baker or a Tom Buchanan. And Gatsby is, frankly, a crook, with underworld associates whose desertion seems to represent the second murdering of Fitzgerald's enigmatic hero. But in the end, Nick Carraway, the narrator, prefers Gatsby to all the rest, and Carraway is a very moral young man who believes that man should use his reason and his inner sense of right to control his passions and to guide his life.

Thus Fitzgerald has shown us a good deal more than a picture of the "roaring twenties." In *The Great Gatsby*, as in a few other works, he has, by holding in the mind at the same time two opposite ideas, met the test of intelligence he himself once prescribed; and in the process he has made a profound insight into the American paradox.

THE GREAT GATSBY
Style and Myth*

by DOUGLAS TAYLOR

Few critics dispute the superbness of Scott Fitzgerald's achievement in *The Great Gatsby*. In precision of workmanship, elegance of prose style, and control of dramatic point of view, it represents to my mind Fitz-

---

* From Douglas Taylor, "*The Great Gatsby*: Style and Myth," *University of Kansas City Review*, XX (Autumn, 1953), 30–37. Reprinted by permission of the publisher.

Passages from *The Great Gatsby* reprinted by permission of Charles Scribner's Sons.

gerald's genius at its sustained best. No other novel of the period, with the exception of *The Sun Also Rises*, can be said to have succeeded so perfectly in transforming the mind and manners of its time into something artistically worthy of the intense moral and social conditions which produced them. The features of the book which stand out most strongly in one's mind—the swirling, sideshow anonymity of Gatsby's Long Island parties, the huge, ominous eyes of the oculist's sign brooding perpetually over the hot, desolate "valley of ashes," the shrill, oppressive atmosphere of Myrtle Wilson's flat, the brutal, cowardly truculence of Tom Buchanan, the poignant dream and pathetic bad taste of Gatsby himself—concentrate a multiple image of an America that had lost its standards and its sense of the moral fitness of things, and had given itself over to a self-deceiving myth that would some day come apart like wet cardboard.

The book is so very good that one is tempted occasionally to go along with the assumption that some influence, other than his own moral growth, operated to aid his imagination in organizing and disciplining his thought and feeling as maturely as it did. Nevertheless, the use of a dramatic narrator to unify a series of swift and intensive scenes was a technique ideally adapted to a talent of Fitzerald's kind, for, aside from the advantages of compositional compactness, such a method allowed his imagination to project in the form and subject of the novel a conception which enabled him to externalize and to exploit simultaneously from within and without both sides of a nature that was split between sentiment and self-criticism. Gatsby and Nick Carraway unquestionably are coextensive with his own feelings about each side of this nature, and are developed within a context of insights which control their precise moral and creative meanings through a bifocal view that manipulates at once the attitudes of intimacy and detachment with a distinctness that is never blurred.

Fitzgerald's bifurcated relation to his experience, so eloquently underscored in *Gatsby*, has been commented upon frequently by his critics, but Malcolm Cowley has provided the perfect figure to concretize the opposition in Fitzgerald's temperament between the wish to belong and the fear of being unaccepted, between the impulse to participate and the tendency to observe, a man who desired to do and yet to become. "He cultivated a sort of double vision," wrote Mr. Cowley—

> It was as if all his novels described a big dance to which he had taken . . . the prettiest girl . . . and as if at the same time he stood outside the ballroom, a little Midwestern boy with his nose to the glass, wondering how much the tickets cost and who paid for the music.[1]

This sense of "double vision" informs both the general organization of *Gatsby* and the arrangement of its smallest thematic details, and, at one point very early in the narrative, Fitzgerald seems to have imbedded in a casual reflection of Nick Carraway's an image which not only emphasizes this double view and represents what may be Fitzgerald's own evaluation of one of the major defects of his earlier novels, but offers a possible esthetic justification for the novel's form as well. It is when Nick, having settled at West Egg and looking forward to the long, quiet days of summer, decides to revive a somewhat neglected habit of reading, doing so with the feeling that ". . . I was going to bring back all such things into my life and become again that most limited of all specialists, the 'well-rounded man.' This isn't just an epigram—*life is much more successfully looked at from a single window, after all.*"[2] Invariably, Nick's experience will demonstrate both

---

[1] "Third Act and Epilogue," *New Yorker*, XXI (June 30, 1945), 54.
[2] F. Scott Fitzgerald, *The Great Gatsby* (New York: Charles Scribner's Sons, 1925), p. 5. (Italics mine.) All references will be made to this edition unless otherwise indicated.

an aspect of his nature and the bifocal continuity of the book itself, as when he pauses wistfully amidst the busy loneliness of the New York evening to watch a thick congestion of crowded taxicabs moving toward the theatre district, and notes how "Forms leaned together in the taxis as they waited, and voices sang, and there was laughter from unheard jokes, and lighted cigarettes made unintelligible circles inside. Imagining that I, too, was hurrying toward gayety and sharing their intimate excitement, I wished them well."[3] The fine control of language in this passage, with its precise use of detail that mingles several qualities of sensation in a swift interplay of mood, feeling, and idea, the tonal proportions of the colloquial rhythms of the first sentence that evoke and lengthen, through its strong liquid properties, the extent of Nick's longing for the warmth and attachment the experience suggests, the sudden withdrawal and running-away of the emotion expressed in the half-nostalgic, half-ironic "I wished them well," indicates the degree to which Fitzgerald's imagination had matured along with the sense of poetic artistry which could compress and modulate variations of action, character, and atmosphere in words that could feel through to the essential quality of a situation and reproduce its most accurate overtones. This flexible and lyrically differentiated kind of prose is duplicated on every page of the novel, and represents a very real development over the confused mixture of tonal and stylistic peccancies that cluttered his earlier writing, where his uncertainty and insufficiency of understanding tended to force him into the use of illegitimate rhetorical and incantatory devices of language in an attempt to communicate intensities of feeling inaccessible to his imagination.

In Nick Carraway, Fitzgerald conceived a figure who was to function as a center of moral and compositional

---

[3] *Ibid.*, p. 70.

activity which fused both the dramatic action and the values it implied. His character, though literally credible, can be regarded as a kind of choric voice, a man who embodies the moral conscience of his race, ". . . a guide, a pathfinder, an original settler,"[4] who ". . . wanted the world to be . . . at a sort of moral attention forever,"[5] but never forgets that ". . . a sense of the fundamental decencies is parcelled out unequally at birth."[6] The very form and larger idea of the novel allows for this possibility, and throughout the narrative, such a relation to the action is suggested both by the nature of his detached moral involvement and by the pitch and timbre of a diction that compels one to have an instinctive faith in his point of view.

Furthermore, it is the position of Fitzgerald to bring out some of the most subtle and ironic proportions of his subject matter by juxtaposing Nick's feelings and the context from which they issue. In the scene, for example, where Daisy and Gatsby meet after five years, Fitzgerald has used the image of a defunct mantelpiece clock to symbolize the discontinuity of time their reunion implies. Gatsby, nervous and miserably uncomfortable, and leaning against the mantel, had almost knocked the clock to the floor—

"I'm sorry about the clock," [Gatsby] said.
My own face had now assumed a deep tropical burn. I couldn't muster up a single commonplace out of the thousand in my head.
"It's an old clock," I told them idiotically.
I think we all believed for a moment that it had smashed in pieces on the floor.
"We haven't met for many years," said Daisy, her voice as matter-of-fact as it could ever be.
"Five years next November."

[4] Ibid., p. 4.
[5] Ibid., p. 2.
[6] Ibid., p. 2.

The automatic quality of Gatsby's answer set us all back at least another minute.[7]

The tonal and compositional elements of this passage develop with faultless imaginative detail a tension between inner feeling and outer statement which generates the most evocative kind of emotional and atmospheric irony: the awkward banality of the conversational surface which runs counter to the seriousness of the subject combines with Nick's "It's an old clock" to carry the irony forward in the phrase "smashed in pieces," and, moving with appropriate figurativeness through the diminishing segments of the remembered time-sequence expressed in "many years" and "five years" to the audacious telescoping of Nick's "set us all back at least another minute," it functions to obliterate artistically the immensity of the moral and psychological distance which separates Gatsby's dream and Daisy's presence, and connects itself dramatically with the image of the defunct clock to complete and reinforce the unsensed irony. This running concentration both of intellect and emotion in Nick's central intelligence thus allowed Fitzgerald to control and intensify the internal and external proportions of his subject in modes which held its values in distinct but inter-animated states of sympathy and evaluation, a method which resulted in a dramatic effectiveness he had never before achieved.

II

Inasmuch as Nick Carraway's point of view represents the significant moral force of *Gatsby*, one is led inevitably to recognize the nature of Jay Gatsby's "incorruptible dream" through the continuous series of moral and emotional insights which reflect Nick's understanding of the importance of the values involved. In spite of the pathetically naive assumptions which lie behind Gatsby's vision

---

[7] *Ibid.*, p.109.

of life, Nick chooses ultimately to commit himself to the beliefs it fosters, because, seen against the callous, destructive charm of Daisy and Tom Buchanan's world, it becomes, to his mind, not the gaudy, unsplendid show-piece which attracts the vagrant and the vulgar, but a creative dream of intense magic and passion of purpose that flows from an innate fineness of heart and feeling. It is the worth and dignity of which the human will and imagination is capable traduced by a specious conviction, inarguably American in character, that the noblest intensities of existence are available if the objects with which they are ostensibly synonymous can be possessed. Such a conviction impels Gatsby to believe that his pink suits and period rooms will somehow secure his dream's right to reality, and to disregard tragically the qualitative points of difference between the self-conscious standards of a superimposed wealth and those ingrained in the certitudes of an aristocratic moneyed class. He assumes, with all the immaturity of his race, that living across the courtesy bay from Daisy entitles him to share the complicated dimensions of her world, but the distance which separates them is of a greater and less tangible kind than any narrow extension of water or the green dock-light toward which he yearns: there are all the years of Daisy's assurance and certainty and self-indulgent pride, a way of life that has made her ignorant of unsatisfied longings and of wishes that could not be had, a whole cynical hierarchy of things taken for granted, like her expensive home in Louisville that always hinted of ". . . bedrooms upstairs more beautiful and cool than other bedrooms. . . ," and seemed ". . . as casual a thing to her as [Gatsby's] tent out at camp was to him."[8] But enchanted by the amenity and charm of Daisy and her world, by the romantic possibilities for subtlety and graciousness of purpose its mystery and mo-

---

[8] *Ibid.*, pp. 177–78.

bility promise, he commits the force of his idealizing imagination to the intense, allusive variousness of its life. His personal tragedy is his failure to understand the complex quality of the mind and motives which go into her fine-seeming world of wealth, for he is captivated by the delightful, exquisitely ordered surface without discerning the behind-the-doors ruthlessness, the years of infinite duplicity and subterfuge that a shrewd, self-preoccupied class has practiced to preserve the power and well-being such a surface implies. Only after the accident, when his vision starts to come to pieces like one of those toy clocks won at carnivals, and he has ". . . lost the old warm world, paid a high price for living too long with a single dream,"[9] does he probably sense how very different the very rich are. "They were careless people," Nick concludes of Tom and Daisy, ". . . they smashed up things and creatures and then retreated back into their money or their vast carelessness, or whatever it was that kept them together, and let other people clean up the mess they had made. . . ,"[10] and the most eloquent irony of the novel is generated by the subtle interplay between, on the one hand, the elegance and charm of Daisy's world as opposed to the cunningness of its inner corruption and, on the other, the gaudy elaborateness of Gatsby's efforts to emulate its surface as contrasted with the uncontaminated fineness of his heart.

In the frantic tenacity of Gatsby's belief that the conditions of both youth and love could be repeated if a way of life commensurate with their particular circumstances could be evolved, the whole complex tissue of Fitzgerald's feeling about time, money, and emotional innocence are developed along with the mixture of sympathy and insight his own divided temperament adopted toward these features of experience. Like Gatsby, Fitzgerald felt very strongly about the sadness and magic of the past and the

[9] *Ibid.,* p. 194.
[10] *Ibid.,* p. 216.

remembrance of the youth and hope and feeling that had gone into its rush of individual moments, as he felt an intense fascination for the life of inherited wealth; but, unlike him, Fitzgerald, though committed imaginatively to both the charm and necessity of such sentiments, understood their value critically and creatively in relation to their total effect on human life and conduct. And in the themes of youth and wealth, two of the most brooding, compulsive images of the American mind, the one with all its overtones of romance, virtue, and emotional intactness, the other with its corresponding associations of happiness and a kind of millennial fulfillment—with the possible irony of corruption—Fitzgerald took hold of the essential qualities by which the American experience could be interpreted and expressed, and the last pages of the novel make explicit the significance of Gatsby as an avatar of a national consciousness that has committed the manifold vastness of its resources to the acquisition of ". . . the orgastic [sic] future that year by year recedes before us."[11] His story takes on the proportions of a mythic or archetypal idea: his dream becomes the tawdry, painted dream of a continent that has forfeited its will to the infinite, deceptive optimisms of film and advertising gauds which have the finality of excommunicatory edicts, while his parties, set in a world that is ". . . material without being real, where poor ghosts, breathing dreams like air, drifted fortuitously about. . . ,"[12] crystallize into the whirling incoherence that stands for the obtrusive, unfeeling largeness of the American social experience itself.

III

In developing the implications of his theme, Fitzgerald seems to have further enriched their quality by uniting them—perhaps unconsciously—with a level of

[11] *Ibid.*, p. 218.
[12] *Ibid.*, p. 194.

social-anagogic meaning that is at once actual and ironic in its dimensions. With frequent scriptural analogies which, though only general in outline, evoke echoes of the Last Supper, the Week of the Passion, and the Crucifixion, as well as numerous other Biblical accounts, Gatsby and the recurring symbols of the novel are given a quality of profane divineness which points ironically toward the idea of a land and people whose actual deification of its aggressive faith in its vision of life has become a formidable secular dogma. The statement that ". . . Jay Gatsby of West Egg, Long Island, sprang from his Platonic conception of himself," that "He was a son of God—a phrase which, if it means anything, means just that—and he must be about His Father's business, the service of a vast, vulgar, and meretricious beauty,"[13] confirms one's feeling that Fitzgerald had in mind the thought of the "self-formed" nation that has made "the American dream" a pageantry and "the success story" an ideal, a nation which is withdrawing progressively from the social, moral, and political reality that surrounds and affects its daily actions into a specious but comforting public image of itself which every popular feature of its cultural life has helped to create and is compelled to maintain. Thus, Gatsby, overtly identified with the figure of Christ, can be regarded as morally and poetically interchangeable with the spirit of a land that believes its destiny to transcend both natural and human limitations, and which, like Simon Magus (Acts 8: 9–24), the sorcerer of Samaria who bewitched the people into thinking he had the power of God, and with whom Fitzgerald seems to have crossed the Christ-image to reinforce the irony of his meaning, is convinced its wealth can buy the mystery of the Holy Ghost.

To realize this aspect of his theme and to engage it cogently with the national drama it signifies, Fitzgerald

---

[13] *Ibid.*, p. 118.

developed the general character of Gatsby's experience to
correspond with that of the life and agony of Christ. From
the moment he boards Dan Cody's yacht on Lake Superior
until his burial and subsequent resurrection in the wonder
of the "Dutch sailors' eyes,"[14] the movement of his life
follows the triadic rhythm of both Christian and pre-Chris-
tian myth: purpose, passion, pain, or insight: Denying his
parents, his symbolic rebirth aboard the yacht, coinciding
with the phrase "His Father's business," parallels Christ's
action at the Temple (Luke 2: 46–49), where he disclaims
Joseph and Mary, saying " 'I must be about My Father's
business,' " while Gatsby's travel with Dan Cody, his almost genuflective feeling for Daisy, his blue, purposive
parties that spin out like cotton-candy the fluff and faith of
a "Universe of ineffable gaudiness"[15] suggest respectively,
and by profane contrast, Christ's temptation on the Mountain (Luke 4: 4–8), when Satan let Him look on "all the
kingdoms of the world in a moment of time," His passionate visionary love of man, and His itinerant dissemination
of an incorruptible, unpretentious faith that offered another kind of mystery and achievement. Moreover, the
rapid unfolding of crucial scenes which lead up to
Gatsby's burial—the furtive, unquiet indefiniteness of his
reunion with Daisy, the ridding of his house of party-
goers, her deliberate words at the luncheon that betray
their liaison to Tom,[16] the struggle, or *agon*, between the
two men in the suite at the Plaza,[17] Daisy's cowardly,
conspiratorial behavior following the accident, Tom's vi-
cious report to Wilson which results in Gatsby's death, the
trial, denial, and flight of Daisy, of Wolfsheim, of Klip-
springer, of the multitude of hangers-on who lived gain-
fully on his dream's outer edges—have their sacred equiva-

---

[14] *Ibid.*, p. 217.
[15] *Ibid.*, p. 119.
[16] *Ibid.*, p. 142.
[17] *Ibid.*, pp. 154-62.

lents in the accounts in the Gospels of the Passion, the Last Supper, and the Crucifixion, which relate variously Christ's precariousness and distress in His final week of life, His purging of the Temple, Judas' apostasy and betrayal, His arraignment before the Pharisaic Sanhedrin and struggle with Caiaphas, the High Priest, His false accusers, the trial, denial, and flight of Peter and the disciples, and His execration and crucifixion by the mob. The scriptural analogy is made complete when Gatsby's father, like the titular Joseph, arrives to bury his son, and by the sudden appearance at the funeral of "Owl-Eyes," whose metonymic name points poetically to the grotesque omniscience of the oculist's sign—the novel's fantastic image of the commercialized desolation of the American spirit—and whose presence corporealizes the symbol of Gatsby's spiritual Father. (Appropriately, both men, each seeming to make tangible a side of Gatsby's antipodal nature—Gatz, his veneration of the vulgar and the ostentatious, "Owl-Eyes," his inner fineness and generous integrity of mind—are brought together at his grave to suggest dramatically the deathly release and return of substance and spirit to their beginnings.) In the final pages, Nick's reflective identification of Gatsby with the Dutch sailors and the American past can be viewed, in a sense, as a resurrection, for it evokes and gives a transient lyric body to the memory of a dead dream that lies ". . . somewhere back in that vast obscurity beyond the city, where the dark fields of the republic rolled on under the night,"[18] reincarnating him in a past he tried so desperately to revive, and uniting its quality with the idea of a nation which persists wistfully and religiously in its belief in the inexhaustible fullness of its native possibilities.

If this hasty and somewhat superficial analogic reading of *Gatsby* is considered as a possible approach to its

---

[18] *Ibid.*, p. 218.

larger moral content, then Gatsby's death, as Christ's, can be understood as a symbolic enactment of the concept of the mythic Scapegoat-Hero but its dramatization in a context which runs against its positive religious implications of rejuvenescence and redemption turns its meaning into one of ironic nullification and defeat. Aside from the literal aspects of Gatsby's preparation for swimming and the manner of his death, the details which invest these final actions have a suggestiveness of tone that accommodates itself tenably to this ritualistic concept of piety and consecration: his bathing trunks, the finality and passivity of his movements, the appropriately autumnal season, his death on water and the slow, symbolic commingling of his blood with the pool's motion to describe within a revolving cluster of dead leaves "a thin red circle" on its surface[19] carry strong overtones of a primitive kind of sacrificial readiness for death which, combined with the immediate factor of natural infertility and decline, echo something of the old animistic response to affliction and unrest, the ceremonious mutilation of life for spiritual salvation and renewal through the reintegrative mystery of death and transfiguration. The circular unity of the image on the surface of the pool, however, confutes whatever expectancy of expiration one traditionally connects with the spirit of such a rite, for, in addition to spelling out the rounded, repetitive pattern of Gatsby's life—his withdrawal and rebirth by water, the circular direction of his dream, his return by water, the foreshadowing of his rain-wet burial—, the image reverberates with an overwhelming connotation of nullity to negate and silence the opposed associations which call up not only the apocalyptic flow of blood and water from the pierced, dying body of Christ, but evoke as well the figure of earth with all its suggestions of efficacy and regeneration, and telescope

---

[19] *Ibid.*, pp. 193-95.

ultimately into the reproductive symbol of the vaginal orifice. Furthermore, this affirmation of nullity is given substantial ironic reinforcement by the artistic fact which identifies Gatsby's death with the autumnal processes of decay (of which the circular image is but a compressed iteration) rather than with the fecund generative powers of spring, as was the case in both the ancient vegetation ceremonies and the greater ritual form of the Crucifixion, a calculated displacement of mythic stress which rounds off the archetypal dimensions of Fitzgerald's irony and points up its relation to a richer and more permanent context of human meaning.

As Yeats and Eliot and Joyce had seized on ancient dignities to gather flux into an "artifice of eternity," so Fitzgerald has used myth in *The Great Gatsby* in a less monumental fashion to alchemize the anarchy of modern life into a unity and permanence. Whatever one may think of the moral beliefs such a device assumes, the manipulation particularly of the novel's climax in ritual terms to dignify a tragic but otherwise commonplace homicide seems to me an extremely effective method for representing, by contrast with the vital social-religious solidarity of antiquity, the contemporary break-up, decline, and disappearance of that intense, imperative kind of spiritual awareness which unifies with its commonly-held hierarchy of values and attachments every layer of a social-cultural complex, and which combines conscience and imagination in the feelings and ideas it projects into the forms and ceremony of religious belief. It is the dramatic postulation of such an awareness which generates in proportion to the degree of its absence in modern American life the ironic moral interplay between the values associated with the symbolic quality of Gatsby's death and the actual remoteness or exclusion of these same values from the moral habits which the American national mind takes for granted. Lacking this awareness, and at best only popularly or unctuously attached to the traditional spiritual resources which nourished and deepened the indefatigable faith of atavistic America, its total national life is given over to a vulgar optimism of illimitableness and extravagance of achievement that ostensibly issues from the composite character of its national past, but to which it bears only the most spurious and distorted kind of relation. Not only does its outlook rest on premises which vitiate the spirit of historical America, but it also has come to acknowledge little more than a perfunctory connection with the moral values which gave a firmness and vitality of purpose to the visionary shapings of the continent by ancestral Americans.

Something of this ambiguous moral reciprocity between modern America and the quality of its national past is sounded throughout the novel in the reiterative "ghost" and its variant "ghostly," verbal motifs which function technically to modulate character and condition, but which, in addition to anticipating and advancing the literal plot element, serve also to strengthen the total aspect of the thematic design. Suggesting, as they do, through an ironic association with the Holy Ghost, the spiritual destitution of a people who, like Dante's Trimmers on the circle outside the Acheron, are rejected both by Heaven and Hell, the motifs lead into the morally related idea of a land which has continued to rely for its identity on a myth of itself and its past until the social-historical reality it reflects has neither the substance of a physical present nor the definiteness of the historical past, but drifts, as intangible and defunct as the dream it seeks to possess, between two modes of reality to neither of which it can ever rightly belong. In this last respect, Fitzgerald has brought into immediate focus a problem which is central to both the novel's theme and to human experience in general—the rich, equivocal reciprocity between two urgent and equally deceptive orders of being: the opposition between the levels of appearance and reality, between mind and activity, between what seems and what is. Does the past have an existential reality to which the novel's characters, as ghosts, do not belong; or is the past a ghost in which the characters, as people, unreally perform? Which reality is more valid from the point of view of moral and emotional experience, the subjective or objective past or present, historical America or its immediately modern counterpart? The problem in its more pandemic sense is one which Lionel Trilling has observed in another context to be the concern of all literature,[20] and in suggesting its nature with reference both to the overall development of his central theme and to the subtle inweaving of his parallels, Fitzgerald achieved a unity and completeness of artistic expression which, in range and depth of general import, gives an encompassing and enduring force to the multiplicity of American moral and social experience. In doing so, he revealed not a romantic limitation of insight, as Mr. Mizener seems to think, in committing Nick Carraway—and himself—to Gatsby's point of view,[21] but rather a discipline and sureness of mind which led him to sense somehow that Jay Gatsby was at once larger and more significant in the issues he dramatized than the literalness concentrated in his "capacity for wonder."

IV

In elucidating above what seemed to me to be the social-anagogic undertones of *Gatsby*, I have attempted to bring into relief a somewhat different set of relations inhering in its content without wishing either to dislocate too severely its superb coördination of thought and feeling or to give the impression of stretching it over a per-

---

[20] "Manners, Morals, and the Novel," *The Liberal Imagination* (New York: The Viking Press, 1950), p. 207.
[21] *The Far Side of Paradise* (Boston: Houghton Mifflin Co., 1951), p. 170.

verse procrustean bed of meaning. Neither has it been my object to claim for such a view an oracular exactness it cannot have, nor to suggest that the relations indicated were to any real extent a defined or consciously controlled part of Fitzgerald's intention. If, as is apparently the case, Fitzgerald was unaware of his theme's connections with religious myth, it does not inevitably mean that these same connections may not have functioned within the deeper ethical folds of his imagination as a quiet archetypal modifier of the known quality of his feelings about his subject.

Over and above this suggested archetypal mode of imagination, however, Fitzgerald, though probably having little more than conversational familiarity with the great anthropological works of his day, with Harrison or Frazer or Jung, assumedly would have had a very natural and fluent understanding of the Bible owing to the early religious training of his Irish-Catholic background, and it is this powerful imaginative influence, as well as the moral atmosphere of which it was a part, that can be said to have contributed largely to the formation of the quality of mind which, as Mr. Mizener has pointed out, makes his ". . . basic feeling for experience . . . a religious one."[22] It is represented with greater dramatic force in the extended irony of *Gatsby*, but it is more or less present in everything he wrote. Thus, fixed, as they were, by an older and more conscionable view of experience, the scrupulous and religiously imbued attitudes which gave to everything he did the seriousness of a canonical imperative set Fitzgerald genuinely apart from the fashionable looseness of his day enabling him to disengage his moral, and hence, his creative, self from the reckless dissipations of an age to which his imprudent, romantic self was at the same time committed. And it is, I think, one of the unfortunate ironies of

---

[22] *Ibid.*, p. 86.

Fitzgerald's career that his life and art should be remembered synonymously with the adulteries and corruptions of the Jazz Age and Boom, when actually he was, like so many other serious writers of his generation, an ethical product of an older order, one which derived its sense of moral conduct from a firm belief in the importance of what he once described as ". . . 'good instincts,' honor, courtesy, and courage,"[23] those ". . . eternal necessary human values"[24] which were fundamentally opposed to the violent indecorums of the age he is popularly supposed to represent.

---

[23] *Tender Is the Night*, p. 266.
[24] "Echoes of the Jazz Age," *The Crack-Up*, p. 22.

THOMAS WOLFE

(1900 – 1938)

Throughout the development of American literature many of our major writers have undertaken in widely different ways to answer Emerson's call for a native literature, one that would give shape to the American experience. One version has been that of writers, like Walt Whitman, who see America itself as "the greatest poem," writers who seek through epic sweep and far-ranging examples, through intimate probing of the consciousness, through symbolic lists and democratic protests to capture the variety and the bigness of America in its intimate meaning to the individual.

Thomas Wolfe, like any writer worth reading, is original, but he belongs nonetheless in this broad tradition. Born and raised in North Carolina, Wolfe studied at the University of North Carolina (B.A., 1920) and at Harvard (M.A., 1922), reading—granted that his claims are exaggerated—prodigiously. A row of books in a library were for Wolfe a challenge, almost an affront. In his passion for learning, as in his hunger for experience, he wanted all and was contemptuous of people satisfied with anything less than all.

Wolfe's insatiable appetite, his tirades and passions, and his capacity for love produced a prose which has been misread by those who are impatient with an artist possessed. It has been said that Wolfe omitted nothing, sought everything, and therefore found nothing; that he was an incurable romantic whose novels are formless and had to be put together by editors. The charge, it must be admitted, does point out his limitation. Wolfe could never understand the word *select*. To him it meant *denial*, an unrealistic and bookish fear of that which stinks or frightens or disgusts or does not fit some pedant's theory of what life ought to be. But the argument between passion and control is as old as man, and it is that old because both sides express a part of that elusive thing we call the truth. (An excellent example of the argument is the famous exchange of letters between Wolfe and F. Scott Fitzgerald, reprinted in Fitzgerald's *The Crack-Up*.) The history of the argument, as a matter of fact, may cause us to misread both sides, expecting no passion in control and no control in passion.

Look Homeward, Angel (1929), Wolfe's first novel, is perhaps a better formed novel than some of the critics have realized. Eugene Gant, the young hero of the novel, is an autobiographical hero. Wolfe has not only admitted it, he has proclaimed it, insisting that all writing is autobiographical. Some critics therefore, and quite understandably, have concluded that the outrages of Gant are the outrages of Wolfe, that the foolish romanticisms of the young hero reveal the shallowness of the mind of his creator. But this reading, however autobiographical the novel, ignores an ironic tone which is successfully blended with a romantic vision. Wolfe, especially in his use of literary allusions, is ironic toward his young hero. The absurdity of the romantic has been seen more clearly by Thomas Wolfe, I think, than by the more unsympathetic of his critics.

Look Homeward, Angel, to put it briefly, is not a novel about an idealized or romanticized world; it is a novel about a naïve and wonderful youth who yearns for an idealized world but who lives in a very realistic world. The rages of W. O. Gant, the hunger of Eugene Gant, the pathos of Ben's wry appearances, the angels and appetites that recur throughout the novel: all are suggestive of an attitude, a symbolical representation of man's nature and of his relationship with the universe. As the title suggests—and as a number of Wolfe's critics have remarked—Wolfe holds that all men are aliens, cast into a world that is antithetical to the human spirit. Our native home lies elsewhere, and until we return we are doomed to wander in search of answers that can be found only in the other land, the home from which we came.

At least in *Look Homeward, Angel* and in *Of Time and the River* (1935) Thomas Wolfe has projected his autobiographical and romantic vision against a background that is ironic, realistic, and objective and is so despite the fact that Wolfe gallantly refused to accept the most factual as the most profound. The realm of art, after all, is not so much the truth as it is our relation to the truth. On the home ground of literature we ignore Thomas Wolfe only at our own loss.

THOMAS WOLFE AND DEATH*

by J. RUSSELL REAVER
and ROBERT I. STROZIER

Wolfe's first novel *Look Homeward, Angel: A Story of the Buried Life* derives its title from Milton's "Lycidas,"

---

* From J. Russell Reaver and Robert I. Strozier, "Thomas Wolfe and Death," *Georgia Review*, XVI, 3 (Fall, 1962), 330–337. Reprinted by permission of the *Georgia Review*.

This is an excerpt from a longer study which traces through Wolfe's novels the "achievement of emotional maturity and shows the corresponding effect that his development had on his stylistic methods." [Editor's note]

Passages from *Look Homeward, Angel* reprinted by permission of Charles Scribner's Sons.

a poem of isolation and the growth of self-awareness. The title is noteworthy because it combines the two central kinds of isolation that troubled Wolfe throughout his life: the inevitable separation of physical death and the agonizing isolation of creative defeat.[1] Wolfe thought of isolation as a kind of death, yet it held a tantalizing promise.

In *Look Homeward, Angel* Eugene Gant's existence becomes an emotional combat against death and the pressures denying him psychological freedom. Eugene's unceasing struggle, from the moment of Grover's death to the awful dying of Ben, makes us aware that isolation and death amount to the same thing for him.

Ironically, his family attachments, which he keenly feels, prevent him from a solitude that might help him realize his creative power. Wolfe could say he cherished as well as feared death because from facing the inevitable he could gain strength. Death must be faced and feared, said Wolfe, claiming those who said they did not fear it were ". . . liars, and fools, and hypocrites" (TWLM, p. 79). In this early fictional version of his youth, Wolfe presents Eugene as deeply involved with a paradox. Separation is to be feared but also to be cherished. Facing death matures Eugene in a very special way. Each death he endures makes him more capable of coping with his next experience with it. But each event also redeems him; it allows

---

[1] See W. P. Albrecht, "The Titles of *Look Homeward, Angel:* A *Story of the Buried Life*," *Modern Language Quarterly*, XI (1950), 50–57. For subsequent references in the text to the titles of Wolfe's writings, the following abbreviations will be used:

LHA: *Look Homeward, Angel* (New York: Charles Scribner's Sons, 1929).

OTAR: *Of Time and the River* (New York: Charles Scribner's Sons, 1935).

TWLM: *Thomas Wolfe's Letters to His Mother, Julia Elizabeth Wolfe,* ed. John Skally Terry (New York: Charles Scribner's Sons, 1951).

LTW: *The Letters of Thomas Wolfe,* ed. Elizabeth Nowell (New York: Charles Scribner's Sons, 1956).

him to begin to understand that death can be seen as something more than a personal experience with the end of a physical process. Gradually from seeing the deaths of loved ones he constructs an analogy that permits him to discern his own life's struggle as a peculiarly personal attempt to conquer death, and at the same time to work his " . . . way toward an essential isolation; a creative solitude; a secret life . . . toward freedom; in a way toward bondage . . . one is as beautiful as the other" (LTW, p. 111). By the time of Ben's death he can look on dying as a redemptive, not a destructive process. "Eugene thought of death now, with love, with joy. Death was like a lovely and tender woman, Ben's friend and lover, who had come to free him, to heal him, to save him from the torture of life" (LHA, p. 560).

But this cherishing of death occurs in Eugene only at the end of *Look Homeward, Angel,* and he arrives at this view slowly. Like his father, Eugene fears physical pain and annihilation. Young Eugene's feelings at Grover's death reflect Oliver Gant's earlier response to the death of his first wife, Cynthia, and closely resemble the father's behavior in the presence of other deaths.

Wolfe shows the childish self-pity of Oliver's reactions to all his personal problems, but the father's immaturity appears most obvious in his reactions to the deaths of his first wife and of his sons Grover and Ben. The imminence of Ben's death stimulates him to depths of mawkish self-pity. In tones of ludicrous pathos he wails that Ben's death has come to torture not Ben, but him. Only shortly before his own death can the father face up to his end, as Wolfe shows in *Of Time and the River:* ". . . he knew that he was done for and he no longer cared" (OTAR, p. 256). But Gant's acceptance of death is an act of precipitate desperation, coming only when he senses ever-nearing Necessity hovering like the Furies about his bed (pp. 258–268).

Not so with Eugene. Since Ben's death he has tried to combat his fear of death by disciplining himself to face it. The degree of maturity he has reached becomes apparent when he decides to break away from home. In his letters Wolfe significantly describes this experience:

> It is like death. I know that people do not die once, but many times, and that life of which they were once a part, and which they thought they could never lose, dies too, becomes a ghost, is lost forever. . . . If, then, I am dead to people who once knew me and cared for me, there is nothing more to say or do— I must go on into a new world and a new life. . . . (LTW, pp. 216–217)

Unlike his father, Eugene matures with experience, each incident building toward his final achievement. Gant's psychic stagnation contrasts with Eugene's growth. Eugene learns to realize how callous and introverted his father's feelings are. The infantile quality of the father's grief over his first wife parallels the shock and grief of the four-year-old Eugene's response to Grover's death. Neither can get beyond the fear and pain of physical loss. And just as the father is saved from an earlier madness by Eliza, who becomes his second wife, so, ironically, the father, though still suffering himself, can save his son from the darkness weighting down his young mind by the cheerful warmth of the family fire and hearty food (LHA, p. 61).

Later when Ben dies, Oliver still shows a pathetic self-centeredness contrasting with Eugene's efforts to gain control of himself. In spite of his fear, Eugene can accept Ben's dying. Alone among the assembly Eugene does not boil over with hate toward others responsible for Ben's death. Only he can quiet his mother whose grief is heightened by Ben's refusal to have her near him. Following their father's example, the others are too concerned with themselves. Although Eugene's "soul plunged downward, drowning in that pit" (p. 548) at his first horror of knowing Ben will die, he controls himself to maintain a selfless awareness of those around him, and from this perception he gains strength. He can finally think of death as a tender, lovely power to be cherished. After this solution Eugene knows the saving grace of humor: he draws the family out of their morbidity soon after Ben's death by reminding them that at least Ben "won't have to drink mama's coffee any more" (p. 559). And he can joke at the artistry of the undertaker who reddens Ben's cheeks with a rouge stick. Wolfe concludes about Eugene in *Look Homeward, Angel*:

> Thus, through the death of his brother, and the sickness that was rooted in his own flesh, Eugene came to know a deeper and darker wisdom than he had ever known before. (p. 587)

This release from his youthful fear of death causes Eugene to think of himself as something unique. He believes that the conquering of his great grief at its very height has made him a new person—a genius, he thinks. From reciting the names of literary greats, military leaders, political emancipators, religious martyrs, he tries to classify himself. The fear of physical death can no longer hold him immobile. After his desperate fantasies conceived to escape from self, he faces the future: "Over that final hedge, he thought, not death, as I once believed—but new life—and new lands" (p. 593).

At this point Eugene benefits further from his father's example. His father had lived a kind of death-in-life since he was unable to escape from the family trap. Eugene must escape this kind of spiritual death that continues to threaten him, for he feels that this death-in-life builds a wall separating him from the new lands. He will not allow himself to sink into the buried life. He must step out of the psychic grave his family lives in (pp. 599–626).

This new life he finds when his mother agrees to send

him to Harvard. He dies to one life hoping to be born again. But this escape paradoxically resembles another death, for it leads to another isolation. Yet he now feels willing to face his destiny alone. If this struggle to survive proves fruitless, he will, if necessary, endure spiritual death.

At the end of the novel Ben's ghost advises Eugene to make the voyage to a new life. From facing isolation he may learn that it will bring life to him. Grasping this hopeful vision, Eugene answers:

> I have lost the blood that fed me; I have died the hundred deaths that lead to life. By the slow thunder of drums, the flare of dying cities, I have come to the dark place. . . . And now prepare, my soul, for the beginning hunt. I will plumb seas stranger than those haunted by the Albatross. (p. 625)

The buried life is over, and the angel can look homeward.

In addition to the direct narrative the gradual maturing of Eugene is revealed by two stylistic devices culminating at the death of Ben, the point of Eugene's greatest maturity.

The first device is the persistent references to various kinds of death in preparation for a death scene. It is used in a pattern of association often enough to seem typical of Wolfe's earlier response to the experience. Prior to a death scene, such associations appear abundantly. Then there is a lull in which these references sharply decline. After this lull the scene of dying is narrated. This stylistic pattern occurs for all the death scenes in *Look Homeward, Angel* except the final one, the death of Ben. This break in method suggests the shift in Eugene's point of view.

Three instances of Wolfe's strict adherence to his pattern should suffice: Grover's death, the death of the young prostitute Lily, and the revelation that Oliver Gant is dying of cancer. The prototype is the preparation for

Grover's death. From incessant references to death, the subject becomes a leitmotif in the poetic themes of the novel. It is mentioned twenty-three times in the first thirty-five pages, including four euphemisms for death like "the gaunt spectre" (pp. 4–35 *passim*). Then occurs the lull of twenty-two pages. The associations with death are allowed to seethe in Oliver Gant's mind. He howls when he learns Eliza plans to leave him since it reminds him of his isolation after his first wife's death. He fears another isolation. Then Grover's death occurs. Although the word "death" is used twice during the four pages narrating Grover's death, it always occurs outside of Eugene's thoughts.

The same pattern leads up to the description of the prostitute's death (pp. 265–269). Since the pattern of Grover's death is developed in a span of fifty-seven pages, the same number is considered in examining this second pattern. In this group of pages, the first thirty-five refer to death fourteen times. The next twenty-two pages have only one mention of death. Again the lull is conspicuous. It is also significant that during this lull the horror of isolation is once more emphasized by Gant's knowing that his children are growing up and leaving him. Immediately following this lull, Gant is told of the death of Lily Reed, a young prostitute he knows. Dreading his own impotence and his sure death, Gant sells his cherished Carrara angel to be used for marking her grave.

The familiar pattern appears prior to the pronouncement that Gant is dying of cancer: references to death are often repeated (pp. 316–358 *passim*) followed by the characteristic lull that prepares for the revelation of death. The pattern here is only slightly modified, the lull with a single mention of death being only twelve pages long (pp. 358–370). The climax arrives when the surgeon tells his assistant to close the wound because Gant is dying of cancer. No details of a death scene are given. The impact of the doctor's announcement is sufficient. Eugene has sensed his father was dying. Further allusions to it would be artistically and psychologically superfluous.

A secondary device that reveals Wolfe's involvement with the theme of death is his use of poetic allusions to the extent that they become refrains. This method of allusion appears later in the novel than the "death" pattern and is used after it. Primarily it serves only to underscore Eugene's experiences with death, which the first pattern has shown.

In the early chapters the references to literary works mainly record the desultory reading habits of Eugene or his father: popular songs and hymns, Stoddard's lectures, *The Iliad* and *The Odyssey*. After Eugene's fourteenth year, however, the allusions are no longer only records of reading habits and tastes. They begin to appear in a stream-of-consciousness style as Eugene's thoughts and speech suggest the death theme or the life-in-death motif dominating his growth toward maturity (pp. 324–411 *passim*).

This device appears most effectively in Chapters XXIV through XXVII. Here Eugene's reading begins to work its way into his conversation and into his subconscious thoughts. Eugene has read heavily in the Romantics (Coleridge, Keats, Wordsworth, Burns, Scott), the Elizabethans (Shakespeare, Jonson, Dekker), and the Metaphysical and Cavalier poets (Donne, Herrick, Carew, Suckling) (pp. 309–315 *passim*). Constant allusions to these poets and their poems show not only how thoroughly he has absorbed his reading but also his preoccupation with death. The allusions forebode the death of Ben Gant, pointing to the climactic scene in the novel with artistic power. The most recurrent allusions in this section are to Ben Jonson and to Robert Herrick's "Ode to Ben Jonson" (pp. 310–344 *passim*). The other poets alluded to more than once are Keats ("Ode to a Nightingale") and Coleridge ("The Rime of the Ancient Mariner"). Both of these references are of course particularly appropriate to the death, death-in-life themes. Poetic allusions appear singularly effective when they occur in the chapter immediately following Ben's death. The references become especially frequent to Keats' "La Belle Dame Sans Merci" and Shelley's "Ode to the West Wind" (pp. 561, 562). These literary echoes serve to intensify the life-in-death, death-in-life thoughts occupying Eugene's mind at the time. Phrasings from these poems course through his mind as Ben's death dominates the scene. These echoes from the emotions of Keats and Shelley richly convey the turbulence and insecurity of the other Gants. Although they have no literary sophistication, they are probed by Eugene's stream-of-consciousness refrain. Wolfe suggests through Eugene the aura hovering over the Gants, the aura of death that will direct their future.

The two devices of using the pattern involving references to death and repeating poetic passages concerning death generally serve to suggest the vestiges of immaturity and the approaching maturity in Eugene's thinking. Overlapping the poetic allusions is the "death" pattern. But the older Eugene becomes, the less occupied he appears to be with the fear of an approaching death. Following the doctor's announcement of Oliver Gant's fatal illness, there is a conspicuous absence of any reference to death. In effect this section of one hundred and five pages is another lull. Following it, the language of the novel becomes filled with "death." The story returns to Gant's pain and his ominous death. Also Ben's existence becomes a virulent sickness; his dark angel hovers above him ceaselessly.

In the meantime, Eugene has gained some maturity. He has gone off to school, has loved both physically and spiritually, carefully and carelessly, has become acutely aware of the lost years, the lost faces. "And there was sorrow in his heart for what would come no more" (p. 474). This maturing process, giving Eugene some of the perspective suggested by the evidence of his intellectual sophistication in his literary responses, occurs during this one-hundred-five-page lull preceding the depiction of Gant's pain, itself a prelude to Ben's death. Only after these experiences is Eugene more able to face life's problems. The psychological involvement with death becomes less evident, and the "death" pattern is not used significantly when Bob Sterling, Eugene's roommate, dies. Eugene is affected by Sterling's death but he does not ponder it. It is almost irrelevant artistically except as a signal of Ben's death.

Although Eugene's feelings about death appear repeatedly through the pages preparing for Ben's death, which Eugene is not sure he can face, Wolfe has revealed Eugene's increasing strength of character. For in the summer before Ben's death Eugene has had experiences that helped him mature even more than his loves and college life have. Alone in Norfolk and Richmond, he has lived through a self-imposed isolation and survived. He has thoughts of his own death during this survival and it has toughened him (LHA, pp. 521–522).

He can face Ben's death not just to fit Wolfe's stylistic scheme of varying intensities in feeling but to discover for himself the real strength he has gained. His response to Ben's death is a final test of character. Wolfe shows the shift in Eugene both narratively and stylistically. Eugene is no longer the child who mourned the loss of physical things and shuddered at " . . . the high horror of death and oblivion, the decomposition of life" (p. 101). He leaves his childhood in which he had mourned that men left nothing behind them to keep their memories alive —something physical, imperishable, like a tombstone. Now he knows that his father's tombstones are perishable. He also outgrows the craning of his neck and the spastic jerks of his foot lifted suddenly in moments of anguish. The spirit is stirred but not the body. He can look on his early thoughts of death as stupid fantasies (p. 331). Wolfe points to this developing maturity through the episodes of his novel and two overlapping stylistic devices. As Eugene increases in maturity the complex patterns of emotional outbursts lessen in number and intensity. After the final death scene Eugene is ready to face life because he has faced death. He has risen from the life that buried him and only appeared to be his real home. He must now search for another father, another brother, another life. This search Wolfe never completed, for it continues as a recurring theme throughout his novels. Eugene in *Of Time and the River* and George Webber in *The Web and the Rock* and *You Can't Go Home Again* discover it is spiritual death that is to be feared more than physical death. In *Of Time and the River* Eugene is seen as struggling to realize spiritual, creative life. Buffeted about for a long time, he finally begins to understand what creativity really is. Then instead of being controlled, he controls. As the record of *Look Homeward, Angel* closes, Wolfe's hero begins this new struggle in utter isolation. He has only the will to survive.

ERNEST HEMINGWAY

(1899–1961)

Ernest Hemingway was born in Oak Park, an upper-middle-class suburb of Chicago. In high school, he became interested in sports, particularly football and boxing, and continued an even earlier interest in fishing and hunting. After working as a reporter for the *Kansas City Star*, he became an ambulance driver in the Italian army during World War I and was seriously wounded in combat. During the twenties and thirties he lived much of his life in Paris—with time also in Spain, Austria, Africa, Cuba, America—and he devoted a great deal of time to deep-sea fishing, big game hunting, and to the study and enjoyment of bullfighting. While working as a foreign correspondent during World War II, he organized a company of irregulars, which participated significantly and extra-legally in front line action. Much of his later life was spent in Cuba, a retreat that allowed him to fish and write with a minimum of disturbance. His finest novels are usually said to be *The Sun Also Rises* (1926), *A Farewell to Arms* (1929), *For Whom the Bell Tolls* (1940), and *The Old Man and the Sea* (1952), with major acclaim also for several short stories.

These facts and others are common knowledge to thousands of readers. Their place in Hemingway's art, however, is often misunderstood. Some of the critics, for example, have been offended by Hemingway's pride in his hunting and fishing abilities and by his boast that he never lost a fist fight. For a man who lived through two world wars and the Spanish Civil War and the depression of the thirties, these critics feel, a self-conscious and almost obsessive interest in sports and in sensuous pleasures suggests a minor vision, a sensibility crippled by immaturity and characterized by the need to escape.

But Hemingway's vision, despite his detractors, is one of the most profound of our times. The many critics who give Hemingway high praise have seen correctly that he does deal with what some of us glibly call "real life," but that he deals with it through a symbolic vision rather than by writing about labor problems or about political knights. The most consistent characteristic of Hemingway's personal and fictive interest in sports and in the sensuous life is a courageous belief in the possibility of a life with meaning, and the emphasis must be on the word *possibility*. Hemingway's heroes awake to a world gone to hell World War I has destroyed belief in the goodness of national governments. The depression has isolated man from his natural brotherhood. Institutions, concepts, and insidious groups of friends and ways of life are, when accurately seen, a tyranny, a sentimental or propagandistic rationalization for those who enjoy a comfortable living room—and would just as soon not look outside.

Yet Jake Barnes, Frederic Henry, Robert Jordan, and Santiago—heroes who do see and feel, and who are deeply wounded by what they know first hand—cannot accept nihilism. They all have the will to believe and the courage to shape that belief in whatever form seems tenable, be it bull ring or boxing ring or in the way you fish.

This is, obviously, an expedient, a conscious and oftentimes desperate struggle. Thus Hemingway's heroes, especially in the earlier novels, are ironic toward themselves and their own best efforts. They wear a wry mask, they make wisecracks, they drink too much, or chase women whose favors can only destroy. The self-conscious pose, however, is born of desperation, of necessity, and not of nihilism. The commitment to belief in a world gone mad requires calculation from those who would like to practice traditional worship (Jake Barnes' effort to pray), from those who would like to keep things simple and natural (the love of Frederic Henry and Catherine Barkeley), from those who want to fight for a cause (Robert Jordan). But man's finest efforts are constantly mocked by the Cosmic and Precinct Joker: Jake Barnes' ironic wound, the biological death of Catherine Barkeley, the bridge in *For Whom the Bell Tolls* that did not need to be blown up after all, the work of the sharks in *The Old Man and the Sea*.

Hemingway's heroes, then, are forced to develop their ethical forms and to avoid the merely personal while doing it. Their check against the pitfall of the merely personal is the discipline of experience: the man who has or is close to a personal form of a universal ethic will be good at his job. It is for this reason that the Hemingway hero learns the language of the country in which he lives, and it is for this reason that Frederic Henry is a good ambulance driver, Pedro Romero a good bullfighter, Santiago a good fisherman. It is a discipline of will, with much danger and only seldom help from one's friends, and at night, or alone, a good man can crack. Few will hear the small sound. But if he can maintain himself, if he can refuse to surrender, his life can testify to a reality that is beyond the individual, to a reality which is described in *Green Hills of Africa* as being permanent.

TRISTAN OR JACOB
The Choice of *The Sun Also Rises**

by ROBERT W. LEWIS, JR.

The Sun Also Rises was Ernest Hemingway's first serious venture into the craft of the novel, and in some ways the 1926 novel may be his best. The style is wonderfully controlled; there is no self-consciousness, no self-imitation; the characters are well-conceived and executed; and there is the feeling if not the certainty of multiple levels of meaning to the story. In short, the novel is an esthetic success.

As a reflection of its time it is also valuable, providing as it does a detailed historical picture of the expatriates and the self-styled lost generation that Hemingway referred to in his epigraph from Gertrude Stein. (In fact, one of his sensitive readers felt compelled to defend himself from a too exact identification of himself with the Robert Cohn of the novel.)[1]

But in terms of Hemingway's present canon and the themes of love in his work as a whole, the interest of the novel is more than esthetic or historical. In *The Sun Also Rises*, the dominant themes that run through all of

---

* From Robert W. Lewis, Jr., "Tristan or Jacob: The Choice of *The Sun Also Rises*," *Hemingway on Love*, Austin, University of Texas Press, 1965. Reprinted by permission of the publisher.

Passages from *The Sun Also Rises* reprinted by permission of Charles Scribner's Sons.

[1] See Harold Loeb, *The Way It Was* (New York, 1959).

Hemingway's novels begin to emerge. The emphases of the different themes will vary as will the images which he will use to convey them, but basically the subject of Hemingway's novels has been chosen in this first novel, and that subject is love. If it were not for gradually changing attitudes toward that subject, the canon might truly be as monotonous as Hemingway's deprecators say it is, but with each novel some changes are evident, though the themes are familiar from *The Sun Also Rises* on.

Further, the method of this first novel is much more heavily ironical than that of the work of the middle and later Hemingway. Thus one can see Hemingway destroying romantic illusions much easier than one can see the construction of positive ideals. In terms of the later Hemingway as well as in terms of the second, more hopeful epigraph from Ecclesiastes, it is possible to read into *The Sun Also Rises* a foreshadowing of the rebirth of love; but mainly the impression of the novel is negative. Loss rather than eternal return and renewal is clearly more strongly felt, in spite of the title and the Biblical epigraph. The irony seems a natural shield for this loss as well as for the novelist's and the hero's sensitivity, self-pity, and lack of a constructive, positive faith to fill the void. To keep from blubbering when a Brett presses against one's sexless body and moans, "Oh, Jake . . . we could have had such a damned good time together," one must hide behind the hard shield of irony and say, as Jakes does, "Isn't it pretty to think so?"[2]

Jake *is* in desperate straits, but Hemingway reminds us, through Bill Gorton, that irony and pity are, after all, a little cheap: "Don't you know about Irony and Pity? . . . They're mad about it in New York. It's just like the Fratellinis [a team of circus acrobats] used to be" (p. 114).

---

[2] Ernest Hemingway, *The Sun Also Rises* (New York, 1962), p. 247. Subsequent references to this novel will be in the text itself. The pagination of the Scribner's Library paperback edition is the same as the 1926 edition.

For all his worldly wisdom, his being an *aficionado*, his wide experience and skills, and his interesting friends, Jake Barnes strikes one as almost deserving of being indicted by Bill's jocular observations:

> "You're an expatriate. You've lost touch with the soil. You get precious. Fake European standards have ruined you. You drink yourself to death. You become obsessed by sex. You spend all your time talking, not working. You are an expatriate, see? You hang around cafes."
>
> "It sounds like a swell life," I said. "When do I work?"
>
> "You don't work. One group claims women support you. Another group claims you're impotent." (p. 115)

In his essay, "The Death of Love in *The Sun Also Rises*," Mark Spilka explains that Jake as well as Cohn is a romantic, but that Jake's romanticism is a partially hidden weakness while Cohn's is public. Jake, Spilka continues, stands as an unhappy medium between the extremes of the Romantic Hero Cohn and the Code Hero Romero, the young bullfighter. The assumption is, of course, that romantic love is dead and that Cohn's clinging to it and Jake's failure to break away from an old reverence for and delight in it are stupid, silly weaknesses with no place in the "real" world.[3]

It would seem more accurate to say that *The Sun Also Rises* is not so much about the death of love as it is about its sickness, a sickness unto death, but by no means a fatal illness. As has been demonstrated most popularly by Denis de Rougemont's book, *Love in the Western*

[3] *Twelve Original Essays on Great American Novels*, ed. Charles Shapiro (Detroit, 1958), pp. 238–256. See, however, the view of Cohn as the real hero of the novel as expressed by Arthur L. Scott, "In Defense of Robert Cohn," *College English*, 18 (March 1957), 309–314. Robert O. Stephens argues in a similar vein that Cohn's idealism is not entirely foolish or outdated: "Hemingway's Don Quixote in Pamplona," *College English*, 23 (December 1961), 216–218.

World, romantic love is still very much alive. More pertinently, in Hemingway's novel the chief proponent of it, Cohn, is complemented by Jake and Brett, whose frustrated love is much more like the traditional love of a Tristan and Iseult than is the idealistic love of Cohn for Brett. Furthermore, Spilka fails to point out the survival and strength of agape, or brotherly love, among the characters. It is a love which is overshadowed by the clearly central romantic love, that is true, but its presence is definite, and in perspective it assumes importance and foreshadows its emergence in the later Hemingway.

The central theme of romantic love is expressed most clearly in the character of Robert Cohn, a well-to-do expatriate and a would-be professional writer. Robert Stephens calls him Hemingway's Don Quixote, but it would be more accurate to call him Hemingway's first Tristan, for he is much more obsessed with love than Don Quixote ever was, and much less concerned with idealism in spheres beyond love's compass. Hemingway explicitly compares Cohn to a medieval chivalric knight when he describes him in the Pamplona brawl with Mike Campbell as "proudly and firmly waiting for the assault, ready to do battle for his lady love" (p. 178). Cohn's view of Brett as a golden-haired angel is of course ridiculous, as Jake and the others see it, but Cohn's whole life with women has been molded on different principles from those of the other expatriates. And Cohn, Jake knows, is very stubborn; he will not surrender his ideals simply because others laugh at him and harbor other (equally misguided) ideals—or anti-ideals.

Lest one think that Cohn is not the pivotal character, if not the central one, Hemingway devotes the first two chapters of this economical novel to a history of Cohn's past and recent life. Like some subsequent Hemingway heroes, from Francis Macomber to Colonel Cantwell, Cohn had been married to a bitch. Presently, he has a mistress, Frances Clyne, to whom Jake satirically refers as Cohn's "lady," and she is another bitch. As Jake views it, Cohn has acquired her, as he did his wife, not because of love, but because of convenience and style; as Frances says, "Robert's always wanted to have a mistress": the idea of a mistress is what appealed to Cohn.

I am sure he had never been in love in his life.

He had married on the rebound from the rotten time he had in college, and Frances took him on the rebound from his discovery that he had not been everything to his first wife. He was not in love yet but he realized that he was an attractive quantity to women, and that the fact of a woman caring for him and wanting to live with him was not simply a divine miracle. This changed him so that he was not so pleasant to have around. (pp. 8-9)

Further, Cohn has, like Don Quixote, learned his way of life from books, specifically W. H. Hudson's *The Purple Land*:

It recounts splendid imaginary amorous adventures of a perfect English gentleman in an intensely romantic land, the scenery of which is very well described. For a man to take it at thirty-four as a guide-book to what life holds is about as safe as it would be for a man of the same age to enter Wall Street direct from a French convent, equipped with a complete set of the more practical Alger books. Cohn, I believe, took every word of *The Purple Land* as literally as though it had been an R.G. Dun report. (p. 9)

It is not unexpected that he would marry the wrong woman and have no forewarning that she might leave him, or that he would acquire Frances, with whom he has so little in common, or that he would fall in love "at first sight" with Brett—like Iseult someone else's woman, and like Quixote's servant girl misunderstood, not seen for the base thing she really is. Love for Cohn, as for all Tristans, is a sickness. It affects the mind and the body. It dominates and one becomes a slave to it. One is in love with love. As in the words of the popular song of the late thirties, "This can't be love because I feel so well." So Jake knows Cohn is in love when the latter's tennis game goes "all to pieces" (p. 45). He must suffer, and the more he suffers, the happier (theoretically) he will be.

Even his break with Frances is needlessly prolonged and painful, almost as if Cohn enjoyed his mistress' acrimony: " 'We have dreadful scenes, and he cries and begs me to be reasonable, but he says he just can't do it [marry Frances]' " (p. 47).

Frances in her turn fails to see the contradiction of her desire to marry Cohn. Now that she sees her prey slipping away, she realizes their two-and-a-half year courtship has been a waste to her; when Jake defends Cohn to her, she replies that he doesn't know the real selfishness of Cohn and then she caustically insults Cohn to his face in Jake's presence. In practical terms, her futile pursuit of security and wealth has been a waste of time, and her labeling of Cohn as selfish and cruel is not simply sour grapes. But how such realistic views, that could be reconciled to marriage, contrast with the ideal of wedded bliss! Frances perceives Cohn's real reason for not marrying his mistress: "If he marries me . . . that would be the end of all the romance" (p. 51). And since Frances, aging a bit, her figure and face fading, sees little future as an Iseult, she is not afraid of touching on the truth of Cohn's actions.

In Book II, Cohn's Tristanizing can have free play. He has had his little fling with Brett (a *real* English lady), and now that the preliminary amour is over, he can get down to serious suffering, which is the joy of romantic love. Where Tristan had but King Mark as a rival, Cohn luxuriates in having as rivals for Brett's love Mike, her fiancé; Pedro Romero, her current lover; Jake, her handi-

capped but constant lover; and assorted peripheral ad-
mirers such as Bill Gorton and the ghost of her first true
love, dead of dysentery in the War. Just as he endured
having Frances berate him in front of Jake, so Cohn endures great abuse from his so-called friends at the
Pamplona fiesta. Brett's lovers have various claims on her,
but Cohn's claim is honored by the tradition with which
he is imbued: he will play his role knowingly and well,
accepting ridicule (pp. 141–142), but at the same time
asserting the superiority earned by his suffering (p.162).
He has no armed battles to fight, no guarded boudoirs to
broach, but he is faithful to the principle of love. Mike
brutally insults him:

> His face had the sallow, yellow look it got when he
> was insulted, but somehow he seemed to be enjoying
> it. The childish, drunken heroics of it. It was his affair
> with a lady of title. (p. 178)

Finally even Brett is rude to him and drives him off. His
best friend, Jake, has come to hate him, and specifically
they hate him because he suffers (p. 182).

When Cohn is finally driven to do real combat for his
lady love, he then discovers the ineffectuality of his role.
Having been a middle-weight boxing champion in college,
Cohn has no trouble winning separate pugilistic jousts
with Jake, Mike, and Pedro Romero, who has displaced
Cohn in Brett's affections, Cohn thinks. But the courageous Romero, though beaten badly, refuses to yield gra-
ciously. He promises to kill Cohn, and Brett refuses to
leave with the Pyrrhic victor. No one plays it as it is in the
movies or in W. H. Hudson's *The Purple Land*. The script
has been rewritten, and no one told Cohn that his role was
thrown out.

> That damn Cohn. He should have hit somebody the
> first time he was insulted, and then gone away. He

was so sure that Brett loved him. He was going to
stay, and true love would conquer all. (p. 199)

Jake makes fun of Cohn's chivalric suffering, but his
and Brett's notions of love are just as insidious, perhaps
more so because of their hyprocrisy and their concealment
of their notions behind a tough façade. Jake clearly views
Cohn as a misguided romantic, and by dating the whore
Georgette he denies to Brett that he is getting romantic (p.
23). But Brett and Jake follow the pattern of Tristan and
Iseult with little variation. Theirs is a hopeless love the
course of which is filled with obstacles of love rivals
aplenty, Jake's maiming wound, and Jake's mixed alle-
giances. Tristan's problems were of the same sort, and if
one imagines Jake as a Tristan, one could imagine Georgette as a type of Iseult of the White Hands, the first
Iseult's (Brett's) rival.

But the chief parallel is not in action or characters
but in the common theme of suffering for love, of being
possessed by love and made its slave, of having no love
except outside the bonds of marriage, and of the spirituali-
zation of love or its severance from man's animal nature.
Cohn's sufferings are academic; he goes literally by the
book, and that is, no doubt, why he is scorned. Brett and
Jake are really sick with love. And thus the essential
comedy of the whole story—of any romantic love story—
in which the lovers claim a special role and ask for a
special sympathy because they are really crazy (only *they*
are entitled, they would seem to plead, to belittle the
scapegoat Cohn who plays at insanity but really isn't
mad, as they are).[4]

The success and continued acclaim of the novel is

---

[4] After extended classroom discussion of *The Sun Also Rises*,
a prettily smiling coed asked, "If Jake and Brett are really in
love, why don't they get married?" More worldly students grinned
and guffawed, but the coed had—inadvertently, no doubt—asked
a very intelligent question.

remarkable in that Hemingway has created such a convincing version of an old theme that is usually read as an attack on that old Tristan and Iseult story—"The death of love in *The Sun Also Rises*"—but this story is of a sick love, a hypochondriac love, of lovers who enjoy poor health, poor love, sick love. But the love never dies.

At Brett and Jake's first meeting in the novel, the lovers escape from their friends at a dance to be alone. The action and tone are greatly restrained, but there is no mistaking the source of Brett's pleading cry: "Oh, darling, I've been so miserable" (p. 24). There is more than frustrated eros in the scenes in which Brett and Jake are alone. After all, Brett has slept with just about whoever pleased her. Jake's wound is presumably not an emasculation but the loss of his penis, and thus he has no accompanying loss or diminution of sexual desire.[5] Tristan's wound was only symbolically castrative, and he voluntarily abstained from intercourse with Iseult even when there were no obstacles to his pleasure. But Jake can never have intercourse with Brett; his predicament is a little laughable, as Jake himself points out (p. 26). And to the ancient Greeks who regarded romantic love as a sickness and a calamity, his wound would be funny, but it is not funny to the romanticist who lives for love.

Brett is compelled by her love for Jake; she has no freedom. She kisses him and then she breaks away from him because she "can't stand it." She turns "all to jelly" when he touches her, and she has a look in her eyes as if she were possessed. Apparently they have tried to find some method of mutual physical relief that was a "hell" that ended in failure, but when Jake suggests that they "keep away from each other," Brett insists, " 'But, darling, I have to see you. It isn't all that [sex] you know.'

[5] See George Plimpton, "Ernest Hemingway," *Paris Review*, 18 (Spring 1958), 61–82. Reprinted in *Writers at Work*, Second Series (New York: The Viking Press, 1963), p. 230.

" 'No, but it always gets to be.' "
Then they discuss Jake's wound:

> "It's funny," I said. "It's very funny. And it's a
> lot of fun, too, to be in love."
> "Do you think so?" her eyes looked flat again.
> "I don't mean fun that way. In a way it's an
> enjoyable feeling."
> "No," she said. "I think it's hell on earth."
> "It's good to see each other."
> "No. I don't think it is."
> "Don't you want to?"
> "I have to." (pp. 26–27)

Brett is compelled to torture herself and to enjoy her
torment. Before rejoining their friends she asks Jake for
just one more kiss.

When he retires that night, he looks at his body in the
mirror, thinks some more of his problem, thinks that Brett
"only wanted what she couldn't have," cries, finally falls
asleep, and is shortly awakened, at four-thirty by the
drunken Brett's arrival with Count Mippipopolous. She
simply must torture herself about Jake, that unattainable
commodity, even it if means being rude and thoughtless,
that is, lacking respect for her love object—in effect, having passion, lacking agape. And Jake, though knowing
Brett for what she is, is still touched by her presence (pp.
30–34).

In short, though Jake perceives the folly of their relationship more sharply than Brett does, he nonetheless
submits to the tyranny of romantic love. Telling Cohn
about Brett, Jake, with conscious irony, says that during
the war Brett's "own true love . . . kicked off with the
dysentery" (p. 39). The idealistic Cohn won't believe Brett
would subsequently marry anyone she didn't love, but
Jake, accepting the terms of the adulterous Tristan-Iseult
love, says that Brett has already married twice without
love.

Later that same day it is Brett's turn to use the phrase "true love," and she of course applies it to Jake during one of their frequent scenes of misery. They avow their love for one another, and they think what a "bad time" they have because of their consummate inconsummable love. With her love vow on her lips and unknown to Jake, Brett is planning her trip to San Sebastian where she will have a brief fling with Robert Cohn, Jake's friend, before her fiancé (whom she later admits she hasn't thought of in a week) returns from Britain! Jake wants to try living together with Brett, but, says Brett, it is better for Jake and better for her that they live apart (p. 55).

Jake hates Cohn and is jealous of him when he learns of his tryst with Brett (she herself casually tells Jake of the affair). A King Mark like Mike Campbell is one thing, but Iseult shouldn't "take up social service," as Jake sarcastically says (p. 84). Yet Jake still "loves" her, and his passion again returns to submerge his irony and bitterness. On his fishing trip with Bill Gorton, he reads a romantic novel by A. E. W. Mason, and once more Jake ironically uses the phrase true love (p. 120). He realizes the comic stupidity of the "wonderful" story in which a man falls into a glacier and his bride waits 24 years "for his body to come out on the moraine," but still he voluntarily chooses to read the story. He begins to protest too much. Like many another denigrator, Jake accompanies his irony with a large amount of pity, in this case, self-pity. Both Jake and Brett have to let others know how they suffer; so Jake tells Bill about his love for Brett, and Brett tells Mike about her affairs, and tells Jake about her new found passion for Pedro Romero. At the same time, she has to know if Jake still loves her (p. 183), for he is still the only person she has (no doubt because he is the only person she has not "had" and never can have). She apparently justifies her promiscuity and torture of Jake, her true love, on the grounds of her unique role; she is the fair lady and, tortured by love herself, her role is to torture, to be, as Cohn calls her, a Circe.

Only after Jake acts as her pimp with Romero does he finally begin to emerge from his passive role, and it is Cohn who has to label Jake for what he is (p. 190). Of course, in resorting to violence, Cohn also plays the fool, but after his Quixotic fights with Jake, Mike, and Romero, Jake's attitudes seem to clear. The progress of the book is toward a frenzied, idiotic climax of action and "romance" at the end of the fiesta. Afterwards there is calmness, cleanliness, catharsis—at least for Jake. His love for Brett has undergone a subtle change. From unreasoning passion it has gone through a period of bitter awareness to an ending which describes a relationship of responsibility and care. Passion is submerged if not subdued.

That is, there is the growing presence of agape in the course of the novel, and it is finally extended to include the two great lovers themselves; the lovers are at least ready to love. In Book I, the epitome of love was Count Mippipopolous, a phony Greek count who is "one of us" (p. 932), as Brett says, because he has taste, manners, the right values, and above all, past sufferings (p. 60). The Count is "always in love" (p. 61), for love too has a place in his system of values. The Count is a charming host, but in spite of his frankness Brett and Jake never become intimate with him. He remains an eccentric.

In Book II, the focus of this other possibility of love is Bill Gorton, Jake's writer friend who goes fishing with him before the fiesta. Gorton is significantly different from the expatriates in that he has remained at home and he works. He is productive as are none of the others except Jake himself. Perhaps the symbol of this difference is the sport of fishing—the fish themselves representing a kind of fertility. Bill and Jake meet a materialistic tourist and a border guard (a representative of authority) who do not care for fishing. Cohn is not keen for it either, and Brett and Mike don't arrive in time to join Bill and Jake as scheduled. Without the parasitic unloving others, Bill and Jake have a splendid, carefree trip. Their mutual affection is complemented by their easy friendship with the pastoral Basques with whom they ride in a bus into the green, undefiled mountains where the fast, cold trout stream runs. They also meet the pleasant Wilson-Harris, another fisherman, another disciple of the sexless brotherhood of man, who is greatly touched by Bill and Jake's friendliness. The trouble is that the Burguete interlude is just that—an idyllic escape into an unreal world of simple military or boyhood relationships. One must go back to work, and one must go back to a more complicated, sexual society where women rather than fish contest with the lovers.

Back at Pamplona, then, Jake assumes a new social role that can be seen as a maturing of the uncomplicated, male love of fellow fishermen. At the fiesta the parallels between Jake and the sexless steers that herd the fertile bulls have been prepared for by the earlier establishment of parallels between Jake and Ecclesiastes, literally the preacher or "steer" of the Old Testament.

Because of the title of the novel and its second epigraph, one may assume that Hemingway read the book of Ecclesiastes. Like the Hebrew writer living in another Waste Land, Hemingway too was skeptical and pessimistic, and his hero Jake Barnes had the same doubts and the same sharp awareness of transiency and death.[6] Learning and wisdom are futile, for God's ways are mysterious, the Preacher says (Eccles. 7:16, 8:17, 11:5, 12:12). "Time and chance happeneth to . . . all" (Eccles. 9:11). In the midst of prosperity and life is the seed of desolation and death (Eccles. 12:1–7). There are, however, some

---

[6] *Ecclesiastes* 3:1, 7:1–4, 8:8, *The Holy Bible*, Oxford University Press (New York, n.d.). Subsequent references to Ecclesiastes will be in the text itself.

positive values to cling to: food and drink are good (Eccles. 2:3, 2:24–26, 5:18–20, 8:15, 9:7, 10:19); companionship and fellowship are good—"two are better than one" (Eccles. 4:9–12); a wise man has heart, but a fool does not (Eccles. 10:2); a good name is desirable—one should live by the "code" (Eccles. 7:1); this means, in part, helping others (Eccles. 11:1–2); in spite of impermanence and futility, life is sweet (Eccles. 9:4–6). The direct parallels are extended and consistent.

Like the author of Ecclesiastes, Jake Barnes is alienated from his faith, Catholicism, which he clings to but cannot sincerely practice. Pragmatically, it does not work, but it seems to offer to fill the void in his spirit, and he wants it to work. In Jake, Hemingway is moving from the even more complete lack of faith of Frederic Henry in *A Farewell to Arms* to the more complete acceptance of Robert Jordan (with a Biblical allusion in his last name) in *For Whom the Bell Tolls* and of the Catholic fisherman Santiago in *The Old Man and the Sea*. The reader is reminded that "Jake" is "a hell of a biblical name" (p. 22), and if one should add up the total of all Hemingway heroes, one could see Jake Barnes as the first stage of the composite hero's parallel to Jacob's life, which ran the cycle of sin and fraud in youth, much suffering and then repentance in maturity, and final exaltation of God's ways in his old age.

Another possible parallel occurs in Book II where the setting shifts to San Sebastian. It is there that Brett goes for her fling with Cohn and later for a pre-honeymoon with Mike. It is also the place where Jake goes after the Pamplona fiesta (Book III). Saint Sebastian and Jake have significant ironic similarities: the saint was martyred during a Roman saturnalia—Jake goes through agony because of his impotence and Brett's great sexuality; after being stoned and shot through with arrows (equal to Jake's suffering), Sebastian was nursed back to health by a devout woman—Brett has not only destructive but recuperative powers upon Jake, Cohn, and Mike.[7]

Jake is the one even mildly religious character in the central group of characters. He is, however, only "technically" Catholic, he explains (p. 124). Like the preacher of Ecclesiastes, he is skeptical and yet devout; he does not believe, but he wants to believe. He goes through the motions of his faith hoping that somehow it will succeed in giving him an anchor in his disintegrating worldly milieu. Jake is world-weary as the preacher is: "All things have I seen in the days of my vanity" (Eccles. 7:15), but, also like the preacher, Jake does not completely abandon his god. Thus Jake, though bitterly, considers the Church's counsel regarding sex—"don't think of it"—and is always noting and visiting churches. Notre Dame in Paris was "squatting against the night sky" (p. 77), a personification picturing Mary in a bestial pose. On his trip to Spain, another Catholic country, he "took a look at the cathedral" in Bayonne, France (p. 90). He notes churches in Spain, and Pamplona is a city of churches with a "great brown cathedral, and the broken skyline of the other churches" (pp. 93–94). A monastery dominates Burguete where Jake and Bill go fishing; it is up in the mountains, like Kilimanjaro "cold" and "high" (p. 108). Jake notes a steel engraving of Nuestra Señora de Roncesvalles in his Burguete room (p. 109), and later Bill, "good old Wilson-Harris," and he visit the monastery. Bill and Harris admit they are "not much on those sort of places," but Jake says nothing (p. 128).

In Pamplona Jake goes to church remarkably often for a skeptic. He first thought the façade of the cathedral ugly, but he later liked it, and it is "dim and dark" and peaceful inside. Jake prays there in a rather naive manner, but at least he prays and thinks about praying, regretting that he is "such a rotten Catholic" but holding out some hope of being a better one in the future (pp. 96–97).

---

[7] Jake met Brett in a hospital during the war. After his wounding, she helped nurse him back to health (p. 38).

After returning to Pamplona, Jake casually mentions going to church "a couple of times, once with Brett" (p. 150). Jake implies that he still confesses himself, for Brett wants to witness his confession. Jake says she could not and adds, significantly, that "it would be in a language she did not know" (p. 151): Both literally—it would be in Spanish—and figuratively the Brett who then goes to the pagan rite of having her fortune told cannot understand his faith. Even in the excitement of the festival, Jake continues to go to church; he goes to mass the first day of the fiesta, noting that the saturnalian "San Fermin is also a religious festival" that begins with a big religious procession which Jake apparently followed (pp. 153, 155). Once more he goes to church with Brett, and once more the pagan fertility bitch-goddess is rejected: she has no hat, no symbol of deference. But outside in the bright sunlight she realizes her role as the dancing Spaniards form a gay circle of homage around her: "They wanted her as an image to dance around" (p. 155). The church remains as a backdrop for the frenzied action. Jake walks as far as the church, once by himself and once with Brett (pp. 156, 182). A third time he and Brett go to church "Where the show started on Sunday" (p. 208). Brett tries to pray for Romero, but she stiffens and becomes "damned nervous. . . . I'm damned bad for a religious atmosphere," she says (p. 208). Jake jokes about praying, but he also says praying works for him (though not for everyone) and he is "pretty religious" (p. 209). Later Jake tells Brett that "some people have God" (p. 245).

Jake also apparently likes to bathe, to purify or re-baptize himself. Brett too rushes off to bathe several times: "Must clean myself. . . . Must bathe," she says after returning from her vacation with Cohn (p. 74), and after a night in a hotel (that looks like a brothel) with her fiancé Mike, she also "must bathe" (p. 83). Twice during the wild fiesta she also has to bathe (pp. 144, 159). The other romantic, Cohn, also tries to wash away his dirt after his brief affair with Brett (pp. 81, 96, 97). But it is Jake who makes almost a ritual, like baptism, out of bathing. After the disappointing, fight-marred end of the partly pagan fiesta, Jake returns to the fertile sea for purification. Hemingway describes at length two swims: the water is green, dark, and cold (p. 235); it is also buoyant—"It felt as though you could never sink" (p. 237). After the renewal of the sea, Jake is ready to answer the call of help from those without even his tentative faith, once more to play the role of sexless priest and steer for his friends, his "parish," his "herd."

In addition to these more or less direct allusions to Ecclesiastes in particular and Judeo-Christian attitudes in general—especially to agape—Jake's relation to bullfighting is also fraught with religious overtones, as is bullfighting itself. As with Saint Sebastian, the Roman, or pagan, and Christian elements overlap. Bullfighting was a favorite sport in imperial Rome, and Pedro Romero's last name hints at a Roman root even if there is no etymological connection. The *espadas* pass through a trying novitiate just as priests do before they may perform publicly. The pomp and brilliance of costume and decoration in the *plaza de toros* parallels the richness of dress and the colorful setting of the Catholic Church. In the *corrida de toros* itself there are the trinities of the triple mule team, of the *espadas*, of the *suertes* or divisions of the fight, and of the bulls, each fighter usually getting three in one afternoon. The *suertes* divide into lancing, planting the darts, and killing, with parallels to the Crucifixion that Hemingway would specifically refer to in the later novels *Across the River and into the Trees* and *The Old Man and the Sea*.

Pedro Romero stays in a room whose two beds are "separated by a monastic partition" (p. 163), and, as with a priest, his retinue believes that women will corrupt the young bullfighter. Montoya, Jake's *aficionado* friend, observes that "He shouldn't mix in that stuff" (p. 172). The very word *aficion*—"aficion means passion" (p. 131)—recalls the similarity of love imagery in the language of the Catholic Church since the Middle Ages. Those who are *aficionados* have a secret fellowship that is discovered by "a sort of oral spiritual examination" concluded by a laying on of hands: "nearly always there was the actual touching. It seemed as though they wanted to touch you to make it certain" (p. 132). If you had *aficion*, like faith, anything could be forgiven you, as Montoya initially forgives Jake his friends who lack it. It seems significant that of Jake's friends it is the Jewish Cohn who is the least interested in the *corrida*; he is even afraid he might be bored (p. 162). Like the revered blood of Christ and the symbolic Communion wine, the blood of the bullfights disturbs only the uninitiated; Brett learns from Jake how to watch and then comments, "Funny. . . . How one doesn't mind the blood" (p. 211). Also remindful of the Passion is the sense of tragedy that the *aficionados* derive from the fights: "People went . . . to be given tragic sensations" (p. 214).

Jake's relation to his friends is paralleled by the steers' role in the *corridas*. The sexless steers—"like old maids"—quiet the bulls in the corrals and keep them from fighting. Sometimes the steers are gored by the bulls. "Can't the steers do anything?" Bill asks. "No," Jake answers. "Must be swell being a steer," Bill later adds (p. 133). At the corral Brett observes that the steers don't look happy, but the bull is "beautiful." The bulls, like Jake's sexually active friends, "are only dangerous when they're alone, or only two or three of them together" (p. 140). Bill makes the analogy clear when he says, "Don't you ever detach me from the herd," and Cohn says, "It's no life being a steer" (p. 141). In the end, Jake's role as a steer is once more demonstrated when he rescues Brett. Jake recalls that he was the one who introduced the bitch-goddess to one bull, Cohn,[8] and later to another bull, Romero. Then he must go fetch her back to the custody of still another bull, Mike (p. 239). The Catholic priest is also celibate, also has a role of explaining ritual to the uninitiated, of confirming and blessing (laying on of hands), and of protecting his flock—his "herd," if you will.

Ecclesiastes once more provides the text and enlightening parallels that Hemingway must have been aware of. Men are like beasts: "they themselves are beasts. For that which befalleth the sons of men befalleth beasts. . . ." (Eccles. 3:18–19). The Biblical Preacher, like Jake, believes it is good to study death, which is the real subject of the bullfight. Further, the Preacher sees that the battle is not to the strong—the bulls—as the race is not to the swift, nor riches to men of understanding (Eccles. 9:11). Thus a good man—a good preacher, a good steer—must help others: "Cast thy bread upon the waters: for thou shalt find it after many days," as Jake does, and a good man must be content in God's wisdom (Eccles. 11:1). All may be vanity, but yet man does not know the ways of God: "thou knowest not what is the way of the spirit . . ." (Eccles. 11:5). Though he may not be a bull, a live steer is better than a dead bull, just as "a living dog is better than a dead lion" (Eccles. 9:4). Even more startling is the suggestion in Ecclesiastes that a man (Jake) is lucky to be sexless, for woman is a trap: "And I find more bitter than death the woman, whose heart is snares and nets, and her hands as bands: whoso pleaseth God shall escape from her; but the sinner shall be taken by her" (Eccles. 7:26). Jake may be unhappy, but he is not tormented by Brett in the way Mike, Cohn, and Romero are; they know they are

---

[8] One of the Pamplona bulls is likened to a boxer, which Cohn once was (139). I am aware of Hemingway's denial that he intended parallels between the bull fight and the characters; see Plimpton's interview.

able to possess Brett. To Cohn, at least, Brett is quite appropriately a Circe, a goddess who turns men into swine (p. 144).

Like the Preacher of Ecclesiastes, and his namesake, the Biblical Jacob, Jake Barnes is passing through a period of doubt and vexation in which superficial values and actions are seen for what they are, even though they may be sanctioned by the Church. One good illustration is the action of the pilgrims who monopolize the dining car on Jake and Bill's train. Neither Jake nor Hemingway nor the Preacher seem quite sure of what is enduring and valuable, but like Jacob they are learning and perhaps will discover a fuller faith as they grow older. The essence of this faith is perhaps imaged in Jake's description of how Romero fought a good bull especially for his loved one Brett:

> Pedro Romero had the greatness. He loved bull-fighting, and I think he loved the bulls, and I think he loved Brett. Everything of which he could control the locality he did in front of her all that afternoon. Never once did he look up. He made it stronger that way, and did it for himself, too, as well as for her. Because he did not look up to ask if it pleased he did it all for himself inside, and it strengthened him, and yet he did it for her, too. But he did not do it for her at any loss to himself. He gained by it all through the afternoon. (p. 216)

This doing for another without individual loss is a sign of agape which the simple uncorrupted Romero possesses. Knowing her own self-centeredness and perhaps perceiving this somewhat paradoxical performance as Jake does, Brett can also make a paradoxical sacrifice. In the quiet but climactic Book III, she knows that her selfishness and her bitchery would eventually hurt Romero, as Montoya predicted, and so she selflessly drives him away (pp. 241–243).

Jake also seems to have come to a greater knowledge of his condition than at any other time. It is true that the concluding note of the novel is still one of irony and pity, but he does not give way to maudlin tears or resort to bitter invective over Brett's cruelty in using him as a pimp and then a rescuer when she is down and out in Madrid. We are not much, they say by their actions, but we are all that we have. Like the polite bartender of the last chapter, they must exercise some devotion to each other by simple acts of kindness. Such is the skeptical but not nihilistic conclusion of Hemingway's first novel.

CRITICISM AND
*A FAREWELL TO ARMS**

by NORMAN FRIEDMAN

The pathetic misfortune which Frederic Henry suffers in losing Catherine through childbirth, at the end of A *Farewell to Arms*, is commonly interpreted as the result of one or the other of two causes, or some combination: he is seen either as the justly punished outlaw for having loved without benefit of clergy, or as the pitiful victim of the arbitrary and remorseless fortunes of war. Either way, what interests modern critics of this novel is, first, its portrait of a generation becoming lost in its conflict with a middle-class industrial society which it cannot accept, and

* From Norman Friedman, "Criticism and the Novel" *Antioch Review*, XVIII, 3 (Fall, 1958). Copyright 1958 by the Antioch Press. Reprinted by permission of the publisher.
This is an excerpt from a longer essay in which Friedman convincingly demonstrates his belief that much modern criticism of fiction has strayed into a dexterity that loses sight of what actually happens in the novel being studied. [Editor's note]

second, the way this portrait suggests the wasteland archetype in its symbolic use of rain and snow, mountain and
plain, lake and river, wound and love, death in birth, and
so on. Thus seen, this book is taken as making a profound
artistic comment on the breakdown of values in the twentieth century: the impossibility of living and loving truly
while following traditional sanctions, the consequent necessity for keeping one's guard up and taking only calculated risks, and the pathos which ensues when one of the
brave is caught with his guard down.[1]

Now all of this may be true in a large and general
way, but even the supporters of this interpretation have
sometimes felt a sense of strain in trying to reconcile the
two obviously discrete portions of the book, which their
punning on its title serves to point up—the "arms" of
battle and the "arms" of a woman. This is clearly, as any
textbook survey will tell you, "a novel of love and war,"
but the relationship between the two has been taken to be
largely associative and symbolic: war destroys lovers just
as society destroys love, or something of the sort.

But let us see what a scrutiny of the actual events and
their connections reveals. Hemingway has divided his story
into five Books, and the central incidents of each may be
outlined as follows:

    I. Henry meets Catherine, goes into battle, and is
       wounded.

   II. He is sent to a hospital, meets her there, and their
       love flowers.

  III. His wound is better, he goes back to the war, is

---

[1] Cf. J. W. Beach, *American Fiction 1920–1940* (New York,
1941), pp. 84 ff.; R. B. West, Jr. and R. W. Stallman, *The Art
of Modern Fiction* (New York, 1949), pp. 622–634: Philip
Young, *Ernest Hemingway* (New York, 1952), pp. 60–66; C. H.
Baker, *Hemingway: the Writer as Artist* (Princeton, 1952),
Ch. V; and H. K. Russell, "The Catharsis in *A Farewell to
Arms*," MFS, I (1955), 25–30.

caught up in a retreat, and is forced to desert.

IV. He finds his way back to Catherine, who is bearing his child.

V. They escape to neutral territory where, after some months, she dies in childbirth.

Notice first of all the proportions devoted to each of the story's two "halves": only the last part of Book I (chs. IX–XIII) and most of Book III deal with the war directly, whereas the remaining three-and-a-half Books deal mainly with the love affair. This suggests that, perhaps because of Hemingway's skill in such writing, we might be overestimating the relative importance of war in the plot as a whole.

A further analysis of the causal connections among these Books bears out this suggestion rather clearly. Since the main culminating incident derives its force and meaning almost entirely from the relationship between the lovers, it would not be an unreasonable hypothesis to assume that the main action of the novel is organized around that relationship. We may ask first, then, what brought about this catastrophe? and secondly, what part does the war play in this sequence?

In the first place, I think it is clear that there is one sufficient cause of Catherine's death, and one only: biology ("You always feel trapped biologically"). That is, her hips were too narrow for a normal delivery—"The doctor said I was rather narrow in the hips and it's all for the best if we keep young Catherine small."—and by the time her doctor decided a caesarian was needed, the baby had strangled itself and she had developed an internal hemorrhage.

Their love for each other, and the fact that they chose to consummate their love physically, is naturally the necessary condition for this effect. But there is no reason whatever in these circumstances as such for so terrible an outcome; nothing prevented a normal delivery except Catherine's unfortunate anatomical characteristics. The same circumstances, given wider hips, could just as easily have ended in a successful delivery; and, by the same token, the same narrowness of hips could just as easily have produced the same catastrophe in the peaceful suburbs.

They could have been married fifty times over, as Henry himself reflects, and thus the theory that he suffers for daring to defy social mores will not bear up under the weight of evidence. Similarly, he could have suffered almost as much if his love had flowered in peacetime, and thus the theory that he is a victim of the war proves equally invalid. Indeed, if we speculate as to what Hemingway could have done had he wanted to do what these theories would have him do, we will see even more clearly the lack, which they ignore, of those causal connections needed. Had Hemingway wanted to make Henry suffer for violating moral conventions, for example, he could have had Catherine's death stem directly from some mischance encountered while loving immorally—she could have contracted a venereal disease from Henry, for instance, or they could have been forced to make love under physical conditions unfavorable to normal conception, and so on. But there is absolutely no hint or implication of anything like this in the narration of the final chapters. Or again, had Hemingway wanted to make Henry suffer as a victim of the war, he could have had Catherine's death result from some contingency of battle, for which any number of gruesome possibilities suggest themselves—she could have been injured while rowing across to Switzerland, or while being caught up in the retreat, or because of having to give birth without medical attention, or under unsanitary conditions, and so on. But the fact is that she had, by and large, a quiet confinement and the best medical care and facilities available. (The possibility that it is the doctor's fault in not operating sooner presents itself, but is not supported by the text; and even if it were, would make very little sense.)

What, then, secondly, *is* the function of the war in relation to this main action? The answer may be discussed under two heads: its causal function, and its intensifying function. Causally, although the war is a sufficient condition of neither their love nor their suffering which is the outcome of this love, it does serve as a necessary condition of this love. Without it, they in all probability would never have met, and even if they had, Catherine would have still had her English fiancé. But the war, in simply bringing them together in a susceptible mood, would not in itself have thrown them in love. Indeed, Catherine met Rinaldi first without being attracted to him at all. The sufficient cause of the love between Henry and Catherine stems primarily from their respective characters and attitudes. The war, further, inflicts a wound upon Henry, which in turn allows him to see more of Catherine and thus to consummate their love; and again, by means of the retreat, the war allows him to return to her and thus to be in attendance when her time arrives. But in each case, its functional role is that of a necessary condition rather than that of a sufficient cause.

As an intensifier, in addition, the war functions to place their doomed love in an emotionally appropriate context. If losing his beloved causes Henry to suffer, how much more does he suffer when she represents all that he has to lose; for the war has placed him in a far country, has disillusioned him in traditional moral values, has wounded him, and has cut him off from his own forces (no one would argue, I think, that he is responsible for his desertion, even though he feels a decent amount of guilt). The war, simply by making it difficult for them to lead a normal life, places an appropriate cloud of doom over their heads and points up the fragility of all human relations. Every move is a gamble involving high stakes, and they are therefore more vulnerable; every decision entails more serious consequences, and thus every failure is more final. Hence the ultimate pathos is intensified.

If all this be so, then we must revise our "war-defeats-love" interpretation of this novel in favor of a "love-causes-sorrow" interpretation, and view the war as playing a strictly subordinate role causally and as serving otherwise mainly as an appropriate background against which the main action unfolds. In this view, Hemingway is not attacking the sterility of war or the breakdown of values, but is rather using them as materials by means of which to achieve his end more effectively, which is simply to draw pathos out of the painful and inevitable limitations under which all human hopes and desires labor. It could be said that his intensifying devices do get out of hand and exceed the needs of his effect, notably in Book III dealing with the famous retreat, but no one would wish them away, I think, except when they mislead critics with special systems to support.

THE OLD MAN AND THE SEA
Hemingway's Tragic Vision of Man*

by CLINTON S. BURHANS, JR.

I

In *Death in the Afternoon*, Hemingway uses an effective metaphor to describe the kind of prose he is trying to

* From Clinton S. Burhans, Jr. "*The Old Man and the Sea*: Hemingway's Tragic Vision of Man," *American Literature*, XXXI (January, 1960), 446–455. Reprinted by permission of Duke University Press and the author.

Passages from *The Old Man and the Sea* reprinted by permission of Charles Scribner's Sons.

write: he explains that "if a writer of prose knows enough about what he is writing about he may omit things that he knows and the reader, if the writer is writing truly enough, will have a feeling of those things as strongly as though the writer had stated them. The dignity of movement of an iceberg is due to only one-eighth of it being above water."[1]

Among all the works of Hemingway which illustrate this metaphor, none, I think, does so more consistently or more thoroughly than the saga of Santiago. Indeed, the critical reception of the novel has emphasized this aspect of it: in particular, Philip Young, Leo Gurko, and Carlos Baker have stressed the qualities of *The Old Man and the Sea* as allegory and parable.[2] Each of these critics is especially concerned with two qualities in Santiago—his epic individualism and the love he feels for the creatures who share with him a world of inescapable violence—though in the main each views these qualities from a different point of the literary compass. Young regards the novel as essentially classical in nature;[3] Gurko sees it as reflecting Hemingway's romanticism;[4] and to Baker, the novel is Christian in context, and the old fisherman is suggestive of Christ.[5]

Such interpretations of *The Old Man and the Sea* are not, of course, contradictory; in fact, they are parallel at many points. All are true, and together they point to both the breadth and depth of the novel's enduring significance and also to its central greatness: like all great works of art

[1] Ernest Hemingway, *Death in the Afternoon* (New York, 1932), p. 183.

[2] On the other hand—though not, to me, convincingly—Otto Friedrich, "Ernest Hemingway: Joy Through Strength," *The American Scholar*, XXVI, 470 (Autumn, 1957), 513-530, sees Santiago's experience as little more than the result of the necessities of his profession.

[3] Philip Young, *Hemingway* (New York, 1952), p. 100.

[4] Leo Gurko, "The Old Man and the Sea," *College English*, XVII, I (Oct., 1955), 14.

[5] Carlos Baker, *Hemingway* (Princeton, 1956), p. 299.

it is a mirror wherein every man perceives a personal likeness. Such viewpoints, then, differ only in emphasis and reflect generally similar conclusions—that Santiago represents a noble and tragic individualism revealing what man can do in an indifferent universe which defeats him, and the love he can feel for such a universe and his humility before it.

True as this is, there yet remains, I think, a deeper level of significance, a deeper level upon which the ultimate beauty and the dignity of movement of this brilliant structure fundamentally rest. On this level of significance, Santiago is Harry Morgan alive again and grown old; for what comes to Morgan in a sudden and unexpected revelation as he lies dying is the matrix of the old fisherman's climactic experience. Since 1937, Hemingway has been increasingly concerned with the relationship between individualism and interdependence;[6] and *The Old Man and the Sea* is the culminating expression of this concern in its reflection of Hemingway's mature view of the tragic irony of man's fate: that no abstraction can bring man an awareness and understanding of the solidarity and interdependence without which life is impossible; he must learn it, as it has always been truly learned, through the agony

---

[6] This direction in Hemingway's thought and art has, of course, been pointed out by several critics, particularly by Edgar Johnson in the *Sewanee Review*, XLVIII, 3 (July-Sept., 1940) and by Maxwell Geismar in *Writers in Crisis* (Cambridge, Mass., 1942). With prophetic insight, Johnson says that "the important thing about Hemingway is that he has earned his philosophy, that he has struggled to reach it, overcome the obstacles to attaining it. . . . He has earned the right to reject rejection. For the good, the gentle and the brave, he now tells us, if they do not try to stand alone and make a separate peace, defeat is not inevitable. His life-blood dripping into the bottom of the boat, Harry Morgan realized it at the end of his career. Philip Rawlings realized it in the blood and terror and tragedy and splendor even of a dying Madrid. Hemingway has realized it there too, and the realization may well be for him the very beginning of a new and more vital career."

of active and isolated individualism in a universe which dooms such individualism.

II

Throughout *The Old Man and the Sea*, Santiago is given heroic proportions. He is "a strange old man,"[7] still powerful and still wise in all the ways of his trade. After he hooks the great marlin, he fights him with epic skill and endurance, showing "what a man can do and what a man endures" (p. 73). And when the sharks come, he is determined to " 'fight them until I die' " (p. 128), because he knows that " 'man is not made for defeat. . . . A man can be destroyed but not defeated' " (p. 114).

In searching for and in catching his big fish, Santiago gains a deepened insight into himself and into his relationship to the rest of created life—an insight as pervasive and implicit in the old fisherman's experience as it is sudden and explicit in Harry Morgan's. As he sails far out on the sea, Santiago thinks of it "as feminine and as something that gave or withheld great favours, and if she did wild or wicked things it was because she could not help them" (p. 33). For the bird who rests on his line and for other creatures who share with him such a capricious and violent life, the old man feels friendship and love (pp. 32, 53). And when he sees a flight of wild ducks go over, the old man knows "no man was ever alone on the sea" (p. 67).

Santiago comes to feel his deepest love for the creature that he himself hunts and kills, the great fish which he must catch not alone for physical need but even more for his pride and his profession. The great marlin is unlike the other fish which the old man catches; he is a spiritual more than a physical necessity. He is unlike the other fish,

---

[7] Ernest Hemingway, *The Old Man and the Sea* (New York: Charles Scribner's Sons, 1952), p. 15.

too, in that he is a worthy antagonist for the old man, and during his long ordeal, Santiago comes to pity the marlin and then to respect and to love him. In the end he senses that there can be no victory for either in the equal struggle between them, that the conditions which have brought them together have made them one (p. 109). And so, though he kills the great fish, the old man has come to love him as his equal and his brother; sharing a life which is a capricious mixture of incredible beauty and deadly violence and in which all creatures are both hunter and hunted, they are bound together in its most primal relationship.

Beyond the heroic individualism of Santiago's struggle with the great fish and his fight against the sharks, however, and beyond the love and the brotherhood which he comes to feel for the noble creature he must kill, there is a further dimension in the old man's experience which gives to these their ultimate significance. For in killing the great marlin and in losing him to the sharks, the old man learns the sin into which men inevitably fall by going far out beyond their depth, beyond their true place in life. In the first night of his struggle with the great fish, the old man begins to feel a loneliness and a sense almost of guilt for the way in which he has caught him (p. 55); and after he has killed the marlin, he feels no pride of accomplishment, no sense of victory. Rather, he seems to feel almost as though he has betrayed the great fish; "I am only better than him through trickery," he thinks, "and he meant me no harm" (p. 110).

Thus, when the sharks come, it is almost as a thing expected, almost as a punishment which the old man brings upon himself in going far out "beyond all people. Beyond all people in the world" (p. 55) and there hooking and killing the great fish. For the coming of the sharks is not a matter of chance nor a stroke of bad luck; "the shark was not an accident" (p.110). They are the direct result of the old man's action in killing the fish. He has driven his harpoon deep into the marlin's heart, and the blood of the great fish, welling from his heart, leaves a trail of scent which the first shark follows. He tears huge pieces from the marlin's body, causing more blood to seep into the sea and thus attract other sharks; and in killing the first shark, the old man loses his principal weapon, his harpoon. Thus, in winning his struggle with the marlin and in killing him, the old man sets in motion the sequence of events which take from him the great fish whom he has come to love and with whom he identifies himself completely. And the old man senses an inevitability in the coming of the sharks (p. 111), a feeling of guilt which deepens into remorse and regret. "I am sorry that I killed the fish . . ." (p. 114), he thinks, and he tells himself that "You did not kill the fish only to keep alive and to sell for food. . . . You killed him for pride and because you are a fisherman" (p. 116).

Earlier, before he had killed the marlin, Santiago had been " 'glad we do not have to try to kill the stars' " (p. 83). It is enough, he had felt, to have to kill our fellow creatures. Now, with the inevitable sharks attacking, the old man senses that in going far out he has in effect tried "to kill the sun or the moon or the stars." For him it has not been "enough to live on the sea and kill our true brothers"; in his individualism and his need and his pride, he has gone far out "beyond all people," beyond his true place in a capricious and indifferent world, and has thereby brought not only on himself but also on the great fish the forces of violence and destruction. " 'I shouldn't have gone out so far, fish . . . ,' " he declares. " 'Neither for you nor for me. I'm sorry, fish' " (p. 121). And when the sharks have torn away half of the great marlin, Santiago speaks again to his brother in the sea: " 'Half-fish,' he said. 'Fish that you were. I am sorry that I went too far out. I ruined us both' " (p. 127).

The old man's realization of what he has done is reflected in his apologies to the fish, and this realization and its implications are emphasized symbolically throughout the novel. From beginning to end, the theme of solidarity and interdependence pervades the action and provides the structural framework within which the old man's heroic individualism and his love for his fellow creatures appear and function and which gives them their ultimate significance. Having gone eighty-four days without a catch, Santiago has become dependent upon the young boy, Manolin, and upon his other friends in his village. The boy keeps up his confidence and hope, brings him clothes and such necessities as water and soap, and sees that he has fresh bait for his fishing. Martin, the restaurant owner, sends the old man food, and Perico, the wineshop owner, gives him newspapers so that he can read about baseball. All of this the old man accepts gratefully and without shame, knowing that such help is not demeaning. "He was too simple to wonder when he had attained humility. But he knew he had attained it and he knew it was not disgraceful and it carried no loss of true pride" (p. 14).

Santiago refuses the young boy's offer to leave the boat his parents have made him go in and return to his, but soon after he hooks the great marlin he wishes increasingly and often that the boy were with him. And after the sharks come and he wonders if it had been a sin to kill the great fish, the old man thinks that, after all, "everything kills everything else in some way. Fishing kills me exactly as it keeps me alive." But then he remembers that it is not fishing but the love and care of another human being that keeps him alive now; "the boy keeps me alive, he thought. I must not deceive myself too much" (p. 117).

As the sharks tear from him more and more of the great fish and as the boat gets closer to his home, the old man's sense of his relationship to his friends and to the boy deepens: "I cannot be too far out now, he thought. I hope no one has been too worried. There is only the boy to worry, of course. But I am sure he would have confidence. Many of the older fishermen will worry. Many others too, he thought. I live in a good town" (p. 127). In the end, when he awakens in his shack and talks with the boy, he notices "how pleasant it was to have someone to talk to instead of speaking only to himself and to the sea" (p. 137). This time he accepts without any real opposition the boy's insistence on returning to his boat, and he says no more about going far out alone.

This theme of human solidarity and interdependence is reinforced by several symbols. Baseball, which the old man knows well and loves and which he thinks and talks about constantly, is, of course, a highly developed team sport and one that contrasts importantly in this respect with the relatively far more individualistic bullfighting, hunting, and fishing usually found in Hemingway's stories. Although he tells himself that "now is no time to think of baseball" (p. 43), the game is in Santiago's thoughts throughout his ordeal, and he wonders about each day's results in the *Gran Ligas*.

Even more significant is the old man's hero-worship of Joe DiMaggio, the great Yankee outfielder. DiMaggio, like Santiago, was a champion, a master of his craft, and in baseball terms an old one, playing out the last years of his glorious career severely handicapped by the pain of a bone spur in his heel. The image of DiMaggio is a constant source of inspiration to Santiago; in his strained back and his cut and cramped left hand he, too, is an old champion who must endure the handicap of pain; and he tells himself that he "must have confidence and . . . be worthy of the great DiMaggio who does all things perfectly even with the pain of the bone spur in his heel" (p. 75).

But DiMaggio had qualities at least as vital to the

Yankees as his courage and individual brilliance. Even during his own time and since then, many men with expert knowledge of baseball have considered other contemporary outfielders—especially Ted Williams of the Boston Red Sox—to be DiMaggio's equal or superior in terms of individual ability and achievement. But few men have ever earned the affection and the renown which DiMaggio received as a "team player"—one who always displayed his individual greatness as part of his team, one to whom the team was always more important than himself. It used to be said of DiMaggio's value as a "team player" that with him in the line-up, even when he was handicapped by the pain in his heel, the Yankees were two runs ahead when they came out on the field. From Santiago's love of baseball and his evident knowledge of it, it is clear that he would be aware of these qualities in DiMaggio. And when Manolin remarks that there are other men on the New York team, the old man replies: " 'Naturally. But he makes the difference' " (p. 23).

The lions which Santiago dreams about and his description in terms of Christ symbols further suggest solidarity and love and humility as opposed to isolated individualism and pride. So evocative and lovely a symbol is the dream of the lions that it would be foolish if not impossible to attempt its literal definition. Yet it seems significant that the old man dreams not of a single lion, a "king of the beasts," a lion proud and powerful and alone, like the one from which Francis Macomber runs in terror, but of several young lions who come down to a beach in the evening to play together. "He only dreamed of places now and of the lions on the beach. They played like young cats in the dusk and he loved them as he loved the boy" (p. 27). It seems also significant that the old man "no longer dreamed of storms, nor of women, nor of great occurrences, nor of great fish, nor fights, nor contests of strength, nor of his wife" (p. 27)—that is that he no longer dreams of great individualistic deeds like the one which brings violence and destruction on him and on the marlin. Instead, the lions are "the main thing that is left" (p. 73), and they evoke the solidarity and love and peace to which the old man returns after hunting and killing and losing his great fish.

These qualities are further emphasized by the symbolic value of the old fisherman as he carries the mast crosslike up the hill to his shack and as he lies exhausted on his bed. His hands have been terribly wounded in catching the great marlin and in fighting the sharks, and as he lies sleeping "face down on the newspapers with his arms out straight and the palms of his hands up" (p. 134), his figure is Christlike and suggests that if the old man has been crucified by the forces of a capricious and violent universe, the meaning of his experience is the humility and love of Christ and the interdependence which they imply.

Such, then, are the qualities which define man's true place in a world of violence and death indifferent to him, and they are the context which gives the experience of the old fisherman its ultimate significance as the reflection of Hemingway's culminating concept of the human condition —his tragic vision of man. For in his understanding that "it is enough to live on the sea and kill our true brothers," the fellow creatures who share life with us and whom he loves, the old man is expressing Hemingway's conviction that despite the tragic necessity of such a condition, man has a place in the world. And in his realization that in going alone and too far out, "beyond all people in the world," he has ruined both himself and also the great fish, the old man reflects Hemingway's feeling that in his individualism and his pride and his need, man inevitably goes beyond his true place in the world and thereby brings violence and destruction on himself and on others. Yet in going out too far and alone, Santiago has found his greatest strength and courage and dignity and nobility and love, and in this he expresses Hemingway's view of the ultimate tragic irony of man's fate: that only through the isolated individualism and the pride which drive him beyond his true place in life does man develop the qualities and the wisdom which teach him the sin of such individualism and pride and which bring him the deepest understanding of himself and of his place in the world. Thus, in accepting his world for what it is and in learning to live in it, Hemingway has achieved a tragic but ennobling vision of man which is in the tradition of Sophocles, Christ, Melville, and Conrad.

III

It is not enough, then, to point out, as Robert P. Weeks does, that "from the first eight words of *The Old Man and the Sea . . .* we are squarely confronted with a world in which man's isolation is the most insistent truth."[8] True as this is, it is truth which is at the same time paradox, for Santiago is profoundly aware that "no man was ever alone on the sea." Nor is the novel solely what Leo Gurko feels it is—"the culmination of Hemingway's long search for disengagement from the social world and total entry into the natural" (p.15). If the old man leaves society to go "far out" and "beyond all people in the world," the consciousness of society and of his relationship to it are never for long out of his thoughts; and in the end, of course, he returns to his "good town," where he finds it pleasant "to have someone to talk to instead of speaking only to himself and to the sea." To go no further than Santiago's isolation, therefore, or to treat it, as Weeks does, as a theme in opposition to Hemingway's concern with society is to miss the deepest level of significance both in this novel and in Hemingway's writing generally.

For, surely, as Edgar Johnson has shown, the true

---

[8] Robert P. Weeks, "Hemingway and the Uses of Isolation," *University of Kansas City Review*, XXIV (Winter, 1957), 125.

direction of Hemingway's thought and art from the beginning and especially since 1937 has been a return to society—not in terms of any particular social or political doctrine, but in the broad sense of human solidarity and interdependence. If he began by making "a separate peace" and by going, like Santiago, "far out" beyond society, like the old man, too, he has come back, through Harry Morgan's " 'no man alone,' " Philip Rawlings's and Robert Jordan's "no man is an island," and Santiago's "no man is ever alone on the sea," with a deepened insight into its nature and values and a profound awareness of his relationship to it as an individual.[9]

In the process, strangely enough—or perhaps it is not strange at all—he has come back from Frederic Henry's rejection of all abstract values to a reiteration for our time of mankind's oldest and noblest moral principles. As James B. Colvert points out, Hemingway is a moralist: heir, like his world, to the destruction by science and empiricism of nineteenth-century value assumptions, he rejects equally these assumptions and the principle underlying them—that intellectual moral abstractions possess independent supersensual existence. Turning from the resulting nihilism, he goes to experience in the actual world of hostility, violence, and destruction to find in the world which destroyed the old values a basis for new ones—and it is precisely here, Colvert suggests, in reflecting the central moral problem of his world, that Hemingway is a significant moralist.[10]

---

[9] This development in Hemingway's thought and art is further illustrated in a story which he wrote in 1939 and which, prompted by the recent Cuban revolution, *Cosmopolitan*, CXLVI, 4 (April, 1959), 78–83, has reprinted. "Nobody Ever Dies!" is the story of a Spanish-speaking young man and a girl who have given themselves with selfless devotion to the cause of social liberty in a revolt in Cuba. The young man is trapped and killed by governmental forces, and the girl faces the torture of questioning with "a strange confidence. It was the same confidence another girl her

But out of this concern with action and conduct in a naturalistic universe, Hemingway has not evolved new moral values; rather, he has reaffirmed man's oldest ones —courage, love, humility, solidarity, and interdependence. It is their basis which is new—a basis not in supernaturalism or abstraction but hard-won through actual experience in a naturalistic universe which is at best indifferent to man and his values. Hemingway tells us, as E. M. Halliday observes, that "we are part of a universe offering no assurance beyond the grave, and we are to make what we can of life by a pragmatic ethic spun bravely out of man himself in full and steady cognizance that the end is darkness."[11]

Through perfectly realized symbolism and irony,[12] then, Hemingway has beautifully and movingly spun out of an old fisherman's great trial just such a pragmatic ethic and its basis in an essentially tragic vision of man; and in this reaffirmation of man's most cherished values and their reaffirmation in the terms of our time rests the deepest and the enduring significance of *The Old Man and the Sea*.

---

age had felt a little more than five hundred years before in the market place of a town called Rouen."

[10] James B. Colvert, "Ernest Hemingway's Morality in Action," *American Literature*, XXVII (Nov., 1955), 372-385.

[11] E. M. Halliday, "Hemingway's Ambiguity: Symbolism and Irony," *American Literature*, XXVIII, 3 (March, 1956).

[12] Halliday's comment on Hemingway's ironic method is particularly applicable to *The Old Man and the Sea:* "the ironic gap between expectation and fulfilment, pretense and fact, intention and action, the message sent and the message received, the way things are thought or ought to be and the way things are— this has been Hemingway's great theme from the beginning; and it has called for an ironic method to do it artistic justice" (*ibid.*, p. 15).

WILLIAM FAULKNER

(1897–1962)

In recent years psychologists have drawn disturbing comparisons between physical causes and personality, between psychic patterns and what we like to think of as our own inner being. Physicists have even upset the theories of absolute time and space, with Einstein, for example, showing that the length of a yardstick and the age of a man depend upon local conditions.

Modern novelists have been alert to such changing views. One result is that time is often seen in fiction as a relative concept, as an integral part of the individual's mode of apprehension. Intelligent men of any age, of course, know that time has also its intimate role within individuals; but for William Faulkner psychological time is central to the human condition.

Faulkner sees psychological time as a series of waves and curves. It may shock, but it is real, and it embarrasses chronological time. Since time, furthermore, is a mode of perception, a framework through which man perceives, one's personal psychology is a part of what he sees when he looks at the universe. The act of perception is colored by the perceiver; thus man is presented with shapes that are beyond the simple concepts of Me, Here, Now. Or again, psychological time may prompt the appearance of images and associations that seem arbitrary. It is the sudden leap of consciousness, however—for Faulkner as for the psychologist—that reveals in mystic shorthand the inner reality.

In *As I Lay Dying*, for example, the title itself suggests a time relative to Addie Bundren. There is a process, in time, most of it occurring after Addie's physical death, but all of it existing as a part of the meaning of her death, of a meaning which *is* even while she retains consciousness. Something like this participation of the past and the future in the meaning of the present must explain, also, the intuitive insight into the future that is the peculiar ability of Darl Bundren. Both the revenge of Addie (as explained in Professor Handy's article) and the foresight of Darl argue against our traditional notion of chronological time. Perception and consciousness participate in actual events, shape man's being in a changing present that comes from the past and contains the future.

And yet time, for Faulkner, as shown especially in *The Bear*, is not merely relative. The other side of individual consciousness is not chaos but timelessness, a frozen eternity that is beyond man, forming a backdrop for the earthly stage on which he moves. Both Jason and Quentin Compson, in *The Sound and the Fury*, are reluctant students of Faulkner's fascinating chronometer: Jason for his selfish rejection of real values which sometimes reverse the masks we wear in a materialistic world, Quentin for his idealistic incapacity to accept history's corruption of the absolute.

The theme of time, which is far more complex than my brief comments suggest, is but one of the many profound insights of William Faulkner. His is a complex vision, and it was not until about fifteen years after his finest period of work that readers and critics began to grasp what he had done. Raised in Oxford, Mississippi, Faulkner was a man who studied in his homeland rather than in the university. He went on hunting trips, listened to stories told in stores and on verandas, and—most important of all—observed with genius the people of the South. And yet he felt, also, the need to gain perspective, to see the rest of the world. After a brief and frustrated career in the Royal

Canadian Air Force, he attended the University of Mississippi (but did not graduate), and then journeyed south to New Orleans, where he met Sherwood Anderson.

After writing some poems, some journalism, and a pair of novels that might best be termed "promising," Faulkner entered a period of incredible productivity: *Sartoris* (1929), *The Sound and the Fury* (1929), *As I Lay Dying* (1930), *Sanctuary* (1931), *Light in August* (1932), *Pylon* (1935), and *Absalom, Absalom* (1936), plus four volumes of short stories and a volume of poems published within the same eight-year period. Until 1945, Faulkner had a few devoted readers but almost no reputation. When mentioned at all, he was usually considered an Erskine Caldwell who wrote bad sentences. After Malcolm Cowley's famous introduction to the Viking Portable Faulkner, critics and students and general readers began to understand him better, and in 1950 he was awarded the Nobel Prize. Among the most significant of his later books are *The Hamlet* (1940), *Go Down, Moses* (1942), *A Fable* (1957), and *The Reivers* (1962). For at least fifteen years now, he has been considered by many discerning critics to be our greatest novelist.

MIRROR ANALOGUES IN
*THE SOUND AND THE FURY**

by LAWRANCE THOMPSON

The concept of holding a mirror up to nature suggests an
attractive, but thorny, path across the history of ideas,
because that trope has lent itself to so many conflicting
usages and interpretations. Yet the persistent allusions to
mirrors in *The Sound and the Fury* would seem to invite
the reader to notice that Faulkner has adapted the ancient
literary mirror device and mirror principle to his own
peculiar purposes, as a means of reflecting various kinds of
correspondences, antitheses, parallelisms, analogues—even
as a means of illuminating certain thematic concerns
which are implicit throughout the total action. At the risk
of oversimplifying Faulkner's elaborately developed meanings, I propose to present in ascending order of significance a few mirror allusions and mirror devices, in the
hope that such a progression may increase our awareness
of certain basic meanings.

Perhaps the first hint or foreshadowing occurs when
the idiot Ben touches a place on a wall where a mirror
used to be. During the late afternoon of Ben's thirty-third
birthday his Negro guardian, Luster, leads him into this
experience:

* From Lawrance Thompson, "Mirror Analogues in *The
Sound and the Fury*," *English Institute Essays*, New York,
Columbia University Press, 1952, pp. 83–105. Reprinted by per-
mission of the publisher.
Passages from *The Sound and the Fury* reprinted by permis-
sion of Random House, Inc.

"We went to the library. Luster turned on the light. The windows went black, and the dark tall place on the wall came and I went and touched it. It was like a door, only it wasn't a door.

"The fire came behind me and I went to the fire and sat on the floor, holding the slipper. The fire went higher. It went onto the cushion in Mother's chair."

Although each of those images in that passage has important associations for Ben, this initial allusion to "the dark tall place on the wall" must strike the first reader as being mysterious, even meaningless, except that the tantalizing phrase does have the effect of creating a tension of interest, a focus of attention, which sharpens the response of the reader to later pertinent passages. For example, the superficial tension is completely resolved when Jason subsequently gives his recollection of a similar situation, and views it from a decidedly different angle.

I went on into the living room. I couldn't hear anything from upstairs. I opened the paper. After awhile Ben and Luster came in. Ben went to the dark place on the wall where the mirror used to be, rubbing his hands on it and slobbering and moaning. Luster begun punching at the fire.

"What're you doing?" I says. "We dont need any fire tonight."

"I trying to keep him quiet," he says.

Even this superficial clarification does not help us to understand the significance to Ben of that "dark place on the wall where the mirror used to be" before some of the furnishings were sold. But through Ben's stream-of-consciousness associations evoked by that "dark place" and that fire, Faulkner proceeds to develop a gradually revealing series of analogues, involving Ben and his sister Caddy and his mother at about the time he had been repudiated by his family through the act of changing his name from Maury to Benjamin. Two brief passages may be quoted to suggest the still enigmatic allusions to mirrors.

> "Versh set me down and we went into Mother's room. There was a fire. It was rising and falling on the walls. There was another fire in the mirror."

Next, and again by association, Ben is reminded of Caddy. " 'Come and tell Mother goodnight.' " Caddy said. We went to the bed. The fire went out of the mirror."

The specific meaning of that final sentence is obvious: as Ben's angle of vision changed, he could no longer see the reflection of fire in the mirror. But the immediate context suggests a symbolic value for that sentence: as Ben turns from Caddy to his mother he suffers a sense of loss which may be symbolized by the disappearance of the reflected fire. His next associational memory dramatizes several reasons why Ben may well have suffered a sense of loss whenever he turned from Caddy to his mother.

> I could see the fire in the mirror too. Caddy lifted me up.
> "Come on, now," she said. "Then you can come back to the fire. Hush now."
> . . . . "Bring him here." Mother said. "He's too big for you to carry."
> "He's not too heavy." Caddy said. "I can carry him."
> "Well, I dont want him carried, then." Mother said. "A five year old child. No, no. Not in my lap. Let him stand up."
> "If you'll hold him, he'll stop." Caddy said. "Hush." she said. "You can go right back. Here. Here's your cushion. See."
> "Dont, Candace." Mother said.
> "Let him look at it, and he'll be quiet." Caddy said. "Hold up just a minute while I slip it out. There, Benjy. Look."
> I looked at it and hushed.
> "You humour him too much." Mother said. "You and your father both. You dont realise that I am the one who has to pay for it. . . ."

"You dont need to bother with him." Caddy said. "I like to take care of him. Dont I, Benjy."

"Candace." Mother said. "I told you not to call him that. . . . Benjamin." she said. "Take that cushion away, Candace."

"He'll cry." Caddy said.

"Take that cushion away, like I told you." Mother said. "He must learn to mind."

The cushion went away.

"Hush, Benjy." Caddy said.

"You go over there and sit down." Mother said. "Benjamin." She held my face to hers.

"Stop that." she said. "Stop it."

But I didn't stop and Mother caught me in her arms and began to cry, and I cried. Then the cushion came back and Caddy held it above Mother's head. She drew Mother back in the chair and Mother lay crying against the red and yellow cushion.

"Hush, Mother." Caddy said. "You go upstairs and lay down, so you can be sick. I'll go get Dilsey." She led me to the fire and I looked at the bright, smooth shapes. I could hear the fire and the roof. . . .

"You can look at the fire and the mirror and the cushion too," Caddy said.

In that little dramatic action is ample evidence that Caddy, motivated by her compassion for her younger brother, has eagerly given Ben the kind of motherly attention previously denied to him because of his own mother's inadequacies. Tenderly, solicitously, Caddy has discovered ways of appealing to Ben's limited responses, to satisfy his instinctive and unreasoning hunger for orderliness, peacefulness, serenity. The fire, the red-yellow cushion, the smooth satin slipper are only a few of the objects used by Caddy to provide him with values which are positive to him because they are somehow sustaining. Then Caddy has also taught Ben the pleasure of multiplying these positive values through their reflections in the mirror. Because she has heightened his awareness of all those symmetrical visions of "bright, smooth shapes" which comfort him, it might be said that Caddy herself has become for Ben a kind of mirror of all his positive values, framed in love: her love for him and his love for her.

Ben's seemingly chaotic reverie in Part One of *The Sound and the Fury* is so contrived by Faulkner as to focus attention, not merely on fragments of the entire Compson story, but particularly on Ben's all-absorbing love for the Caddy who was and (like the mirror) is now gone. Her presence was Ben's joy; her absence his grief; her possible return his hope. The arrangement of these fragments in Part One enables Faulkner to withhold conclusive information as to how it happened that the finely sensitive and mothering child Caddy has so completely disappeared. The reader's tension of interest concerning that question is gradually resolved through various later uses of mirror analogues which disclose related aspects of Faulkner's complex theme.

Throughout *The Sound and the Fury* Faulkner employs the convention of using some of his characters to serve as mirrors of other characters; mirrors set at different angles so that they provide contrasting angles of vision. For example, we have already had occasion to observe two contrasting images of Ben: the image reflected in the articulated consciousness of Caddy, as differing from the image reflected in the articulated consciousness of Mrs. Compson. Although various characters in the narrative reflect various images of Ben, all these images may be reduced to two roughly antithetical categories: most of the characters view Ben as a disgrace, a menace, or at least as a slobbering idiot. By contrast, those who genuinely love Ben (particularly Caddy and the Negro servant Dilsey) insist that Ben has certain peculiar and extraordinary powers of perception. As Roskus phrases it, "He know lot more than folks thinks." Repeatedly Ben is represented as having the instinctive and intuitive power to differentiate between objects or actions which are life-encouraging and others which are life-injuring, and these are used by Faulkner to symbolize the antithesis between good and evil. In this limited sense, then, Ben serves as a kind of moral mirror, in which the members of his own family may contemplate reflections of their own potentialities, their own moral strengths and weaknesses. Most of them naturally refuse to acknowledge this power in Ben, because they do not wish to see themselves in any light other than that of self-justification.

Appropriately, Caddy is represented as having the greatest sensitivity to her brother's power of serving as a kind of moral mirror, and her sensitivity is heightened by her unselfish love for him. Faulkner develops this aspect of Ben's significance in four episodes which illuminate the progressive phases of Caddy's growth. When she is old enough to be interested in adolescent courtship, she discovers that Ben's unreasoning reaction against the smell of perfume gives her a sense of guilt and prompts her to wash herself clean—a primitive ritual repeatedly correlated with Ben's potential for serving as moral agent and moral conscience in his family. Later, when Ben escapes from the house one night, to find Caddy and Charlie kissing in the swing on the lawn, Caddy leaves Charlie, ostensibly to quiet Ben, but also because Ben has again evoked in her a sense of guilt.

> We ran out into the moonlight, toward the kitchen. . . . Caddy and I ran. We ran up the kitchen steps, onto the porch, and Caddy knelt down in the dark and held me. I could hear her and feel her chest. "I wont." she said. "I wont anymore, ever. Benjy. Benjy." Then she was crying, and I cried, and we held each other. "Hush." she said. "Hush. I wont anymore." So I hushed and Caddy took the kitchen soap and washed her mouth at the sink, hard.

The third time when Ben is represented as a moral

mirror occurs as Caddy returns home immediately after her first complete sexual experience. In that scene Faulkner correlates two implicit analogues which complement each other: first, the analogue of Ben as a moral mirror; secondly, the analogue between simple physical vision and conscious moral vision, suggested by the persistent recurrence of the word "eyes" and the cognate words, "looking" and "seeing," as Ben again evokes in Caddy a deeper sense of guilt.

> Caddy came to the door and stood there, looking at Father and Mother. Her eyes flew at me, and away. I began to cry. It went loud and I got up. Caddy came in and stood with her back to the wall, looking at me. I went toward her, crying, and she shrank against the wall and I saw her eyes and I cried louder and pulled at her dress. She put her hands out but I pulled at her dress. Her eyes ran. . . . We were in the hall, Caddy was still looking at me. Her hand was against her mouth and I saw her eyes and I cried. We went up the stairs. She stopped again, against the wall, looking at me and I cried and she went on and I came on, crying, and she shrank against the wall looking at me. She opened the door to her room, but I pulled at her dress and we went to the bathroom and she stood against the door, looking at me. Then she put her arm across her face and I pushed at her, crying.

Each of these three closely related episodes (involving Ben as moral mirror and also involving the symbolic and penitent ritual of washing away guilt with water) are associated in Ben's recollection with his ultimate reaction, at the time of Caddy's fake wedding, where the sense of guilt was ironically washed away with champagne until the celebration was terminated by Ben's unreasoning and bellowing protest. This fourth episode represents the end of the period in Ben's life when Caddy had been able to help him by bringing relative order out of his relatively chaotic experience, and the end of the period when Ben had served as moral mirror for Caddy. Notice that these two endings are obliquely suggested by reiterative mirror imagery in

Quentin's recollection of that incident which broke up the wedding celebration.

> She ran right out of the mirror, out of the banked scent. Roses. Roses. . . . Only she was running already when I heard it. In the mirror she was running before I knew what it was. That quick, her train caught up over her arm she ran out of the mirror like a cloud, her veil swirling in long glints her heels brittle and fast clutching her dress onto her shoulder with the other hand, running out of the mirror the smells roses roses the voice that breathed o'er Eden. Then she was across the porch I couldn't hear her heels then in the moonlight like a cloud, the floating shadow of the veil running across the grass, into the bellowing.

Caddy goes away after the fake wedding ceremony, leaving a double image of herself as reflected in the consciousness of her family. The reader's initial image of Caddy has been that reflected repeatedly in the consciousness of Ben: the sensitive and mothering Caddy whose love for Ben evoked his love for her and gave meaning to his life. That image remains. Antithetically, the second image of Caddy is that soon reflected (with only minor variations) in the consciousness of Mrs. Compson, Quentin, and Jason: the image of the member of the family whose fall from innocence is said to have brought a peculiar disgrace on the entire family; a disgrace considered equal to, or even greater than, that of Ben's idiocy. Gradually, however, the reader appreciates that Mrs. Compson, Quentin, and Jason, each motivated by different kinds of need for self-justification, have first made a scapegoat of Ben and have then made a scapegoat of Caddy, so that they may heap on these two scapegoats the ultimate blame for the disintegration within the Compson family. Although this suggests one further aspect of Faulkner's complex theme, further elaboration of this central meaning may be postponed until we have considered other varieties of mirror analogues.

In Part Two of *The Sound and the Fury* Faulkner gradually suggests antithetical contrasts between Ben's pre-occupation with mirrors and Quentin's preoccupation with mirrors. At one point in his reverie Quentin makes this sequence of observations.

> I could smell the curves of the river beyond the dusk and I saw the last light supine and tranquil upon the tide-flats like pieces of broken mirror . . . Benjamin the child of. How he used to sit before that mirror. Refuge unfailing in which conflict [was] tempered silenced reconciled.

Quentin is (if we may borrow a phrase which Faulkner affords to Quentin himself) "a sort of obverse reflection" of Ben. By contrast with Ben's instinctive response to objects used to symbolize positive values in human experience, Quentin serves to dramatize a consciously willed and obsessive love for negative values which are life-injuring, life-destroying, and which in turn are nicely symbolized by his elaborately planned act of suicide by drowning. Throughout *The Sound and the Fury* a recurrent motif, suggested by the title itself, is the traditional convention of conflict between order-producing forces and chaos-producing forces in human experience, here represented in part by the gradual drift of the Compson family from remembered dignity and order toward disgrace and chaos. Quentin is represented as one whose disordering self-love motivates not only his masochistic delight in creating inner chaos but also his erotic lust for his own death. Structurally, then, the juxtaposition of Ben's thirty-third birthday against Quentin's death day accentuates the contrasting life-visions symbolized by Ben (who is ironically the shame of the Compsons) and by Quentin (who is ironically the pride of the Compsons). The two brief passages which constitute, respectively, the end of Ben's day and the beginning of Quentin's day may be quoted to suggest, once again, Faulkner's fondness for the technical principle of antithesis, here used to illuminate obliquely the basic ways in which these two brothers serve as obverse reflections of each other. Ben's day ends with these words:

> Caddy held me and I could hear us all, and the darkness, and sometimes I could smell. And then I could see the windows, where the trees were buzzing. Then the dark began to go in smooth, bright shapes, like it always does, even when Caddy says that I have been asleep.

There, implicitly, recurs the thematic suggestion that Ben, with the aid of Caddy, has developed the ability to find within himself the power to convert even darkness into a pattern of meaningful and soothing symmetry, serenity, order: "refuge unfailing, in which conflict [was] tempered silenced reconciled," as Quentin phrased it. By contrast, Quentin begins his day with an irritated resentment of sunlight and with an insistence on finding within himself the power to convert even the life-giving value of sunlight into a reminder of time. After the manner of his father, Quentin has already endowed time with ugly and chaotic significance: "When the shadow of the sash appeared on the curtains it was between seven and eight o'clock and then I was in time again, hearing the watch."

For immediate purposes the pivotal image there is "shadow," an image subsequently enriched by Faulkner to represent Quentin's *alter ego*, his own reflected image of himself, developed by Quentin as an elaborate mirror analogue. Quentin's reasoning, obliquely suggested by his numerous references to his own mirror analogue, may be paraphrased briefly. To achieve his willed act of self-destruction, he is aware that he must cope with that other side of self which is represented by his physical being or body, which intuitively or instinctively clings to life while resisting the death-will of his mind. To insult and belittle that resisting other-self (the body), Quentin identifies his body with his sun-cast shadow. Because the sun is repeatedly represented as creating the shadow of his body, this shadow might be considered poetically as the body's tribute to the life-giving power of the sun. But this is exactly the kind of tribute which Quentin wishes to deny. His inverted attitude toward the instinctive life-wish of his body is nicely reflected in the following poetic sentence, so rich in suggested extensions of meanings: "There was a clock, high up in the sun, and I thought about how when you don't want to do a thing, your body will try to trick you into doing it, sort of unawares."

At first glance, this echo of the traditional body-versus-spirit antithesis suggests Quentin's warped Calvinistic Presbyterian heritage. On reconsideration, it becomes obvious that the thing which Quentin does not want to do is to live; that which his body tries to do is to resist Quentin's obsessive and erotic lust for death. Consequently Quentin perversely views the body's natural death-resistance as the body's attempt to "trick" him. This inverted concept evokes his further conviction that he must counterattack that body-impulse by managing somehow to subdue and "trick" his shadow. Four very brief utterances of Quentin's may be quoted here to demonstrate the ironically enriching effects achieved by Faulkner in permitting this shadow-reflection of Quentin's body to represent Quentin's other-self opponent.

[1] I stepped into the sunlight, finding my shadow again.
[2] Trampling my shadow's bones into the concrete with hard heels. . . .
[3] The car stopped. I got off, into the middle of my shadow . . . trampling my shadow into the dust.
[4] The wall went into shadow, and then my shadow, I had tricked it again.

Obviously, Quentin's ultimate tricking of his "shadow" must be the destruction of his body in the planned act of suicide by drowning. In developing the double significance of this act (as being desired by the will and as being not desired by the body), Faulkner makes pertinent use of Quentin's initial experience on a bridge over the Charles River, where he stands contemplating his own shadow mirrored on the surface of the water below.

> The shadow of the bridge, the tiers of railings, my shadow leaning flat upon the water, so easily had I tricked it that it would not quit me. At least fifty feet it was, and if I only had something to blot it into the water, holding it until it drowned, the shadow of the package like two shoes wrapped up lying on the water. Niggers say a drowned man's shadow was watching for him in the water all the time. . . . I leaned on the railing, watching my shadow, how I had tricked it. I moved along the rail, but my suit was dark too and I could wipe my hands, watching my shadow, how I had tricked it.

Later, from another bridge, Quentin blindly contemplates another symbolic shadow: the trout, instinctively fulfilling its potentialities as it swims against the destructive element in which it has its being.

> I could not see the bottom, but I could see a long way into the motion of the water before the eye gave out, and then I saw a shadow hanging like a fat arrow stemming into the current. Mayflies skimmed in and out of the shadow of the bridge just above the surface. . . . The arrow increased without motion, then in a quick swirl the trout lipped a fly beneath the surface. . . . The fading vortex drifted away down stream and then I saw the arrow again, nose into the current, wavering delicately to the motion of the water above which the Mayflies slanted and poised. . . . Three boys with fishing poles came onto the bridge and we leaned on the rail and looked down at the trout. They knew the fish. He was a neighborhood character. . . . "We dont try to catch him anymore," he said. "We just watch Boston folks that come out and try."

That little parable or implicit mirror of meaning, wasted on Quentin, helps to correlate several different aspects of Faulkner's steadily developing emphasis on the value of certain kinds of instinctive response in human experience. There is even a suggested analogy between the instinctive action of the trout and the instinctive action of the sea gull which Quentin also blindly contemplates: each in its own discrete element instinctively uses the current or stream of its own element to achieve poise, even as the Mayflies do. Consider these two quotations in their relation to each other.

> . . . rushing away under the poised gull and all things rushing.
> . . . the arrow again, nose into the current, wavering delicately to the motion of the water above which the Mayflies slanted and poised.

Quentin's element is time, and instead of building on his own innate and instinctive potentialities for achieving poise against the motion of "all things rushing," he is represented as having deliberately chosen to pervert and destroy those potentialities. The trout, the gull, the Mayflies, along with Ben, make available to the reader the kinds of metaphorical "mirrors" of meaning which Quentin refuses to understand. By contrast with Ben, Quentin has a tendency to use all mirrors (literal or figurative) to multiply negative values, particularly those disordered and chaotic values symbolized by the reflection of his own death-obsessed face. On the evening of his death day, as he continues his chaotically systematic ritual of death courtship, Quentin momentarily finds in a window of a trolley car a mirror of things broken: "The lights were on in the car, so while we ran behind trees I couldn't see anything except my own face and a woman across the aisle with a hat sitting right on top of her head, with a broken feather in it."

Having established that mirror-image of the trolley

car window, Faulkner subsequently develops extensions of meaning from it. Quentin, after returning to his dormitory room to clean himself up for death, stands before a conventional mirror, brushing his hair, troubled at the thought that Shreve, his roommate, may return in time to spoil his plans. Or perhaps, he thinks, Shreve may be coming in to town on a trolley, just as Quentin is again going out on another trolley, and if so their faces will be momentarily juxtaposed and separated only by the two windows and the space between. The elliptical passage containing hints of these thoughts is of particular interest here, because it suggests a basic mirror principle, namely, Quentin's use of phrases which have only a superficial value for him, but a far deeper thematic suggestion for the reader. Here is the passage.

> While I was brushing my hair the half hour went. But there was until the three quarters anyway, except supposing seeing on the rushing darkness only his own face no broken feather unless two of them but not two like that going to Boston the same night then my face his face for an instant across the crashing when out of the darkness two lighted windows in rigid fleeing crash gone his face and mine just as I see saw did I see.

The potentials of meaning which go far beyond Quentin's immediate meaning there may be passed over to let us concentrate particularly on that striking phrase, less applicable to Shreve than to the total action of Quentin: "seeing on the rushing darkness only his own face." That again strongly suggests not only the conflict between Quentin's two opposed consciences but also the total contrast between Quentin's uses of mirrors and Ben's uses of mirrors.

Faulkner's most elaborately contrived mirror analogue, in the presentation of Quentin's death day, stands out as technically different from any mirror analogue we

have yet considered. It is a figurative or symbolic mirror-
ing of the meaning of a past action in a present action: the
parallelism between the way Quentin plays big brother to
the little Italian girl and the way Quentin previously
played big brother to Caddy. Another kind of "broken
mirror" effect is achieved by scattering through the entire
episode involving the Italian girl evoked fragments of
memories concerning earlier and related episodes involving
Quentin and Caddy. This twofold sequence of analogous
actions is much too long to be analyzed here. Yet it deserves to be mentioned as an extremely important example
of a mirror analogue, in which Faulkner at least suggests
that Caddy's love for her younger brother Ben and for her
older brother Quentin was soiled, stained, and perverted
by Quentin's self-love until Caddy, trying to keep up with
her brother, got into trouble. To a large degree, Quentin is
represented as having been personally responsible for the
change which occurred in the character of Caddy. Yet,
even as Quentin rejects as ridiculous the charge of the
Italian brother, "You steela my sister," so he also rejects
and ignores even the suggestions made by his own conscious or subconscious associations that he was, indeed, in
some way responsible for what happened to Caddy. In this
immediate context there is a highly ironic significance in
the fact that Caddy should have chosen to name her
daughter Quentin, even though her brother was not physically the father of her child.

Faulkner seems to have saved two oblique and "gathering" metaphors or symbolic actions for use in the concluding pages of *The Sound and the Fury*, and in this
context it may be permissible to consider those two actions
as mirror analogues, figuratively speaking. The first of
these occurs in the episode involving Dilsey and Ben at the
Easter service in the Negro church, and Faulkner begins it
by making technical use, once again, of two contrasting or antithetical attitudes toward one person,

namely, the monkey-faced preacher, who undergoes a metamorphosis, as he loses himself in the meaning of an action symbolizing self-sacrificial love:

> And the congregation seemed to watch with its own eyes while the voice consumed him, until he was nothing and they were nothing and there was not even a voice but instead their hearts were speaking to one another in chanting measures beyond the need for words, so that when he came to° rest against the reading desk, his monkey face lifted and his whole attitude that of a serene, tortured crucifix that transcended its shabbiness and insignificance and made of it no moment, a long expulsion of breath rose from them.

Faulkner would seem to be dramatizing in that symbolic action a key aspect of his central theme, always pivoting, as it does, on various possible meanings for the single word "love." For that reason the responses of Dilsey and Ben to that action are pertinent.

> Dilsey sat bolt upright, her hand on Ben's knee. The tears slid down her fallen cheeks, in and out of the myriad coruscations of immolation and abnegation and time. . . . In the midst of the voices and the hands Ben sat, rapt in his sweet blue gaze. Dilsey sat bolt upright beside, crying rigidly and quietly in the annealment and the blood of the remembered Lamb.

The second of these gathering metaphors also illuminates and accentuates the implicit thematic antithesis between two kinds of vision. This time the extensions of meaning are ironically suggested through Luster's saucy analogy between how he does something and "how quality does it." While entertaining Ben by taking him for his customary ride to the cemetery on Easter Sunday, Luster decides to show off, for the benefit of some loitering Negroes. He merely proposes a simple violation of a simple law when he says, "Les show dem niggers how quality does it, Benjy." Instead of driving around the monument in the accustomed way, he starts Queenie the wrong way.

Ben, instinctively feeling the difference between right and wrong even in such a trivial situation, begins to bellow and continues until the minor chaos of that situation (ironically corrected by Jason, out of mere embarrassment) has given way to the ritual of orderly return. So the total action of the narrative ends with the implicit and symbolic reiteration of the part Ben has played throughout, in terms of the antithesis between the human power to create chaos and the human power to create order.

> Queenie moved again, her feet began to clop-clop, steadily again, and at once Ben hushed. Luster looked quickly back over his shoulder, then he drove on. The broken flower drooped over Ben's fist, and his eyes were empty and blue and serene again, as cornice and façade flowed smoothly once more, from left to right; post and tree, window and doorway, and signboard, each in its ordered place.

Faulkner's choice of title deserves to be viewed figuratively as suggesting one further kind of mirror analogue, because the attitude of Macbeth, as dramatized in the familiar fifth-act soliloquy, nicely reflects an important element in the attitudes of Faulkner's three major protagonists of chaos, Mrs. Compson, Quentin, and Jason. All of these characters have this much in common: each is intent on self-pitying self-justification. All are certain that they have become victimized by circumstances beyond their control, and all of them project outward on life their own inner chaos, which has its roots in a perversion of love, through self-love. Similarly, in the fifth act, Macbeth is represented as refusing to recognize that he has been in any way to blame, or responsible, for what has happened to him. Instead, he also projects his own inner chaos outward, self-justifyingly, to make a scapegoat of the whole world, even of time, and to view life itself as a walking "shadow." Now consider the ironies of situation implicit in that passage which Faulkner's title suggests as a pertinent

mirror of the attitudes not only of Quentin and Jason but
also of Mr. and Mrs. Compson.

> Tomorrow, and tomorrow, and tomorrow,
> Creeps in this petty pace from day to day,
> To the last syllable of recorded time.
> And all our yesterdays have lighted fools
> The way to dusty death. Out, out, brief candle!
> Life's but a walking shadow, a poor player
> That struts and frets his hour upon the stage,
> And then is heard no more. It is a tale
> Told by an idiot, full of sound and fury,
> Signifying nothing.

Finally, the meaning of Faulkner's total structure
may be suggested by one last mirror analogue. As narrator, he would seem to be intent on achieving a high
degree of detachment by arranging his four separate parts
in such a way that they do not tell a story in the conventional sense. Faulkner neither invites nor permits the
reader to look directly at the total cause-and-effect sequence of events, as such. Instead, each of the four parts
provides a different aspect, a different view, a different
angle of vision, a different reflection of some parts of the
story. Each of these four structural units, thus contiguous,
hinged, set at a different angle from the others, might be
called analogous to those hinged and contiguous haber-
dashery mirrors which permit us to contemplate the immediate picture reflected in any single one of those mirrors, and then to contemplate secondary or subordinate
pictures which are reflections of reflections in each of the
separate mirrors.

In Faulkner's four structural mirrors (the four
parts), the first picture (or pictures) may be said to be
provided through Ben's reflecting angle of vision. Although the reader's initial impression of Ben's reverie may,
indeed, provide a sense that the tale is told by an idiot,
signifying nothing, the ultimate impression is that Ben's

angle of vision concentrates our attention symbolically on certain basic and primitive powers of perception, available even to an idiot; powers of perception which enable even a severely handicapped individual to create, from his own experience and with the aid of his instincts and intuitions, some forms of order which can give positive values to human experience.

Structurally, the second set of pictures is provided through Quentin's reflecting angle of vision. This time, although the reader's early impression of Quentin's reverie may provide a preliminary sense of a highly sensitive and Hamlet-like character, who views himself as intent on holding up to nature his own idealistic mirror, the ultimate impression is that Quentin's angle of vision reflects, by contrast with Ben's, several important aspects of the negative or obverse side of Faulkner's theme. Psychologically unbalanced by his own inner and outer conflicts, Quentin is represented as being partly responsible not only for what has happened to himself but also for what has happened to some other members of his family. He has permitted his warped and warping ego to invert exactly those basic and primitive and positive values symbolized by that which Ben instinctively and intuitively cherished.

The third set of images is provided by Jason's reflecting angle of vision, and even though Jason sees himself as the only sane Compson, the reader quickly becomes convinced that Jason's sadistic scale of values is more nearly analogous to the values of Iago than to those of the almost Hamlet-like Quentin. The irony of the total situation involving Jason culminates in a ridiculously fine burlesque of poetic justice when Faulkner permits Jason's golden fleece of Caddy to be avenged by Caddy's daughter's golden fleece of Jason. Even as Caddy's brother Quentin has somehow been at least partially responsible for the moral degeneration of Caddy, so Jason is represented as being at least partially responsible for the moral degeneration of Caddy's daughter.

The fourth set of images is provided through Dilsey's reflecting angle of vision. Implicitly and symbolically there is an analogous relationship between Dilsey's emphasis on certain basic, primary, positive values throughout and Ben's intuitive sense of values. Thus, the positive angles of vision, mirrored by Ben and Dilsey most sharply in the first and fourth structural parts of *The Sound and the Fury*, may be considered literally and symbolically as bracketing and containing the two negative angles of vision mirrored by Quentin and Jason in the second and third parts. Taken in this sense, the structural arrangement of these four hinged mirrors serves to heighten the reader's awareness of Faulkner's major thematic antithesis between the chaos-producing effects of self-love and the order-producing effects of compassionate and self-sacrificial love in human experience.

AS I LAY DYING
Faulkner's Inner Reporter*

by WILLIAM J. HANDY

Perhaps with the exception of *The Sound and the Fury*, Faulkner's *As I Lay Dying* remains the most baffling of his works. As an account of a somewhat pathetic family of southern poor whites compelled to undertake a journey beset with hardships, in subject matter it resembles *The Grapes of Wrath*. But Faulkner's novel is much more

* From William J. Handy, "*As I Lay Dying*: Faulkner's Inner Reporter," *The Kenyon Review*, XXI (Summer, 1959), 437–451. Reprinted by permission of the publisher and the author.

Passages from *As I Lay Dying* reprinted by permission of Random House, Inc.

complex than Steinbeck's, its subject matter much more inclusive. In moving from the consciousness of one character to that of another, Faulkner is concerned not so much with a pattern of events as he is with a pattern of individual existences. His intention in this respect is closer to that of Joyce and Henry James than it is to that of Steinbeck. That is, for Faulkner, as for Joyce and James, the emphasis on inner awareness reflects an interest in the intensity of human experience, not in its order of succession.

In *As I Lay Dying* the Darl of event is not the Darl of consciousness, for the former is presented primarily through the eyes of others. Similarly with each of the other characters—their existence as participants in a journey is generically different from their existence as living, experiencing beings. What Faulkner offers us is the ironic quality of the difference.

But Faulkner's technique, like that of Joyce, demands a degree of alertness by the reader that is not required by the techniques of James. In *As I Lay Dying* as in *Ulysses*, the point separating the objective reporter from the inner reporter is disarmingly close. In *The Ambassadors*, on the other hand, James passes clearly and with good warning from one to the other. Yet it is in the rapid movement from the world of objective experience to the world of inner experience that the real quality of Faulkner's novel resides, and the reader must constantly bear this in mind.

To the extent that we can view Darl objectively—as one who is different from the others, as one slightly peculiar at times, at times quite insane—to the extent that such a view is possible, we are aware of Darl as a case history. But the objective view of Darl is not our only account. What Darl is essentially, in his inner experiencing, pervades the entire book. Nearly one-third of the sixty-odd sections are devoted to presenting the inner Darl.

Faulkner is nowhere more successful than in depicting this complex individual. The reader's comprehension moves from the Darl of action and event to the Darl of inner consciousness. The paradoxical quality of the real Darl resides finally in the tension between these two different aspects of human experience. The Darl who taunts his brother with the fact of their mother's death because to his brother Addie's dying is too painful to face, the Darl who sees his sister's dilemma but offers only silent repudiation, the Darl who sets fire to the stock-filled barn of a helpful farmer in order to cremate his mother—such a Darl is easy to judge. He is jealous and vindictive, lacking in family responsibility, socially incompetent, and even felonious.

But the Darl of being, the Darl we know by Faulkner's discovery of a way "to see into the heart," is not easy to judge. Indeed, we are not moved to judgment. It is enough that we understand. Darl's *doing*, his external acts, the part he plays in the unfolding of events, become understandable in the light of our insight into the reality of his felt experience.

Faulkner's portrayal of such a character as Darl changes our most fundamental ideas about character and characterization. We are no longer so concerned with the unfolding of events, with the question, "Then what happened?" as we are with the presentation of being, with the question, "What is man's real experience?" Between Anse's simple question, "Where's Jewel?" and Darl's answer, "Down to the barn," we will experience something of the quality of Darl's living awareness.

When I was a boy I first learned how much better water tastes when it has set awhile in a cedar bucket. Warmish-cool, with a faint taste like the hot July wind in cedar trees smells. It has to set at least six hours, and be drunk from a gourd. Water should never be drunk from metal.

And at night it is better still. I used to lie on the pallet in the hall, waiting until I could hear them all asleep, so I could get up and go back to the bucket. It would be black, the shelf black, the still surface of the

> water a round orifice in nothingness, where before I
> stirred it awake with the dipper I could see maybe a
> star or two in the bucket, and maybe in the dipper a
> star or two before I drank.

The writing here is exceptionally vivid; the images are
lucid and flawless. But the intention of the imagery is not
to describe a Mississippi boy's pleasure in drinking cool
water on a hot summer night. Rather the passage means to
objectify the strange quality of the boy's sensibility. That
is, we are not so much concerned with the particular experience as we are with the consciousness which was capable
of it.

The consciousness marking the greatest contrast with
Darl's is that of Cora Tull. It affects our own sensibilities.
Our interest is not with Cora's chickens and eggs, with her
baking cakes to sell to wealthy ladies; rather we are interested in how these things objectify her preoccupations,
reveal to us the quality of her conscious experience, and
express Cora's world, her values, and her relationship to
the action of the novel. It is what Cora essentially *is* as
that *isness* comes into immediate relation to the Bundren
family, that causes Jewel's explosive utterance in the only
section in which he is the viewpoint figure, and to Vardaman's disgust when he throws into the dust the fish which
he was proudly carrying to his mother.

Cora is important. Her facile moral pronouncements
become the ironic expression of some of the central meanings of the novel. In an early section she declares,

> The Lord can see into the heart. If it is his will that
> some folks has different ideas of honesty from other
> folks, it is not my place to question his decree.

Many ironic ambiguities are present here. It is immediately apparent that Cora is blinded by her moral preconceptions from ever seeing into the heart of any human
being—especially herself. Further, the passage is related to

Faulkner's technique and the meaning which he is able to formulate through that technique. Cora's utterance is an objective symbol of her values which ironically enables the reader to "see into the heart."

Ultimately, the passage is related to the total meaning of the work: the sympathetic narrative, devoid of moral preconceptions, of living, experiencing mankind. For it is Faulkner's chief task to present what he has found man's nature to be—to present the "different ideas of honesty" which define the human situation. And his presentation is necessarily varied and complex—from the spiritually blind Cora Tull to the supersensitively aware Darl—a range that encompasses a world of humanity in its scope and requires a boldness of fictional technique such as we have found in the most successful experiments of modern fiction.

The scene in which Cora visits Addie just before Addie's dying is characteristic. Cora is a spectator at Addie's bedside from curiosity more than sympathy. The face she presents to the ladies of the sick room is conventional enough. She believes she is doing her duty as friend and comforter. But in objectifying her inner awareness, Faulkner presents her with a much more real face. Here is her consciousness reporting:

> The quilt is drawn up to her chin, hot as it is, with only her two hands and her face outside. She is propped on the pillow, with her head raised so she can see out the window, and we can hear him every time he takes up the adze or the saw. If we were deaf we could almost watch her face and hear him, see him.

This is the Cora who has come to witness the approaching death of another being, to watch and note the face of the dying woman as she hears her coffin being built. Faulkner finds effective symbolic correlatives for her real feeling in concise successive images. We do not see Addie in them; we see Addie as Cora sees her; we see one aspect of Cora's essential self:

Her face is wasted away so that the bones draw just
under the skin in white lines. Her eyes are like two
candles when you watch them gutter down into the
sockets of iron candlesticks.

Then in one unexpected stroke, Faulkner gives us a deeper
insight into Cora's being as she pronounces judgment:

But the eternal and everlasting salvation and grace is
not upon her.

And we see that, for Cora, Addie is not Addie; she is the
violation of Cora's understanding of a moral principle.
Cora has labeled the picture she comes each day to witness
and what is Addie has long since dissolved into Cora's
label. Here is justification for Jewel's cry.

Like the buzzards that will circle the coffin throughout its long journey, the ladies of the sick-room are at
once a presence which is both ludicrous and ominous—
comic in what they suggest of gossipy, dissembling
women, but tragically ominous in what they suggest of
man's relationship to his fellow man. The unique quality
of Faulkner's meaning resides neither in what Cora voices
nor in what she thinks but in the tension between the
two:

"They turned out real nice," I say. "But not like the
cakes Addie used to bake." You can see that girl's
washing and ironing in the pillow slip, if ironed it ever
was. Maybe it will reveal her blindness to her, laying
there at the mercy and ministration of four men and a
tomboy girl.

Cora, Kate, and Eula are an essential part of the
scene as Addie Bundren lies dying. Cora's mind wanders
from the real image of Addie:

Under the quilt she makes no more of a hump than a
rail would, and the only way you can tell she is
breathing is by the sound of the mattress shucks.—

Then her concern is as to the propriety of Eula's necklace

which cost only twenty-five cents—abruptly she reflects on her own loss of the money for the cakes and finally on Eula's real reason for being present, which is to catch the attention of Darl. In carrying out the death-bed ritual the ladies are fulfilling the requirements of the country mores. But in exposing their real feelings, their sometimes trivial and sometimes vindictive preoccupation, Faulkner has passed judgment on one aspect of man's essential nature. They are as blameless for their activity as are the buzzards but, in the real quality of their consciousness, no less repulsive.

The fact of Darl's insanity raises the question of just how valid his insights are intended by Faulkner to be. And it is not merely a matter of the insanity's occurring at the end of the journey. Anse, in his opening section, makes an indirect allusion to it:

> And Darl, too. Talking me out of him, durn them. It ain't that I am afraid of work; I always have fed me and mine and kept a roof above us; it's that they would shorthand me just because he tends to his own business, just because he's got his eyes full of the land, because the land laid up-and-down ways then; it wasn't till that ere road come and switched the land around longways and his eyes still full of the land, that they begun to threaten me out of him, trying to shorthand me with the law.

And so it is established early in the novel that Darl's sanity is suspect, even, it is suggested, to the point where incarceration is considered. Ironically it is Anse's selfish concern with being shorthanded that keeps Darl out of the asylum from the outset.

Yet Darl's inner experiences are never presented as mere fantasy. They seem to be offered not only as adequate expressions of what is happening but also as matter-of-fact instances of Darl's incredible sensitivity. The section dealing with the death of Addie is perhaps the most successful instance of the technique. In the preceding section Peabody, the doctor, has been dismissed from the sick room by the silent repudiation of the dying woman. In the final lines of his section he reports:

> Beyond the porch Cash's saw snores steadily into the board. A minute later she calls his name, her voice harsh and strong,
> "Cash," she says; "you, Cash!"

In the next section, which is Darl's report, there is a detailed account of Addie's death. It is Darl's imagined account, his experienced vision of the scene which is presented. Darl and Jewel are miles away at the time, Darl having succeeded in keeping Jewel and Addie apart at the time of her death by urging the need for the three dollars which could be earned by hauling a wagonload of lumber. Anse, always greedy for another dollar, was an easy prey to Darl's intention. Jewel, refusing to admit that his mother's death was imminent and unable to face the possibility of it, had also consented to Darl's suggestion. Three short passages of the section are in italics. They serve to locate Darl's actual position, far removed from the room in which Addie lay dying. The first begins:

> *Jewel, I say. Overhead the day drives level and grey, hiding the sun by a flight of grey spears. In the rain the mules smoke a little, splashed yellow with mud, the off one clinging in sliding lunges to the side of the road above the ditch. The tilted lumber gleams dull yellow, water-soaked and heavy as lead, tilted at a steep angle into the ditch above the broken wheel; about the shattered spokes and about Jewel's ankles a runnel of yellow neither water nor earth swirls. . . .*

It is at this moment, having succeeded not only in separating Jewel from Addie but in rendering him completely impotent of action, that Darl's authentic vision of Addie's death occurs. Here is the scene as Faulkner accepts its existence in the mind of Darl:

Pa stands beside the bed. From behind his leg Vardaman peers, with his round head and his eyes round
and his mouth beginning to open. She looks at pa; all
her failing life appears to drain into her eyes, urgent,
irremediable. "It's Jewel she wants," Dewey Dell
says.

"Why, Addie," pa says, "him and Darl went to
make one more load. They thought there was time.
That you would wait for them, and that three dollars
and all. . . ."

He stoops, laying his hand on hers. For a while
yet she looks at him, without reproach, without anything at all, as if her eyes alone are listening to the
irrevocable cessation of his voice. Then she raises
herself, who has not moved in ten days. Dewey Dell
leans down, trying to press her back.

"Ma," she says; "ma."

She is looking out the window, at Cash stooping
steadily at the board in the failing light, laboring on
toward darkness and into it as though the stroking of
the saw illumined its own motion; board and saw
engendered.

"You, Cash," she shouts, her voice harsh, strong,
and unimpaired. "You, Cash!"

Here is ample justification for accepting Darl's subjective
experience as a valid account of what actually occurred.
For Darl's report of Addie's last utterance is the same as
Peabody's. The fact makes credible Darl's amazing insight.

Darl's sensibility is most acute when it is focused on
Jewel. Every nuance of Jewel's discernible emotion and
action registers upon Darl's awareness. When Anse asks
"Where's Jewel?" Darl pictures his brother and replies:

Down there fooling with that horse. He will go on
through the barn into the pasture. The horse will not
be in sight. . . .

Then abruptly Faulkner changes from the future tense
reflecting Darl's imagined view of the scene to the present
tense—as if Darl were actually reporting the scene. Again

what is most important is not the event itself but the actuality which Darl experiences in it:

> . . . [the horse] is up there among the pine seedlings, in the cool. Jewel whistles, once and shrill. The horse snorts, then Jewel sees him, glinting for a gaudy instant among the blue shadows.

The meaning which Faulkner is able to achieve through this technique is very complex. Darl suddenly becomes the author of Jewel's experience. We accept the viewpoint as Jewel's, that the horse for Jewel is "glinting for a gaudy instant among the blue shadows." Yet we are aware that this is a projection of Darl's imagination. Darl's acute sensitivity has invaded the awareness of his brother, so that not only is Darl constantly aware of his brother's external actions but of Jewel's inner experience.

The reason for Darl's obsession with his brother is not presented for some hundred pages, but, until the reader becomes acquainted with it, Darl remains an inexplicable figure. When Jewel was fifteen Darl, then slightly older, came to the realization of Addie's infidelity—and to the realization of her love for Jewel. Here was the experience that conditioned what he was during the time of the story, the time of Addie's death and the journey. All of his feelings have become centered by now on his deep resentment of Jewel—the objectification of his grief and incompleteness.

In a story by D. H. Lawrence, "The Rocking Horse Winner," the deep, primal need of a boy for the love of his mother, a need which her nature is incapable of satisfying, expresses itself in violent and desperate action to remove the obstacle between himself and his mother: her obsessive craving for money. Lawrence's story suggests the slumbering forces in man's nature—forces which come into being when psychical development is threatened by the nonfulfillment of a vital need. Love, too, becomes a force, measurable only because of its absence. The effect on Lawrence's boy and the effect on Darl show remarkable similarities: both withdraw into a lonely isolation and introspection; both develop a heightened sensitivity and awareness; in both appears an obsessive preoccupation with the obstacle that blocks their completeness. For the boy the embodiment of the obstacle is money; for Darl it is Jewel, the symbol of his frustration.

Nearly every one of Darl's nineteen viewpoint sections is in some way an expression of Darl's obsessive preoccupation with his brother. Eleven open with this preoccupation, and five others are centrally concerned with it. Some examples of these openings reveal the way Faulkner builds this important expressive symbol of Darl's inner world. The book begins with a Darl section:

> Jewel and I come up from the field, following the path in a single file.

Darl's third section opens:

> We watch him come around the corner and mount the steps. He does not look at us. "You ready?" he says.

And his fourth section:

> He has been to town this week: the back of his neck is trimmed close, with a white line between hair and sunburn like a joint of white bone. He has not once looked back.

As Darl and Jewel return to the family who have been waiting to begin the long journey to the cemetery in Jefferson, Darl's obsessive hatred for his brother emerges in the first of the bitter taunts he is to voice throughout the journey. The section opens:

> "It's not your horse that's dead, Jewel," I say.

It picks up the earlier phrase, "Jewel, I say," which had

not been voiced but had been significantly a part of Darl's conscious thought. Darl's taunts continue as he points to the buzzards circling the house containing the body of the dead Addie. He has succeeded not only in keeping Jewel from the side of his dying mother, but in delaying for two additional days the departure for the cemetery. The buzzards are an added affront to the pride and dignity of Jewel who, in his one viewpoint section, had lashed out at the indignities attending the dying of Addie; such as Cash's construction of the coffin in Addie's presence, the neighboring women "sitting like buzzards in the sick room," and Dewey Dell's "keeping the air always moving so fast on her face that when you're tired you can't breathe it." It is these violations of pride that give rise to Jewel's tragic outburst:

> It would just be me and her on a high hill and me rolling the rocks down the hill at their faces, picking them up and throwing them down the hill, faces and teeth and all by God until she was quiet and not that goddamn adze going one lick less. One lick less and we could be quiet.

Darl is fully aware of his brother's values, and now is moved to play on them in his taunts:

> "See them?" I say. High above the house, against the quick thick sky, they hang in narrowing circles. From here they are no more than specks, implacable, patient, portentous.

And then, aware that Jewel through prolonged effort had succeeded in establishing the horse as a surrogate for his mother, as a way of release from the overwhelming intensity of their relationship, Darl probes the psychical wound in Jewel's personality:

> "But it's not your horse that's dead." "Goddamn you," he says. "Goddamn you."

Immediately juxtaposed is Darl's pathetic motive:

I cannot love my mother because I have no mother.

To understand Darl's loneliness, and his obsession with his brother, it is necessary to examine his relationships with Addie, the one who determined the direction his psychical development would take. The single section which Faulkner assigns to the consciousness of Addie has no location within the unfolding events of the story. It is the voice of one giving an account of her life, explaining and justifying her action in an existence which is no longer capable of action. She begins with a reminiscence of her experiences with the children in her schoolroom just before her marriage to Anse.

> In the afternoon when school was out and the last one had left with his little dirty snuffling nose, instead of going home I would go down the hill to the spring where I could be quiet and hate them.

The passage resembles the beginning of a confession. The speaker offers her real feelings toward the children. There is no circumlocution for "hate," because there is no recognition of the conventional preconceptions toward hating which one finds and expects in the values of Addie's moralistic neighbor, Cora Tull. Addie's values are offered at once. We see before long that her hatred of the children is not for their runny noses or unfinished lessons, but for their individuation, their withdrawal into their secret selves, their native instinct to refuse communion with another by shutting that other out of their awareness. For Addie such individuation meant death in life:

> I could just remember how my father used to say that the reason for living was to get ready to stay dead a long time. And when I would have to look at them day after day, each with his and her secret and selfish thought, and blood strange to each other blood and strange to mine, and think that this seemed to be the only way I could get ready to stay dead, I would hate my father for having ever planted me.

In her marriage to Anse, Addie had the great disappointment of her life. Like the children's, his world was completely self-centered, shared with no one and kept impregnable by the conventional abstractions and labels which could readily be attached to any act or intention. For Addie there was no marriage of real selves, no violation of her aloneness, no real communion with another.

> He had a word, too. Love, he called it. But I had been used to words for a long time. I knew that that word was just like the others: just a shape to fill a lack. . . .

Throughout her long confession, we have the gradual development of an image of a woman of great physical and spiritual vitality, dedicated to a conviction that life must be shared to be meaningful, that withdrawal meant rejection of one's responsibility to live meaningfully and that the reason for living was to get ready to stay dead a long time. Addie's disappointment with her marriage to Anse reaches a climax after the unexpected and unwanted birth of Darl:

> He [Anse] did not know that he was dead, then. Sometimes I would lie by him in the dark, hearing the land that was of my blood and flesh, and I would think: Anse. Why Anse. Why are you Anse. I would think about his name until after a while I could see the word as a shape, a vessel, and I would watch him liquefy and flow into it like cold molasses flowing out of the darkness into the vessel, until the jar stood full and motionless: a significant shape profoundly without life like an empty door frame.

It was at this point that Addie abandoned her marriage to Anse. Though she continued to stay with the family, she no longer considered Anse and the children who were to follow from their spiritually sterile relationship as her children. She had admitted her acceptance of her first born, Cash:

. . . that when the right time came, you wouldn't need a word [love] for that any more than for pride or fear. Cash did not need to say it to me nor I to him.

But Darl was rejected:

Then I found that I had Darl. At first I would not believe it. Then I believed that I would kill Anse. It was as though he had tricked me, hidden within a word like within a paper screen and struck me in the back through it.

The product of her relationship with Whitfield, the minister, was Jewel, the object of her full acceptance and love.

And so I have cleaned my house. With Jewel—I lay by the lamp, holding up my own head watching him [the doctor] cap and suture it before he breathed—the wild blood boiled away and the sound of it ceased.

Addie's final pronouncement reveals the reason for Darl's pathetic situation:

I gave Anse Dewey Dell to negative Jewel. Then I gave him Vardaman to replace the child I had robbed him of. And now he has three children that are his and not mine. And then I could get ready to die.

Darl is one of the "three children that are his and not mine."

Addie's conviction that the purpose in human existence is to be found in relationships which are experienced rather than those which are sterilized through abstractions gives us insight into her individual values. We understand her special "hate" for the school children and the violence of her behavior toward them.

I would look forward to the times when they faulted, so I could whip them. When the switch fell I could feel it upon my flesh; when it welted and ridged it was my blood that ran, and I would think with each blow of the switch: Now you are aware of me! Now I am

> something in your secret and selfish life, who have
> marked your blood with my own for ever and ever.

And presently:

> I knew that it had been, not that they had dirty noses,
> but that we had had to use one another by words
> like spiders dangling by their mouths from a beam,
> swinging and twisting and never touching, and that
> only through the blows of the switch could my blood
> and their blood flow as one stream.

Having this account of her action, we can understand
Darl's plaintive observation of Jewel's relationship with
Addie: "Ma always whipped and petted him more." It
accounts for Darl's insight into Jewel's semi-violent relationship with the horse, the violence recognizable as an
essential part of the love between man and animal.

> He enters the stall and waits until it kicks at him so
> that he can slip past and mount on to the trough and
> pause, peering out across the intervening stalltops to-
> ward the empty path, before he reaches into the
> loft.
> "Goddamn him. Goddamn him."

For Darl there has been no such relationship with another,
and his cry of hatred is understandable as the expression
of his pathetic lot rather than an evidence of some perverse vindictiveness.

Similarly, we can understand the promise which
Addie elicited from Anse that she would be buried in
Jefferson. The exacted promise is Addie's revenge for the
destruction of her life by the clash between her own and
Anse's values. His shallow concept of love and her deep
desire for an experienced love meant only frustration and
unfulfillment for Addie:

> But then I realized that I had been tricked by words
> older than Anse or love, and that the same word had
> tricked Anse too, and that my revenge would be that
> he would never know I was taking revenge. And when

Darl was born I asked Anse to promise to take me back to Jefferson when I died.

Here is the real motive for the promise, a motive that is rooted in Addie's values. She knows that Anse who lives by words will remain consistent with his ways. The irony is that those ways have been responsible not only for Addie's situation but for the tragic lives of those children whom her feelings toward her husband had obliged her to repudiate.

In *As I Lay Dying* Faulkner is not writing simply out of a belief that man will endure in the face of hardship. He is writing out of a conviction that what is most real in human experience is the kind of inner world man inhabits —a world wherein is determined man's feelings, hopes, desires, aspirations, compulsions and obsessions, and ultimately his attitudes and actions towards his fellow man.

JOHN STEINBECK
(1902–   )

John Steinbeck's values—those fundamental beliefs which are the necessary framework within which we understand concrete words and events—are not commonly known to his readers. His most typical subject, by contrast, is common knowledge; and thus it is that Steinbeck came to be known, during the thirties, as a proletarian novelist. *Tortilla Flat*, published in 1935, was judged by most critics to be a novel that needed more economic realism and less sentimentality; but Steinbeck, unlike Fitzgerald and Hemingway and others, was at least concerned with the poor and with socio-economic problems in a time of national depression and ought, consequently, to be granted some indulgences.

The Grapes of Wrath (1939), generally conceded to be Steinbeck's best novel, was taken to be a fitting achievement, for it concentrated, more successfully than any other novel, on the depression and on the need for economic and social reforms. Since the 1940 award of the Pulitzer Prize for *The Grapes of Wrath*, however, Steinbeck's reputation has declined. The Nobel Prize (in 1962) has sparked some new attention, but the general feeling is that novels like *East of Eden* (1952) and *The Winter of Our Discontent* (1961) ought to be like *The Grapes of Wrath* but are not. The proletarian novelist is not writing proletarian novels: *East of Eden* is vaguely mystical; *The Winter of Our Discontent* is about a faded aristocrat back East. Neither novel comes to grips with the problems handled so courageously in *The Grapes of Wrath*.

The error, however, is not Steinbeck's. It is the reader's. Steinbeck has used proletarian subjects, but he has never been a proletarian novelist. His values are not liberal, as opposed to traditional; but *sacred*, as opposed to *profane*, in the sense that these terms are defined by Mircea Eliade in *The Sacred and the Profane*. The selection of a home site, for example, is to the profane person a matter of traditional values, practical values, aesthetic considerations, perhaps a way to rebel against social enemies; but for Steinbeck, as in *To a God Unknown* (1933), to select your home is to designate the center of your universe. The act is successful insofar as it re-creates the primordial and sacred selection of place. Kinship, as in *East of Eden*, is also sacred. Brother stands to brother as Cain stood to Abel. It has been done before, will be done again, and is the necessary and circular framework within which we live. Herein, also, is the appropriate context for Steinbeck's bawdy. To the sacred mind, the body is an absurd home, though a sacred one, for the spirit of man; body functions are a spiritual irony, funny perhaps, but not dirty. And thus it is, finally, that Steinbeck has an interest in economics and science; for no one is more capable of realism than the truly sacred sensibility, who can even reject his gods when they become irrelevant to actuality.

In the more characteristic mainstream of American life, there is always a temporal purpose, a democratic end forecast by the myth of the promised land. One works to pay for his house, to get somewhere, to become somebody; and his earthly endeavor is what keeps his faith honest, is realistic testimony to belief in a higher teleology. But for Steinbeck, life is non-teleological, as he states, somewhat ineptly, in *The Log From the Sea of Cortez*; and as he says, most expertly, in *The Grapes of Wrath*, *The Red Pony*, *The Winter of Our Discontent*, and in other works.

Within this framework we can see more accurately a novel like *In Dubious Battle* (1936), Steinbeck's most "reformist" novel. The labor union is described as a worthwhile activity that gives direction and meaning to the lives of its supporters, but throughout the novel dedication to the cause of labor requires men to use one another, to sacrifice the individual to the mass, to rationalize cruelty as the only means to a just end, to lose sight of a sacrality that is without end. Those who lack the sense of sacrality may find themselves with achieved ends that have no meaning.

Appropriately, Steinbeck's personal life is characterized by variety rather than by single-minded consistency. Born in Salinas, California—which has become a central symbol in his works—he lives now in New York. He attended Stanford University, but not as a degree candidate. He worked, in his early years, as a bricklayer, reporter, caretaker; and his interests have included biology, labor unions, script-writing for Hollywood, travel to Russia, travels over America, playwrighting, satire, humor, propaganda for the war effort, and primitivism. Most important, the variety of his mind has helped him to shape an American version of Eastern thought which will endure, I think, through the strictures of those who believe it is incoherent to write of both the sacred and the economic.

THE GRAPES OF WRATH
AS FICTION*

by PETER LISCA

When *The Grapes of Wrath* was published in April of
1939 there was little likelihood of its being accepted and
evaluated as a piece of fiction. Because of its nominal
subject, it was too readily confused with such high-class
reporting as Ruth McKenny's *Industrial Valley*, the WPA
collection of case histories called *These Are Our Lives*,
and Dorothea Lange and Paul S. Taylor's *An American
Exodus*. The merits of *The Grapes of Wrath* were debated
as social documentation rather than fiction. In addition to
incurring the disadvantages of its historical position, coming as a kind of climax to the literature of the Great
Depression, Steinbeck's novel also suffered from the pe-
rennial vulnerability of all social fiction to an attack on its
facts and intentions.

The passage of eighteen years has done very little to
alter this initial situation. Except for scattered remarks,
formal criticism of *The Grapes of Wrath* is still pretty
much limited to a chapter by Joseph Warren Beach, a
chapter by Harry Thornton Moore, a few paragraphs by
Kenneth Burke, part of a chapter by the French critic

* From Peter Lisca, "*The Grapes of Wrath* as Fiction,"
PMLA, LXXII, 1 (March, 1957), 296–309. Reprinted by permission of the Modern Language Association of America.

Claude-Edmonde Magny, and an essay by B. R. Mc-
Elderry, Jr.[1] In a period of such intensive analysis of the
techniques of fiction as the past fifteen years, the dearth of
critical material on *The Grapes of Wrath* must indicate an
assumption on the part of critics that this novel cannot
sustain such analysis. The present paper is an attempt to
correct this assumption by exploring some of the techniques by which John Steinbeck was able to give significant form to his sprawling materials and prevent his novel
of social protest from degenerating into propaganda.

The ideas and materials of *The Grapes of Wrath*
presented Steinbeck with a problem of structure similar to
that of Tolstoy's in writing *War and Peace*. Tolstoy's materials were, roughly, the adventures of the Bezukhov,
Rostov, and Bolkonski families on the one hand, and the
Napoleonic Wars on the other. And while the plot development brought these two blocks of material together,
there was enough about the Napoleonic Wars left over so
that the author had to incorporate it in separate philosophic interchapters. Steinbeck's materials were similar.
There were the adventures of the Joads, the Wilsons, and
the Wainwrights; there was also the Great Depression.
And like Tolstoy, he had enough material left over to write
separate philosophic interchapters.

In the light of this basic analogy, Percy Lubbock's
comments on the structural role of these two elements in
War and Peace become significant for an understanding of
structure in *The Grapes of Wrath*: "I can discover no
angle at which the two stories will appear to unite and
merge in a single impression. Neither is subordinated to
the other, and there is nothing above them . . . to which

---

[1] *American Fiction 1920–1940* (New York: Macmillan, 1941),
pp. 327–347; *The Novels of John Steinbeck* (Chicago: Nor-
mandie House, 1939), pp. 54–72; *The Philosophy of Literary
Form* (Louisiana State Univ. Press, 1941), p. 81; *L'Age du roman
américain* (Paris: Editions du Sueil, 1948), pp. 178–195; "*The
Grapes of Wrath:* In the Light of Modern Critical Theory,"
College English, v (March 1944), 308–313.

they are both related. Nor are they placed together to illustrate a contrast; nothing *results* from their juxtaposition. Only from time to time, upon no apparent principle and without a word of warning, one of them is dropped and the other is resumed."[2] In these few phrases Lubbock has defined the aesthetic conditions not only for *War and Peace* but for any other piece of fiction whose strategies include an intercalary construction—*The Grapes of Wrath*, for example. The test is whether anything *results* from this kind of structure.

Counting the opening description of the drought and the penultimate chapter on the rains, pieces of straightforward description allowable even to strictly "scenic" novels (Lubbock's term for materials presented entirely from the reader's point of view), there are in *The Grapes of Wrath* sixteen interchapters, making up a total of just under a hundred pages—almost one sixth of the book. In none of these chapters do the Joads, Wilsons, or Wainwrights appear.

These interchapters have two main functions. First, by presenting the social background they serve to amplify the pattern of action created by the Joad family. Thus, for example, Chapter i presents in panoramic terms the drought which forces the Joads off their land; Chapters vii and ix depict, respectively, the buying of jalopics for the migration and the selling of household goods; Chapter xi describes at length a decaying and deserted house which is the prototype of all the houses abandoned in the Dust Bowl. In thirteen such chapters almost every aspect of the Joads's adventures is enlarged and seen as part of the social climate. The remaining interchapters have the function of providing such historical information as the development of land ownership in California, the consequent development of migrant labor, and certain economic aspects of the social lag. These three informative chapters

<hr>

[2] *The Craft of Fiction* (New York: Peter Smith, 1945), p. 33.

make up only nineteen of the novel's six hundred-odd pages. Scattered through the sixteen interchapters are occasional paragraphs whose purpose is to present, with choric effect, the philosophy or social message to which the current situation gives rise. For the most part these paragraphs occur in four chapters—ix, xi, xiv, and xix.

While all of these various materials are obviously ideologically related to the longer narrative section of the novel (five hundred pages), there remains the problem of their aesthetic integration with the book as a whole. Even a cursory reading will show that there is a general correspondence between the material of each interchapter and that of the current narrative portion. The magnificent opening description of the drought sets forth the condition which gives rise to the novel's action; Highway 66 is given a chapter as the Joads begin their trek on that historic route; the chapters dealing with migrant life appear interspersed with the narrative of the Joads's actual journey; the last interchapter, xxix, describes the rain in which the action of the novel ends.

A more careful reading will make evident that this integration of the interchapters into a total structure goes far beyond this merely complementary juxtaposition. There is in addition an intricate interweaving of specific details. Like the anonymous house in the interchapter (v), one corner of the Joad house has been knocked off its foundation by a tractor (pp. 52–53, 54).[3] The man who in the interchapter threatens the tractor driver with his rifle becomes Grampa Joad, except that whereas the anonymous tenant does not fire, Grampa shoots out both headlights (pp. 53, 62). The tractor driver in the interchapter, Joe Davis, is a family acquaintance of the anonymous tenants, as Willy is an acquaintance of the Joads in the

---

[3] This and all subsequent references are to the 1st ed. of *The Grapes of Wrath* (New York: Viking Press, 1939).

narrative chapter (pp. 50, 62). The jalopy sitting in the Joads's front yard is the same kind of jalopy described in the used-car lot of Chapter vii. Chapter viii ends with Al Joad driving off to sell a truckload of household goods. Chapter ix is an interchapter describing anonymous farmers selling such goods, including many items which the Joads themselves are selling—pumps, farming tools, furniture, a team and wagon for ten dollars. In the following chapter Al Joad returns with an empty truck, having sold everything for eighteen dollars—including ten dollars for a team and wagon. Every interchapter is tied into the book's narrative portion by this kind of specific cross reference, which amplifies the Joads's typical actions to the level of a communal experience.

Often, this interlocking of details becomes thematic or symbolic. The dust which is mentioned twenty-seven times in three pages of Chapter i comes to stand not only for the land itself but also for the basic situation out of which the novel's action develops. Everything which moves on the ground, from insects to trucks, raises a proportionate amount of dust: "a walking man lifted a thin layer as high as his waist" (p. 4). When Tom returns home after four years in prison and gets out of the truck which had given him a ride, he steps off the highway and performs the symbolic ritual of taking off his new, prison-issue shoes and carefully working his bare feet into the dust. He then moves off across the land, "making a cloud that hung low to the ground behind him" (p. 23).

One of the novel's most important symbols, the turtle, is presented in what is actually the first interchapter (iii). And while this chapter is a masterpiece of realistic description (often included as such in freshman English texts), it is also obvious that the turtle is symbolic and its adventures prophetic allegory. "Nobody can't keep a turtle though," says Jim Casy. "They work at it and work at it, and at last one day they get out and away they go . . ." (p.

28). The indomitable life force that drives the turtle drives the Joads, and in the same direction—southwest. As the turtle picks up seeds in its shell and drops them on the other side of the road, so the Joads pick up life in Oklahoma and carry it across the country to California. (As Grandfather in "The Leader of the People" puts it, "We carried life out here and set it down the way those ants carry eggs.") As the turtle survives the truck's attempts to smash it on the highway and as it crushes the red ant which runs into its shell, so the Joads endure the perils of their journey.

This symbolic value is retained and further defined when the turtle enters specifically into the narrative. Its incident with the red ant is echoed two hundred and seventy pages later when another red ant runs over "the folds of loose skin" on Granma's neck and she reaches up with her "little wrinkled claws"; Ma Joad picks it off and crushes it (p. 286). In Chapter iii the turtle is seen "dragging his high-domed shell across the grass." In the next chapter, Tom sees "the high-domed back of a land turtle" and picking up the turtle, carries it with him (p. 24). It is only when he is convinced that his family has left the land that he releases the turtle, which travels "southwest as it had been from the first," a direction which is repeated in the next two sentences. The first thing which Tom does after releasing the turtle is to put on his shoes, which he had taken off when he left the highway and stepped onto the land (p. 60). Thus, not only the turtle but also Tom's connection with it is symbolic, as symbolic as Lennie's appearance in *Of Mice and Men* with a dead mouse in his pocket.

In addition to this constant knitting together of the two kinds of chapters, often the interchapters are further assimilated into the narrative portion by incorporating in themselves the techniques of fiction. The general conflict between small farmers and the banks, for example, is presented as an imaginary dialogue, each speaker personifying the sentiments of his group. And although neither speaker is a "real" person, both are dramatically differentiated and their arguments embody details particular to the specific social condition. This kind of dramatization is also evident in such chapters as those concerning the buying of used cars, the selling of household goods, the police intimidation of migrants, and others.

Because Steinbeck's subject in *The Grapes of Wrath* is not the adventures of the Joad family so much as the social conditions which occasion them, these interchapters serve a vital purpose. As Percy Lubbock has pointed out, the purely "scenic" technique "is out of the question . . . whenever the story is too big, too comprehensive, too widely ranging to be treated scenically, with no opportunity for general and panoramic survey. . . . These stories, therefore, which will not naturally accommodate themselves to the reader's point of view, and the reader's alone, we regard as rather pictorial than dramatic—meaning that they call for some narrator, somebody who *knows*, to contemplate the facts and create an impression of them" (pp. 254–255).

Steinbeck's story certainly is "big," "comprehensive," and "wide ranging." But although he tried to free his materials by utilizing what Lubbock calls "pictorial" as well as "scenic" techniques, he also took pains to keep these techniques from breaking the novel in two parts. The cross reference of detail, the interweaving symbols, and the dramatization are designed to make the necessary "pictorial" sections of the novel tend toward the "scenic." Conversely, an examination of the narrative portion of *The Grapes of Wrath* will reveal that its techniques make the "scenic" tend toward the "pictorial." Steinbeck worked from both sides to make the two kinds of chapters approach each other and fuse into a single impression.

That the narrative portion of *The Grapes of Wrath*

tends toward the "pictorial" can be seen readily if the book is compared to another of Steinbeck's social novels, *In Dubious Battle*, which has a straightforward plot development and an involving action. Of course things happen in *The Grapes of Wrath*, and what happens not only grows out of what has gone before but grows into what will happen in the future. But while critics have perceived that plot is not the organizational principle of the novel, they have not attempted to relate this fact to the novel's materials as they are revealed through other techniques, assuming instead that this lack of plot constitutes one of the novel's major flaws. Actually, this lack of an informing plot is instrumental in at least two ways. It could reasonably be expected that the greatest threat to the novel's unity would come from the interchapters' constant breaking up of the narrative line of action. But the very fact that *The Grapes of Wrath* is *not* organized by a unifying plot works for absorbing these interchapters smoothly into its texture. A second way in which this tendency of the "scenic" toward the "pictorial" is germane to the novel's materials becomes evident when it is considered that Steinbeck's subject is not an action so much as a situation. Description, therefore, must often substitute for narration.

This substitution of the static for the dynamic also gives us an insight into the nature and function of the novel's characters, who often have been called "puppets," "symbolic marionettes," and "symbols," but seldom real people. While there are scant objective grounds for determining whether a novel's characters are "real," one fruitful approach is to consider fictional characters not only in relation to life but in relation to the *rest* of the fiction of which they are a part.

In his Preface to *The Forgotten Village*, which immediately followed *The Grapes of Wrath*, Steinbeck comments on just these relationships.

A great many documentary films have used the generalized method, that is, the showing of a condition or
an event as it affects a group of people. The audience
can then have a personalized reaction from imagining
one member of that group. I have felt that this was
the more difficult observation from the audience's
viewpoint. It means very little to know that a million
Chinese are starving unless you know one Chinese
who is starving. In *The Forgotten Village* we reversed
the usual process. Our story centered on one family in
one small village. We wished our audience to know
this family very well, and incidentally to like it, as we
did. Then, from association with this little personalized group, the larger conclusion concerning the racial
group could be drawn with something like participation.[4]

This is precisely the strategy in *The Grapes of Wrath*.
Whatever value the Joads have as individuals is "inci-
dental" to their primary function as a "personalized
group." Kenneth Burke has pointed out that "most of the
characters derive their role, which is to say their personality, purely from their relationship to the basic situation"
(p. 91). But what he takes to be a serious weakness is
actually one of the book's greatest accomplishments. The
characters are so absorbed into the novel's "basic situation" that the reader's response goes beyond sympathy for
individuals to moral indignation about their social condition. This is, of course, precisely Steinbeck's intention.
And certainly the Joads are admirably suited for this purpose. This conception of character is parallel to the fusing
of the "scenic" and "pictorial" techniques in the narrative
and interchapters.

Although the diverse materials of *The Grapes of
Wrath* made organization by a unifying plot difficult, nevertheless the novel does have structural form. The action
progresses through three successive movements, and its

---

[4] *The Forgotten Village* (New York: Viking Press, 1941).

significance is revealed by an intricate system of themes and symbols.

The Grapes of Wrath is divided into thirty consecutive chapters with no larger grouping; but even a cursory reading reveals that the novel is made up of three major parts: the drought, the journey, and California. The first section ends with Chapter x (p. 156). It is separated from the second section, the journey, by *two* interchapters. The first of these chapters presents a final picture of the deserted land—"The houses were left vacant on the land, and the land was vacant because of this." The second interchapter is devoted to Highway 66. It is followed by Chapter xiii which begins the Joads's journey on that historic highway—"The ancient overloaded Hudson creaked and grunted to the highway at Sallisaw and turned west, and the sun was blinding" (p. 167). The journey section extends past the geographical California border, across the desert to Bakersfield (pp. 167–314). This section ends with Chapter xviii—"And the truck rolled down the mountain into the great valley"—and the next chapter begins the California section by introducing the reader to labor conditions in that state. Steinbeck had this tripartite division in mind as early as September of 1937, when he told one interviewer that he was working on "the first of three related longer novels."[5]

This structure has its roots in the Old Testament. The novel's three sections correspond to the oppression in Egypt, the exodus, and the sojourn in the land of Canaan, which in both accounts is first viewed from the mountains. The parallel is not worked out in detail, but the grand design is there: the plagues (erosion), the Egyptians (banks), the exodus (journey), and the hostile tribes of Canaan (Californians).

This Biblical structure is supported by a continuum

---

[5] Joseph Henry Jackson, "John Steinbeck: A Portrait," *Sat. Rev. of Lit.*, XVI (Sept. 25, 1937), 18.

of symbols and symbolic actions. The most pervasive symbolism is that of grapes. The novel's title, taken from "The Battle Hymn of the Republic" ("He is tramping out the vintage where the grapes of wrath are stored"), is itself a reference to Revelation: "And the angel thrust in his sickle into the earth, and gathered the vine of the earth, and cast it into the great winepress of the wrath of God" (xiv.19). Similarly in Deuteronomy: "Their grapes are grapes of gall, their clusters are bitter. Their wine is the poison of serpents" (xxxii.32); in Jeremiah: "The fathers have eaten sour grapes, and their children's teeth are set on edge" (xxxi.29). Sometimes these aspects of the symbol are stated in the novel's interchapters: "In the souls of the people the grapes of wrath are filling and growing heavy, heavy for the vintage" (pp. 447, 388).

But Steinbeck also uses grapes for symbols of plenty, as the one huge cluster of grapes which Joshua and Oshea bring back from their first excursion into the rich land of Canaan, a cluster so huge that "they bare it between two on a staff" (Num. xiii.23). It is this meaning of grapes that is frequently alluded to by Grampa Joad: "Gonna get me a whole big bunch of grapes off a bush, or whatever, an' I'm gonna squash 'em on my face an' let 'em run offen my chin" (p. 112). Although Grampa dies long before the Joads get to California, he is symbolically present through the anonymous old man in the barn (stable), who is saved from starvation by Rosasharn's breasts: "This thy stature is like to a palm tree, and thy breasts to clusters of grapes" (Cant. vii.7).[6] Rosasharn's giving of new life to the old man is another reference to the ortho-dox interpretation of Canticles: "I [Christ] am the rose of

---

[6] One of the oddest interpretations of this scene is Harry Slochower's in *No Voice is Wholly Lost* (New York: Creative Age Press, 1945), p. 304, n. Mr. Slochower uses this incident to explain the novel's title: "The grapes have turned to 'wrath,' indicated by the fact that the first milk of the mother is said to be bitter."

Sharon, and the lily of the valleys" (ii.1); and to the Gospels: "take, eat; this is my body." Still another important Biblical symbol is Jim Casy (Jesus Christ), who will be discussed in another connection.

Closely associated with this latter symbolic meaning of grapes and the land of Canaan is Ma Joad's frequent assertion that "We are the people." She has not been reading Carl Sandburg; she has been reading her Bible. As she tells Tom when he is looking for a suitable verse to bury with Grampa, "Turn to Psalms, over further. You kin always get somepin outa Psalms" (p. 195). And it is from Psalms that she gets her phrase: "For he is our God; and we are the people of his pasture, and the sheep of his hand" (xcv.7). They are the people who pick up life in Oklahoma (Egypt) and carry it to California (Canaan) as the turtle picks up seeds and as the ants pick up their eggs in "The Leader of the People." These parallels to the Hebrews of Exodus are all brought into focus when, near the end of the novel, Uncle John sets Rose of Sharon's stillborn child in an old apple crate (like Moses in the basket), sets the box in a stream "among the willow stems" and floats it toward the town saying, "Go down an' tell 'em" (p. 609).

As the Israelites developed a code of laws in their exodus, so do the migrants: "The families learned what rights must be observed—the right of privacy in the tent . . . the right of the hungry to be fed; the right of the pregnant and the sick to transcend all other rights" (p. 265). Chapter xvii can be seen as the "Deuteronomy" of *The Grapes of Wrath*. It is this kind of context which makes of the Joads's journey "out west" an archetype of mass migration.[7]

---

[7] In a recent article Bernard Bowron fails to perceive this larger significance of the Joads's journey and attempts to make far too much out of some obvious similarities to the Covered Wagon genre. "*The Grapes of Wrath*: A 'Wagons West' Romance," *Colorado Quart.*, III (Summer 1954), 84–91.

The novel's Biblical structure and symbolism are supported by Steinbeck's skillful use of an Old Testament prose. The extent to which he succeeded in recreating the epic dignity of this prose can be demonstrated by arranging a typical passage from the novel according to phrases, in the manner of the Bates Bible, leaving the punctuation intact except for capitals.

> The tractors had lights shining,
> For there is no day and night for a tractor
> And the disks turn the earth in the darkness
> And they glitter in the daylight.
>
> And when a horse stops work and goes into the barn
> There is a life and a vitality left,
> There is a breathing and a warmth,
> And the feet shift on the straw,
> And the jaws champ on the hay,
> And the ears and the eyes are alive.
> There is a warmth of life in the barn,
> And the heat and smell of life.
>
> But when the motor of a tractor stops,
> It is as dead as the ore it came from.
> The heat goes out of it
> Like the living heat that leaves a corpse. (p. 157)

The parallel grammatical structure of parallel meanings, the simplicity of diction, the balance, the concrete details, the summary sentences, the reiterations—all are here. Note also the organization: four phrases for the tractor, eight for the horse, four again for the tractor. Except for the terms of machinery, this passage might be one of the psalms.

It is this echo—more, this pedal point—evident even in the most obviously "directed" passages, which supports their often simple philosophy, imbuing them with a dignity which their content alone could not sustain. The style gives them their authority:

> Burn coffee for fuel in the ships. Burn corn to keep warm, it makes a hot fire. Dump potatoes in the rivers

and place guards along the banks to keep the hungry people from fishing them out. Slaughter the pigs and bury them, and let the putrescence drip down into the earth.

There is a crime here that goes beyond denunciation. There is a sorrow here that weeping cannot symbolize. There is a failure here that topples all our success. The fertile earth, the straight tree rows, the sturdy trunks, and the ripe fruit. And children dying of pellagra must die because a profit cannot be taken from an orange. (p. 477)

These passages are not complex philosophy, but they may well be profound. The Biblical resonance which gives them authority is used discreetly, is never employed on the trivial and particular, and its recurrence has a cumulative effect.

There are many other distinct prose styles in the interchapters of *The Grapes of Wrath*, and each is just as functional in its place. There is, for example, the harsh, staccato prose of Chapter vii, which is devoted to the sale of used cars.

Cadillacs, La Salles, Buicks, Plymouths, Packards, Chevvies, Fords, Pontiacs. Row on row, headlights glinting in the afternoon sun. Good Used Cars.

Soften 'em up Joe. Jesus, I wisht I had a thousand jalopies! Get 'em ready to deal, an' I'll close 'em.

Goin' to California? Here's jus' what you need. Looks shot, but they's thousan's of miles in her.

Lined up side by side. Good Used Cars. Bargains. Clean runs good. (p. 89)

A good contrast to this prose style is offered by Chapter ix, which presents the loss and despair of people forced to abandon their household goods. Here the prose style itself takes on their dazed resignation.

The women sat among the doomed things, turning them over and looking past them and back. This book. My father had it. He liked a book. *Pilgrim's*

Progress. Used to read it. Got his name in it. And his pipe—still smells rank. And this picture—an angel. I looked at that before the fust three come—didn't seem to do much good. Think we could get this china dog in? Aunt Sadie brought it from the St. Louis Fair. See? Wrote right on it. No, I guess not. Here's a letter my brother wrote the day before he died. Here's an old-time hat. These feathers—never got to use them. No, there isn't room. (p. 120)

At times, as in the description of a folk dance in Chapter xxiii, the prose style becomes a veritable chameleon: "Look at that Texas boy, long legs loose, taps four times for ever' damn step. Never see a boy swing aroun' like that. Look at him swing that Cherokee girl, red in cheeks and her toe points out" (p. 449). No other American novel has succeeded in forging and making instrumental so many prose styles.

This rapid shifting of prose style and technique has value as Americana and contributes to a "realism" far beyond that of literal reporting. Also, this rapid shifting is important because it tends to destroy any impression that these interchapters are, as a group, a separate entity. They are a group only in that they are not a direct part of the narrative. They have enough individuality of subject matter, prose style, and technique to keep the novel from falling into two parts, and to keep the reader from feeling that he is now reading "the other part."

In addition to the supporting Biblical structure and context, the interchapters and narrative section are held together by an interweaving of two opposing themes which make up the "plot" of *The Grapes of Wrath*. One of these, the negative one, concerns itself with the increasingly straitened circumstances of the Joads. At the beginning of their journey they have $154, their household goods, two barrels of pork, a serviceable truck, and their good health. As the novel progresses they become more and more impoverished until at the end they are destitute, without food, sick, their truck and goods abandoned in the mud, without shelter, and without hope of work. This economic decline is paralleled by a disintegration of the family's morale. The Joads start off as a cheerful group full of hope and will power and by the end of the novel are spiritually bankrupt. As Steinbeck had noted about the migrants around Bakersfield three years earlier, they "feel that paralyzed dullness with which the mind protects itself against too much sorrow and too much pain."[8] When the Joads enter their first Hooverville they catch a glimpse of the deterioration which lies ahead of them. They see filthy tin and rug shacks littered with trash, the children dirty and diseased, the heads of families "bull-simple" from being roughed-up too often, all spirit gone and in its place a whining, passive resistance to authority. Although the novel ends before the Joads come to this point, in the last chapter they are well on their way.

And as the family group declines morally and economically, so the family unit itself breaks up. Grampa dies before they are out of Oklahoma and lies in a nameless grave; Granma is buried a pauper; Noah deserts the family; Connie deserts Rosasharn; the baby is born dead; Tom becomes a fugitive; Al is planning to leave as soon as possible; Casy is killed; and they are forced to abandon the Wilsons.

These two negative or downward movements are balanced by two positive or upward movements. Although the primitive family unit is breaking up, the fragments are going to make up a larger group. The sense of a communal unit grows steadily through the narrative—the Wilsons, the Wainwrights—and is pointed to again and again in the interchapters: "One man, one family driven from the land; this rusty car creaking along the highway to

---

[8] "The Harvest Gypsies," *San Francisco News*, Oct. 6, 1936, p. 3.

the west. I lost my land, a single tractor took my land. I
am alone and I am bewildered. And in the night one
family camps in a ditch and another family pulls in and
the tents come out. The two men squat on their hams and
the women and children listen. . . . For here 'I lost my
land' is changed; a cell is split and from its splitting grows
the thing you [owners] hate—'We lost *our* land' " (p.
206). Oppression and intimidation only serve to strengthen
the social group; the relief offered by a federal migrant
camp only gives them a vision of the democratic life they
can attain by cooperation, which is why the local citizens
are opposed to these camps.

Another of the techniques by which Steinbeck develops this theme of unity can be illustrated by the Joads's
relationship with the Wilson family of Kansas, which they
meet just before crossing the Oklahoma border. This relationship is developed not so much by explicit statement, as
in the interchapters, as by symbols. Grampa Joad, for
example, dies in the Wilsons' tent and is buried in one of
the Wilsons' blankets. Furthermore, the epitaph which is
buried with Grampa (in Oklahoma soil) is written on a
page torn from the Wilsons' Bible—that page usually re
served for family births, marriages, and deaths. In burying
this page with Grampa the Wilsons symbolize not only
their adoption of the Joads, but their renouncing of hope
for continuing their own family line. Also, note it is the
more destitute Wilson family which embraces the Joads.
Steinbeck makes of the two families' relationship a
microcosm of the migration's total picture, its human significance.

This growing awareness on the part of the people en
masse is paralleled by the education and conversion of
Tom and Casy. At the beginning of the book, Tom's attitude is individualistic. He is looking out for himself. As he
puts it, "I'm still laying my dogs down one at a time," and
"I climb fences when I got fences to climb" (p. 237). His

first real lesson comes when Casy strikes out against the trooper to save his friend and then gives himself up in his place (p. 361). The section immediately following is that of the family's stay in a federal migrant camp, and here Tom's education is advanced still further. By the time Casy is killed, Tom is ready for his conversion, which he seals by revenging his mentor. While Tom is hiding out in the cave after having struck the vigilante, he has time to think of Casy and his message, so that in his last meeting with his mother, in which he asserts his spiritual unity with all men, it is evident that he has moved from material and personal resentment to ethical indignation, from particulars to principles. It is significant that this last meeting between mother and son should take place under conditions reminiscent of the prenatal state. The entrance to the cave is covered with black vines and the interior is damp and completely dark, so that the contact of mother and son is actually physical rather than visual; she gives him food. When Tom comes out of the cave after announcing his conversion it is as though he were reborn. When Tom says, "An' when our folks eat the stuff they raise an' live in the houses they build—why I'll be there," he is paraphrasing Isaiah: "And they shall build houses and inhabit them, they shall not build and another inhabit; they shall not plant and another eat" (LXV, 21–22).

The development of Jim Casy is similar to that of Tom. He moves from Bible-belt evangelism to social prophecy. At the beginning of the book he has already left preaching and has returned from "in the hills, thinkin', almost you might say like Jesus went into the wilderness to think His way out of a mess of troubles" (p. 109). But although Casy is already approaching his revelation of the Over-Soul, it is only through his experiences with the Joads that he is able to complete his vision. As Tom moves from material resentment to ethical indignation, so Casy moves from the purely speculative to the pragmatic. Both

move from stasis to action. Casy's Christlike development
is complete when he dies saying, "You don' know what
you're a doin' " (p. 527). Those critics are reading super-
ficially who, like Elizabeth N. Monroe, think that Steinbeck "expects us to admire Casy, an itinerant preacher,
who, over-excited from his evangelistic revivals, is in the
habit of taking one or another of the girls in his audience
to lie in the grass."[9] Actually, Casy himself perceives the
incongruity of this behavior, which is why he goes "into
the wilderness" and renounces his Bible-belt evangelism
for a species of social humanism, and his congregation for
the human race. His development, like that of Tom, is
symbolic of the changing social condition which is the
novel's essential theme, paralleling the development of the
Joad family as a whole, which is, again, but a "personalized group." (See p. 181 above.) Casy resembles Ralph
Waldo Emerson more than he does Lewis' Elmer Gantry
or Caldwell's Semon Dye. For like Emerson, Casy discovers the Over-Soul through intuition and rejects his congregation in order to preach to the world.[10]

Because these themes of education and conversion
are not the central, involving action of the novel, but grow
slowly out of a rich and solid context, the development of
Tom and Casy achieves an authority lacking in most proletarian fiction. The novel's thematic organization also
makes it possible for Steinbeck successfully to incorporate
the widest variety of materials, and with the exception of
romantic love, to present a full scale of human emotions.

This ability of Steinbeck's thematic structure to absorb incidents organically into its context is important for

---

[9] *The Novel and Society* (Univ. of North Carolina Press,
1941), p. 18.
[10] Further parallels between Casy and Christ: see Martin
Shockley's "Christian Symbolism in *The Grapes of Wrath*," *CE*,
XVIII (Nov., 1956), 87–90.

an understanding of the novel's last scene, of which there has been much criticism. The novel's materials do make a climactic ending difficult. The author faced three pitfalls: a *deus ex machina* ending; a summing up, moral essay; and simply a new level of horror. But the novel's thematic treatment of material made it possible for Steinbeck to end on a high point, to bring his novel to a symbolic climax without doing violence to credulity, structure, or theme.

This climax is prepared for by the last interchapter, which parallels in terms of rain the opening description of the drought. The last paragraphs of these chapters are strikingly similar:

> The women studied the men's faces secretly. . . . After a while the faces of the watching men lost their bemused perplexity and became hard and angry and resistant. Then the women knew that they were safe and that there was no break. (p. 6)

> The women watched the men, watched to see whether the break had come at last. . . . And where a number of men gathered together, the fear went from their faces, and anger took its place. And the women sighed with relief, for they knew it was all right—the break had not come. (p. 592)

With this latter paragraph, a recapitulation of the novel's two main themes as they are worked out in three movements, *The Grapes of Wrath* is brought full circle. The last chapter compactly reenacts the whole drama of the Joads's journey in one uninterrupted continuity of suspense. The rain continues to fall; the little mud levee collapses; Rosasharn's baby is born dead; the boxcar must be abandoned; they take to the highway in search of food and find instead a starving man. Then the miracle happens. As Rose of Sharon offers her breast to the old man the novel's two counter themes are brought together in a symbolic paradox. Out of her own need she gives life; out of

of the novel, we shall be in a position to see exactly what the author intended when he remarked recently of *All the King's Men*: "The book . . . was never intended to be a book about politics. Politics merely provided the framework story in which the deeper concerns, whatever their final significance, might work themselves out."[2]

According to the generally accepted interpretation, "the King" in *All the King's Men* is the protagonist Willie Stark, an interpretation which derives from the fact Willie is governor of the state, a man the other characters in the novel refer to as "the Boss." "The King's Men," on the other hand, are assumed to be all the people who in one way or another serve the Boss—Jack Burden, Willie's research man; Tiny Duffy, the lieutenant governor; Sugar Boy, Willie's bodyguard, etc. Then, too, there are "the King's women," the mistresses of the governor's palace—Sadie Burke, Anne Stanton, Willie's wife Lucy. As tidy as this interpretation undoubtedly is, something more than a casual reading of the story will show Willie Stark was never intended to be "the King" in *All the King's Men*, and that the title of the novel has a meaning more significant than critics have hitherto realized.

There are a number of reasons why Willie Stark cannot be "the King" in *All the King's Men*. There is, first, the nursery rhyme from which the title was derived: Willie is Humpty Dumpty, not "King." Like Humpty Dumpty, Willie "sat on a wall" when he rose to become governor and "had a great fall" when shot down by Adam Stanton. Willie is, like his legendary counterpart, a synthetic creation, a grotesque composite of the abstract needs of the people who have shaped him. As Warren has pointed out, Willie's "power was based on the fact that somehow he could vicariously fulfill the secret needs of the people

---

[2] Introduction, *All the King's Men* (Modern Library, 1953), vi. All quotations are from this edition.

about him."[3] Hence the principal characters in *All the King's Men*, like Mr. Munn in Warren's *Night Rider* (1939), attempt to find themselves by merging their identities with another person. In Willie Stark the people of the state satisfy their craving for justice—hence Willie's easy political slogan "Your need is my justice"—while to the narrator, Jack Burden, Willie fulfills Jack's need of a father, his need of the purpose and direction and decisive authority which have been lacking in his aimless life. To Adam Stanton, "the man of idea" who eventually destroys him, Willie represents the concrete power to accomplish the idealistic, humanitarian good which Adam has dedicated his whole life to achieve. In short, it is an obvious truism to say that to Sadie Burke, to Anne Stanton—to virtually every character in the novel—Willie Stark represents the fulfillment of some secret compulsion, some indigenous shortcoming or incompleteness, and in this sense, most of all, Willie is Humpty Dumpty—an artificial composite of the needs inherent in the society which has created him. After Willie's assassination Tiny Duffy performs the futile ritual of attempting to put Humpty Dumpty "back together again" when he seeks to employ Jack Burden, Sadie Burke, and Sugar Boy, Willie Stark's political aides.

But if Willie Stark is Humpty Dumpty, who then is king? In view of the nursery rhyme it is difficult to see how Willie can be Humpty Dumpty and king, too. Part of a solution to our problem is to be found in Warren's introduction to the Modern Library Edition, where he states that in *All the King's Men* he tried to "avoid writing a straight naturalistic novel, the kind of novel the material so readily invited." By the phrase "straight naturalistic novel" Warren apparently intended the bleakly deterministic and materialistic novel which portrays its characters as being

---

[3] *Ibid.*, i.

merely biological organisms attracted and repelled by hereditary or environmental forces over which they have no control. As we shall see, the "material" of *All the King's Men* "readily invited" a novel of this description, for there is a temptation to think of Willie Stark as an ineluctible demi-urge riding the beast of the people to their moral collapse while the rider himself is pulled to destruction by a gloomy necessity. And yet one of Warren's main problems in writing *All the King's Men* was, I think, to avoid any implications of determinism, to establish a sure balance between the fact of Willie's diabolic attraction for others and the fact of their free wills; for it was essential to Warren's moral purpose, to his whole concept of man, that his characters exercise free will, that Willie Stark remain, after all, only Humpty Dumpty and not king—not Necessity, not God. In Warren's teleology only God is King, and we are all of us "all the King's men."

God is not only King but absolute monarch informing every moment of life with His purposive Will, and this predestination, which under Warren's hand becomes something quite different from determinism of a theological order, is "the material" that "readily invited" what Warren calls "the straight naturalistic novel," the novel which, in the tradition of Zola and Crane and Dreiser, is informed by biological necessitarianism and psychological behaviorism. This naturalistic tradition is emphatically repudiated in *All the King's Men* when determinism, a chief characteristic of "the straight naturalistic novel," is sardonically labeled "The Big Twitch" by Jack Burden, who abjures it as totally inadequate to explain the events that take place in the story. The philosophy Jack Burden does come to accept, however, is one which has to do with the enigmatic paradox of Christianity—the omnipotence of God and the moral responsibility of man. And if at the end of the novel Jack's acceptance of this view of life is not without some reservations, we must remember that the paradox is baffling, is one that derives not from a spontaneous rational acquiescence but from a hard discipline of faith.

If omnipotent God has power over everything, how can man be said to have respon ity for anything? *All the King's Men* confronts this ation cautiously, with a full cognizance of the critical sions created by Darwin, Marx, Freud, and the holocaust of two world wars. From these spirit-shattering, enervating experiences, we must preserve, Warren tells us, what is most distinctive, significant and compelling about man, his consciousness and spirituality. According to Warren, man has moral choice, lives in an "agony of will," but, paradoxically, he has no choice, no power whatever, in the consequences of his moral life. To put it another way, in Original Sin—which looms darkly in the background of all Warren's novels from *Night Rider* to *Band of Angels*—Adam and Eve devoured a fruit of agony when they ate of the Tree of the Knowledge of Good and Evil, for in that fatal act they took upon themselves the knowledge of what was right and wrong, and consequently the responsibility for their actions; but they were denied the divinity which Satan had promised them, the power to transcend time and perceive, as God perceives, the ultimate consequences of good and evil. (In Milton's *Paradise Lost,* for example, a travesty on those supernal powers promised to Adam and Eve by Satan is implicit when Michael comes to inform them of the Atonement, of the *real* consequences of the Fall which only God can know.)

Ironically, then, the Fall simultaneously gave man moral vision and struck him blind: it gave him an immediate, a priori knowledge of good and evil as it related to any moral decision, to any incoherent fact, but it left him blind to the ultimate purpose of direction or consequences of the fact. As an individual, he is the master of his soul in a moment of crucial moral decision; as a species, he is a pawn in a cosmic game the ultimate meaning or purpose of which he can never know. In *All the King's Men* Hugh

Miller expresses the human viewpoint, indeed the only view man has capacity for, when he remarks at the end of the novel that "History is blind, but man is not."

This concept of history as a fleeting montage of ingly purposeless causes and effects, of good and events so complex and confoundingly intermingled man cannot perceive the *ultimate* good or evil of anything, is profoundly confirmed in *All the King's Men*. Several years before the story of Willie Stark unfolds, Judge Irwin accepted a bribe which Irwin's friend Jack Burden uncovers in one of his investigations as Willie Stark's research man. This bribe, a completely voluntary act, sets off a chain reaction of mediate causes and effects. First, her discovery that her father concealed Irwin's crime so disillusions Anne Stanton that she becomes Willie Stark's mistress, while her brother Adam so modifies his militant idealism that he agrees to accept Willie's offer of the directorship of the Willie Stark Memorial Hospital. When Adam learns of Anne's affair, he assassinates Willie. But Irwin's bribe has even more far-reaching consequences. Jack's discovery of the bribe leads to Irwin's suicide, to Jack's realization that Irwin is his real father, to a reconciliation of Jack and his estranged mother. Was Judge Irwin's crime an evil? Although Warren is neither a weak-headed immoralist nor a sentimental relativist, his answer remains ambiguous. For his crime Irwin suffers guilt, repentance, absolution by atonement, just as do the other characters, whose particular crimes have been the indirect result of Irwin's: Jack Burden for uncovering Irwin's bribe, Anne Stanton for her adulterous relationship with Willie, Sadie Burke for her malicious jealousy of Anne and betrayal of Willie, and Lucy Stark for her pride of virtue and weakness of mind. Irwin's crime is evil because it results in the destruction of Willie, of Adam, of Irwin himself, and yet it has the undeniably good effects of saving Mrs. Burden's soul, of uniting her with her son, of bringing together Anne and Jack, and finally—if the reader chooses to remain skeptical of Willie's deathbed assurance that "things might have been different"—of freeing the people of the state from the grip of an unscrupulous demagogue. Hence Judge Irwin's crime and its results confirm what Jack Burden describes as the "moral neutrality of history." As an isolated, incoherent fact it is evil, but as a part of history, as one stitch in a complex, variegated tapestry, it has shades of both good and evil.

Willie Stark expresses a profound truth when he insists throughout the novel that good must come from evil because "evil is all you have to work with," while Adam Stanton, the more conventionally "noble" of the two, lives a dangerous error when he arbitrarily separates people and events into moral categories. The point is made by Jack Burden at the conclusion of the story: "As a student of history, Jack Burden could see that Adam Stanton, whom he came to call the man of idea, and Willie Stark, whom he came to call the man of fact, were doomed to destroy each other, just as each was doomed to try to use the other and to yearn toward and try to become the other, because each was incomplete with the terrible division of their age."[4] Willie brings about his own destruction when he tries to be like Adam, when, like "the man of idea" that he is not, he sets out to create something which is completely devoid of evil. Inconsistent with his own philosophy that any good there is must come from evil, Willie dreams of building a magnificent hospital that will stand as the

---

[4] Page 462. In a recent article ("The Failure of Robert Penn Warren," *College English*, XXVIII [April, 1957], 359), Norman Kelvin argues that there is no basis for Warren's distinction between Willie as "the man of fact" and Adam Stanton as "the man of idea": "The Willy [sic] Stark we met in the novel was as much a man of ideas as was the puritanical, compulsive Dr. Stanton. They merely held to *different* ideas, and while some of Willy's were outrageous, so were some of Adam's." But this appears to be a very literal reading of what, after all, is only a pair of arbitrary metaphors. It matters not, really, what phrases Warren employs to describe Willie and Adam so long as we recognize his meaning.

purely good achievement of his political administration, and yet, unknown to Willie, the hospital is tainted by evil in the moment of its conception, for the idea of the hospital is really the result of Willie's unconscious effort to compensate for the guilt he feels in protecting from prosecution his corrupt state auditor, Bryam B. White. The hospital becomes an instrument of Willie's downfall when he refuses to permit the venal Gummy Larson from having the contract to construct it, when he refuses, in other words, to allow the good he dreams of achieving to be contaminated by evil, and this refusal prompts Tiny Duffy to inform Adam of Willie's affair with Anne. In shooting Willie Stark, Adam becomes himself "the man of fact," acknowledging Willie's dictum that the end justifies the means, but more than that, he proclaims by his act that he has God's knowledge, a final knowledge of good and evil. In his arrogant effort to usurp divinity, Adam repeats the folly of the Fall.

The fact that Willie's hospital is never built underscores man's tragic limitations. Confined to a tenuous reality of isolated facts, hemmed in by illusory absolutes of good and evil, man cannot perceive the transcendent reality, the ultimate moral purpose and direction of life. Willie, "the man of fact," thinks he knows how things really are, and Adam Stanton, "the man of idea," thinks he knows how things ought to be, but both are incomplete, both presumptuous. So man lives on one moral level of reality, where he suffers an "agony of will," of personal responsibility, and God exists on another, the level of "history" or "direction," a level unknown to man, who yearns toward the fulfillment of some ideal good which in the "moral neutrality of history" has no objective existence.[5]

---

[5] In a very interesting article ("The Meaning of Robert Penn Warren's Novels," *Kenyon Review*, X [Summer, 1948], 417), Eric Bentley describes Warren as "utterly empirical." This is of course true; nevertheless, Professor Bentley does not appear to be sufficiently aware of how in Warren's novels the facts of experi-

On God's level, good and evil are not as inseparable as man persists in making them. What man conceives as a completed moral action is, in God's omniscient comprehension, merely another phase in man's continuous struggle to create some good in a fallen world he only faintly understands. Warren's concept of man as a fallen, debased, limited, and therefore heroic, creature working out moral decisions in an "agony of will" yet oblivious to the eventual good or evil of those decisions is one which recalls St. Augustine and medieval nominalists like Duns Scotus (the analogues of Warren's Puritanism), who stressed God's awful power and mystery, and man's irrationality and impotence. Like these medieval nominalists who reacted against the liberal rationalism of the Scholastics, Warren has repudiated the optimistic rationalism of the liberal reformers, just as he has repudiated their scientism and materialism—what Jack Burden refers to as "the dream of our age."

In *All the King's Men* man finds solace not in the liberal experience, not in the nineteenth-century dream of power through reason, but in the more ancient Christian experience of humility, repentance and hope; for Warren sees this world as a Dantesque purgatory where man works out his salvation by a process of transgression, acknowledgement of guilt, and contrition. Every character in *All the King's Men* who is worth saving eventually submits to this tortuous ritual of life: Cass Mastern, Judge Irwin, Willie Stark, Jack Burden, Mrs. Burden, Sadie Burke, and Anne Stanton. Tiny Duffy, like his friend Gummy Larson, is a mere shade, an abstraction, while Adam Stanton, paradoxically the "noblest" character in the novel, is, by the fact of his fierce and intransigent pride in virtue, quite beyond all hope of redemption. For the remainder of the

---

ence and Christian orthodoxy coalesce. Of how, in other words, empiricism confirms Warren's essentially Christian philosophy of life.

characters in *All the King's Men*, however, the epigraph to the novel applies. Appropriately, the epigraph to *All the King's Men* is Manfred's tortured cry of hope in Canto III of Dante's *Purgatorio:* "Mentre che la speranze ha fior del verde."*

As if to turn back at the end of the novel to interpret his story, Warren spells out these ideas about God and man in a religious tract dictated to Jack by Ellis Burden:[6]

> The creation of man whom God in His fore-knowledge knew doomed to sin was an awful index of God's omnipotence. For it would have been a thing of trifling and contemptible ease for Perfection to create mere perfection. To do so would, to speak truth, be not creation but extension. Separateness is identity and the only way for God to create, truly create, man was to make him separate from God Himself, and to be separate from God is to be sinful. The creation of evil is therefore the index of God's glory and His power. But by His help. By His help and in His wisdom.

Jack Burden tentatively concurs in Ellis Burden's credo. "I did so to keep his mind untroubled," he says, "but later I was not certain that in my own way I did not believe what he had said." Jack's statement, although not an unqualified affirmation, is nevertheless a long step away from his earlier cynicism and philosophical determinism. It signifies a gradual awakening of Jack's spirituality, the beginning of an unconscious application of Cass Mastern's story to his

---

* "So long as hope retaineth aught of green." [Editor's note]

[6] Page 462. I am not suggesting that Ellis Burden is a mouthpiece through which Warren expresses his views, nor that this religious tract is a violation of the novel's dramatic integrity. Ellis Burden is a fully developed, integrated character, and his tract does have a certain dramatic inevitability. Nevertheless, Ellis Burden, and to a less extent perhaps, Hugh Miller, function in a way reminiscent of a Sophoclean chorus: they may have their etiology in Warren's pseudo-Greek drama *Proud Flesh*, which, written in 1938, was the germinal beginning of *All the King's Men*.

own tragic experience in life. In his diary, which Jack had studied but could not understand until his own experiences confirmed its views, Cass Mastern had written: "I do not question the Justice of God, that others have suffered for my sin, for it may be that only by the suffering of the innocent does God affirm that men are brothers in His Holy Name" (p. 199). Cass Mastern sees the world as a vast spider web of intersecting lives:

> Your happy foot or your gay wing may have brushed it ever so lightly, but what happens always happens and there is the spider, bearded black and with his great faceted eyes glittering like mirrors in the sun, *or like God's eye*, and the fangs dripping. (Italics mine, p. 200.)

Because the Cass Mastern episode was printed as an independent story before the publication of *All the King's Men*, some critics have been quick to regard it as an extraneous feature, as a brilliant but irrelevant *tour de force*, and yet, as Eric Bentley has pointed out, it is really Warren's effort to "put the whole theme of a work into one short and strongly symbolic interlude."[7] It supplies not only an inverted contrast to Jack's own story, a contrast between a crime of commission and one of omission, but plainly underlines the dominant themes of the omnipotence of God, and the utter helplessness and brotherhood of men. Cass Mastern tripped the gossamer threads of the spider web when he seduced his best friend's wife;

---

[7] "The Meaning of Robert Penn Warren's Novels," 415–16. It ought to be mentioned, however, that the Cass Mastern episode is not completely successful. For one thing, it invites comparison with the adulterous relationship between Irwin and Mrs. Burden rather than with the Platonic romance of Jack and Anne. Hence at the end of the novel Warren felt it necessary to have Jack Burden point out that Judge Irwin bears no resemblance to Cass Mastern: "For Judge Irwin and Cass Mastern do not resemble each other very closely. If Judge Irwin resembles any Mastern it is Gilbert, the granite-headed brother of Cass." (p. 464)

Judge Irwin when he accepted the bribe; Willie Stark when he refrained from prosecuting Bryam B. White; and Jack Burden when he revealed the truth about Irwin. That Jack comes to accept Cass Mastern's view of the world is suggested when he observes toward the end of the story that "each of us is the son of a million fathers" (p. 462), but more pointedly, when Jack, who has always been lashed by a compulsion to seek and reveal the truth, tells his mother an outright lie rather than impart to her the cause of Irwin's suicide, and when he lies to Sugar Boy rather than name the man who was indirectly responsible for Willie Stark's death. On both occasions Jack's prevarication, like Marlow's lie to Kurtz's intended in Conrad's *Heart of Darkness*, is an honest man's acknowledgement and atonement. Now sharing Cass Mastern's vision of the world as a web of humanity, Jack dares not assume responsibility for awakening the drowsy spider. He has come to see the brotherhood of men and the universality of guilt.

To assume, then, that Willie Stark is "the King" in *All the King's Men* is to ignore the meaningful symbolism of the title, to lose sight of Warren's basic idea. As I have attempted to show, *All the King's Men* portrays a world which Willie could not have ruled; for in that world of Warren's thoughtful creation there is but one King and we are all of us "all the King's men." From first to last, Willie Stark is but Humpty Dumpty, whose fall is a form of triumph for those who survive him. As Ellis Burden states in another context, "Separateness is identity," and with the death of Willie those who involved their identities in him must find completion within themselves or not at all. As in any great tragedy, there is loss, there is gain: they have lost Willie but have gained the power to find themselves. It may not be a coincidence, therefore, that the conclusion to *All the King's Men* is reminiscent of the ending to another great tragedy as Jack Burden and Anne Stanton, like

Adam and Eve departing from the Garden after the Fall, prepare to leave Burden's Landing forever to "go into the convulsion of the world, out of history into history and the awful responsibility of Time."

J. D. SALINGER
(1919–   )

J. D. Salinger is one of the most controversial writers of the past fifteen years. Seldom has a writer's work been greeted with such extremes of praise and condemnation. Critics oriented toward the socio-economic have said that his heroes are self-righteous and self-centered misfits who reveal the immaturity and preciosity of Salinger's vision. At the opposite pole are critics—more concerned with language analysis and with psychology—who have said that Salinger's insight into contemporary man is one of the most brilliant yet achieved. On at least one score, however, there is widespread agreement: critics from both camps have remarked Salinger's ability to capture the idiom of contemporary speech.

Talking is extremely important to Salinger, and he has used his ear for human speech to shape a theme and a technique that is central to his art. Holden Caulfield, hero of *The Catcher in the Rye*, will hang fire at an awkward moment, but he is a great talker. Along with Holden's psychological imbalance and immature judgments there is a childish and slangy rhetoric which graphically expresses his frustrated, brilliant insights into the human condition. Seymour Glass—the stoop-ball mystic, quiz kid, English professor, poet, and suicide who occupies so much of Salinger's attention—is "an inspired non-stop talker," and he lives in a family of "naturally profuse verbalizers and expounders." Buddy Glass, Salinger's alter-ego, claims that he speaks nine languages, "incessantly"; and all of the Glass siblings are said to learn foreign languages with ease.

Verbal ability, for Salinger, is basically a performance, a pouring out from an inner and excessive richness
of spirit that seeks shape in words. It is part ecstasy (especially for Seymour Glass), part torment (especially for
Buddy Glass), and always part irony; for Salinger holds
that the truest expression of our deepest self is a bit insane,
a bit freakish. This explains, I think, the heritage of the
Glass children. They are "descended from an astonishingly
long and motley double-file of professional entertainers,"
jugglers and hoofers; and they are themselves precocious
radio entertainers. The performance is, in short, a balanc-
ing act, a hoax of spiritual ecstasy, a trick of man's fated
commitment to the dust of flesh, and thus a trick of
truth.

Critics unfriendly to Salinger, I think, have not read
with sufficient clarity the central image of the non-stop
talker. Holden's verbal thrusts bring him to imbalance, but
this is not evidence of Salinger's supposed immaturity. The
subject, rather, is the human condition as seen by Salinger,
a condition which forces virtue into the obsessive, on the
edge of insanity. The "true artist-seer," says Buddy Glass,
"the heavenly fool . . . is mainly dazzled to death by his
own scruples, the blinding shapes and colors of his own
sacred human conscience." And this is the reason for
Buddy's dislike of psychologists, whom he calls "a peerage
of tin ears." They cannot hear through preconceptions and
pseudo-science the real voice of the juggler, the non-stop
talker who commits himself to the insanity of loving spirits
trapped in clay houses.

The biographical critic will want to suggest other
reasons, for Salinger himself has had, apparently, some of
Buddy's psychological problems. Born in New York City,
Salinger attended Valley Forge Military Academy and
three colleges. He served in the U.S. Army from 1942 to
1946 and was awarded five battle stars. Perhaps his most
important publications to date are *The Catcher in the Rye*

(1951); *Nine Stories* (1953); *Franny and Zooey* (1961); and *Raise High the Roof Beam, Carpenters* and *Seymour —An Introduction* (1963). For a time, in the early fifties, Salinger was available, at least to very young people in his neighborhood; but he has become something of a recluse, burying himself in a vault-like study where he works long hours in moods that are, apparently, much like those of Buddy Glass in *Seymour—An Introduction.* The works that result (especially "Hapworth 16, 1924," in the June 19, 1965, *New Yorker*) will be too mystical for many a practical American; but for others Salinger's attempt to discover man's "spiritual mechanism" through a rhetoric of slang will be considered one of the boldest attempts of our times.

NO CATCHER IN THE RYE*

by J. D. O'HARA

The Catcher in the Rye has been read more widely and discussed more thoroughly than any other contemporary novel; teenagers, professors, and professional critics alike express their admiration for it. And yet in some ways it is an unsuccessful book, it would seem, since even now, some twelve years after its publication, scarcely anyone can be found to answer such simple questions as these: at the end of the book, is Holden a catcher? How does Salinger feel about the idea of a catcher in the rye? The

* From J. D. O'Hara, "No Catcher in the Rye," *Modern Fiction Studies* IX, 4 (Winter, 1963–1964), 370–376. Reprinted by permission of Purdue Research Foundation, and the author.

Passages from *The Catcher in the Rye* reprinted by permission of Little, Brown & Co.

answers, usually reluctant, to these questions often suggest embarrassment, as if a weakness had been found in the novel; they are summed up by Ihab Hassan's objections to "the avoidance of conversion" in the story and to "Salinger's failure to modify Holden's point of view by any other."[1]

Certainly the questions raised above are central to the meaning of the novel, at least from Salinger's point of view, since much of the story is devoted to answering them. When they are both answered, the work comes to a close—abruptly, on the narrative level, when Holden remarks during the carrousel scene, "I really did go home afterward";[2] but satisfactorily, so far as the questions are concerned, because the carrousel scene answered them. The theme of the novel, then, is based on Salinger's examination of the attitude toward life represented by Holden's picture of a catcher on the edge of a cliff, protecting innocent children from a fall. When we follow this theme through the story we discover the answers to the two questions: Salinger opposes Holden's "catcher" attitude throughout the story; at the end of it, Holden himself abandons that attitude, converted by his experiences to a morally sounder acceptance of life.

The development of the "catcher" theme is most clearly revealed in the five related pictures of life through which Salinger describes the "catcher" attitude toward life, attacks it, and finally replaces it with a better one. The first picture is Holden's description of the predicament faced by the ducks in Central Park; this picture is supplanted by the cab driver Horwitz's comments on the fish in the Central Park lagoon. Phoebe provides the third picture when she tells Holden about "The Doctor," a movie she has seen;

---

[1] *Radical Innocence: Studies in the Contemporary American Novel* (Princeton: Princeton University Press, 1961), pp. 274 f.

[2] *The Catcher in the Rye* (Boston: Little, Brown, 1951), p. 274.

and Holden's catcher in the rye idea is the fourth. The climactic scene, in which Phoebe rides the carrousel and Holden decides to return home, resolves the thematic conflicts by presenting the fifth and final picture of life.

All five pictures describe life in the same terms. In each, we are shown an innocent in danger, a threat, and a potential savior. It is an appropriate description of the world, from Holden's point of view, since he would like to be a savior and he certainly seems to need saving.

We first hear about this attitude toward life in chapter two, when Holden is being advised and bullied by his history teacher at Pencey. His thoughts turn to the lagoon in Central Park: "I was wondering where the ducks went when the lagoon got all icy and frozen over. I wondered if some guy came in a truck and took them away to a zoo or something. Or if they just flew away" (p. 18). Here, of course, the ducks are the endangered innocents; ice, winter, and death are the threat; and the man in a truck is the potential savior. The situation is Holden's, as well as the ducks'; through most of the novel he looks for rescue from his wintry life or plans to fly from it. In fact, however, the ducks have another alternative. Holden never thinks of it, but Salinger surely expects the reader to. What *do* ducks do in the winter? Sometimes they are protected, certainly; sometimes they do fly away; but sometimes they stay where they are, keeping a small part of the pond clear of ice by swimming around in it.

That Salinger had in mind this unstated alternative to flight or protection is suggested by the next image of life. In chapter twelve, Holden asks Horwitz what the ducks do in the winter, and the cab driver switches the topic from ducks to fish. "The *fish* don't go no place," he points out. "They live right *in* the goddam ice. It's their nature, for Chrissake" (pp. 107f.). Then he makes clear the connection between Holden and the fish: "If you was a fish, Mother Nature'd take care of *you*, wouldn't she? Right?

You don't think them fish just *die* when it gets to be winter, do ya?" (p. 109). In fact, of course, fish sometimes do die in the winter, just as ducks sometimes freeze in the ice and innocents like Holden's brother Allie sometimes succumb to the dangers of life. Nevertheless, Horwitz's comments are significant. We see that the idea of a human savior is made to seem impractical, at least; the possibility of an inhuman savior, Mother Nature, is suggested; and Horwitz argues that the innocents need not escape, since they are capable of surviving by themselves. (We learn in chapter twenty that the Central Park lagoon is not completely frozen over.)

The next attack on Holden's understanding of life is made in chapter twenty-one through Phoebe, who provides Holden and the reader with an unspoiled, natural acceptance of life. Her version of the innocent-danger-savior theme, more complex than Horwitz's, is contained in her approving description of "The Doctor":

> It was all about this doctor in Kentucky and everything that sticks a blanket over this child's face that's a cripple and can't walk. Then they send him to jail and everything. It was excellent.. . .
> He feels sorry for it, the doctor. That's why he sticks this blanket over her face and everything and makes her suffocate. Then they make him go to jail for life imprisonment, but this child that he stuck the blanket over its head comes to visit him all the time and thanks him for what he did. He was a mercy killer. Only, he knows he deserves to go to jail because a doctor isn't supposed to take things away from God. (p. 211)

Phoebe accepts the dangers of life that Horwitz had denied, as well as the attractiveness of escape and protection; the child is grateful for being saved. But the morality of life is sterner in this story, and the human savior recognizes, despite the child's thanks, that he was wrong in playing God. Where Holden might have put the stress on *mercy,* Phoebe accepts the punishment of the *killer:* "Then they send him to jail and everything. It was excellent." There is a notable lack of piety in Phoebe's summary of the moral; the idea of God is expressed as conventionally and unconvincingly as Horwitz's reliance on Mother Nature. "The Doctor" pictures a painful world, but one that cannot be improved by human intervention.

It seems clear, then, that Salinger does not share Holden's attitude toward life, since he has taken pains to prepare the reader not to accept Holden's idea of a catcher in the rye when he describes it to Phoebe. She rejects it even before it is stated, of course:

> "You know that song 'If a body catch a body comin' through the rye'? I'd like—"
> "It's 'If a body *meet* a body coming through the rye'!" old Phoebe said. . . .
> She was right, though, It *is* "If a body meet a body coming through the rye." I didn't know it then, though. (p. 224)

Holden's comment suggests that he has now (while telling his story) accepted Phoebe's understanding of life, in which people meet as equals in the rye field of life and there are no human saviors.

When Holden concludes his description of the catcher in the rye by saying, "I know it's crazy, but that's the only thing I'd really like to be. I know it's crazy," Salinger has prepared the reader to agree. Life might be better if there were a catcher in the rye ("Isn't it pretty to think so," as Jake said), but such a life is not humanly possible. The novel thoroughly explores the idea, both before and after its statement by Holden, and suggests that the dangers are real enough, but the innocents are not so badly off as Holden thinks (and not always so innocent, either). The possibility of a human savior is given special attention. Several people, including Holden himself, attempt to play God—attempt, that is, to assume a position of superiority from which they offer advice and assistance. Mr. Spencer and Mr. Antolini give sensible lectures, but lectures are not what Holden needs; and both men are all too fallible human beings. We hear about another kind of savior indirectly, since Carl Luce's father is a psychiatrist. Luce himself suggests the uselessness of that kind of saving; his father has not helped him, and we are not led to believe at the end of the story that the doctors are helping Holden. Holden's own attempts to save are for the most part pathetic or futile. His lie to Mrs. Morrow, the money he gives to the nuns, his erasure of obscenities—they are no more than token gestures of his desire to protect the innocent.

Sometimes, as in the case of the crippled girl in "The Doctor," the innocent wants to be saved; Holden did when he was leaving his home: "I didn't give much of a damn any more if they caught me. I really didn't. I figured if they caught me, they caught me. I almost wished they did, in a way" (pp. 233f.). For the most part, however, the innocents prefer not to be protected. The little girl in Central Park accepts Holden's offer to tighten her skate, but refuses his offer of hot chocolate because "she had to meet her friend" (the word *meet* reminds us of Phoebe's insistence on meeting, not catching, in the rye). The little boy singing "Comin' Through the Rye" is equally happy in his dangerous world. And there is something rather unpleasant in Holden's gallant defense of Jane's honor after Stradlater has taken her out; it never occurs to Holden that she could or would resist Stradlater's charms.

Salinger also suggests that life in a protected world might be rather unpleasant. He shows us such an existence when Holden evokes the atmosphere of the Museum of Natural History, concluding that "the best thing, though, in that museum was that everything always stayed right where it was" (p. 157). The museum is a tempting refuge from life, but Holden resists the temptation: "when I got to the museum, all of a sudden I wouldn't have gone inside for a million bucks. It just didn't appeal to me" (p. 159). Given a choice between a cosy, static unreality and the potential unpleasantness of "that damn date with Sally," Holden chooses the world. The final image of a protected life, the sanatorium, is equally unappealing to him, but perhaps the best glimpse into such an existence is given us when Holden, delivering a note to Phoebe's school, sees "one little kid, a colored kid, on his way to the bathroom. He had one of those wooden passes sticking out of his hip pocket, the same way we used to have, to show he had permission and all to go to the bathroom" (p. 259).

The structure of *The Catcher in the Rye*, then, is controlled by Salinger's examination of the attitude toward life summed up by Holden's comments about the ducks and his desire to be a catcher in the rye. The second image of life is the dominant one, of course, and the novel is filled with references to falling and catching. As an innocent, Holden is aware of falls around him, notably James Castle's fall from the window; and he falls frequently himself. As a catcher, he retains a vivid memory of Allie's baseball glove, and he wears his hunting hat backwards, as a catcher wears his cap. But Holden's acceptance of life, which provides the climax of the novel, is predicated on his abandonment of this "catcher" attitude—an abandonment for which Salinger has prepared the reader throughout the story.

It is not clear exactly when Holden changes his mind. After all, Salinger is describing a young boy; to make Holden analytical and conscious of his motives would be unrealistic. We can see that Holden gives up catching before he gives up his desire to be caught, but neither change is specifically located. He throws away his money even before he sees Phoebe; he leaves his hat with her and never wears it again until she puts it on his head in the carrousel scene. (Which way did she put it on him? Salinger leaves the question open. Holden comments that, although the hat gave him a lot of protection, he got soaked by the rain, "especially my neck and my pants." Since Phoebe never saw Holden with his hat on backwards, we can probably assume that she dressed him as a hunter, not a catcher.)

Despite these preliminary indications that his attitude is changing, Holden intends to fly away from his cold world until his second meeting with Phoebe. Their tentative reconciliation and Salinger's exploration of the "catcher" attitude reach their climax as Holden watches his sister riding on the carrousel:

> All the kids kept trying to grab for the gold ring, and so was old Phoebe, and I was sort of afraid she'd fall off the goddam horse, but I didn't say anything or do anything. The thing with kids is, if they want to grab for the gold ring, you have to let them do it, and not say anything. If they fall off, they fall off, but it's bad if you say anything to them. (pp. 273 f.)

Here we have the familiar pattern—innocent, danger, and savior. But the catcher is refusing to catch, and the possibility of falling is now accepted. Not on easy terms, of course; but "it's bad if you say anything to them." Holden's acceptance of the situation clearly indicates his renunciation of his earlier attitude, and there can be no doubt that Salinger approves of his character's change. Furthermore, something new has been added to the description of life: a chance at the gold ring, a purpose in life, the possibility of a reward. The interpretation must be made cautiously, however. After all, the gold ring only entitles one to another ride, not a still point outside the turning world; and Holden himself is not yet willing to take a chance.

The final chapter of the novel, then, is thoroughly (but not bitterly) ironic. The man in the truck has come to protect the ducks; the doctor has saved Holden from the real world; the child is protected from the dangers of

the rye field. But he no longer wants to be caught; he has
reconciled himself to life in a world full of people like
Stradlater and Maurice. Lots of problems remain un-
solved, of course, and Phoebe's return of the cap suggests
that Holden still has some hunting to do.

Salinger's emphasis on meeting, rather than catching,
and his acceptance of the possibility of falling are not
characteristic of The Catcher in the Rye alone. In "For
Esmé—with Love and Squalor," to take an early example,
Esmé meets Sergeant X as an equal, out of love, and her
brother Charles emphasizes the theme with his riddle
(what did one wall say to the other wall? Meet you at the
corner) and his addition to Esmé's letter: twelve
HELLO's, followed by LOVE AND KISSES. Seven years
later, in "Zooey" (1957), Salinger still preached the doctrine of acceptance. Franny Glass, overcome like Holden
by an increasingly unpleasant existence, had passed out
just as Holden did, and then had retreated from life to the
security of her home. Salinger also suggests a comparison
between her and Phoebe: where Phoebe was reaching for
the gold ring, at the risk of falling, Franny dreamed of
diving into a swimming pool repeatedly, in spite of
threatening people around her, in search of a can of
Medaglia d'Oro coffee. "Zooey" is concerned with her
brother Zooey's successful attempt to force Franny out of
her retreat and into life again. In a letter to Zooey, Buddy
Glass had urged him to "Act, Zachary Martin Glass, when
and where you want to, but do it with all your might."[3]
Zooey passes the advice on to Franny: "The only thing
you can do now, the only religious thing you can do, is
act" (p. 197). In both cases the reference is specifically to
acting in the theater, but the implications go beyond that.
Salinger makes the connection between Franny's fainting,
her retreat, and the necessity for remaining active most

---

[3] Franny and Zooey (Boston: Little, Brown, 1961), p. 68.

explicitly when Zooey tells his mother about *The Way of a Pilgrim* and the Jesus Prayer, which combine a religious attitude with an active life. It is significant that Zooey begins his description by telling his mother that "Christ himself, as a matter of fact, says, 'Men ought always to pray and not to faint'" (p. 110). The religious understanding of goodness, Salinger suggests, must not be accompanied by a retreat from the evil world. Franny's return to life is anticipated by Salinger's description of her treatment of the cat: "She was still stroking Bloomberg, still succoring him, forcibly, into the subtle and difficult world outside warm afghans" (p. 133). The same combination of love and force might bring Holden safely out of the sanatorium and into the world again.

SAUL BELLOW
(1915–   )

Born in Quebec, Canada, Saul Bellow was raised in Chicago, his family having moved there when he was nine. After two years at the University of Chicago, he transferred to Northwestern, where he majored in anthropology and sociology, graduating with honors in 1937. Since then, Bellow has received numerous awards (including the Guggenheim Fellowship) and held various positions (including professorships), and he has come to be recognized as perhaps the most successful of a new generation of writers.

He is associated with the post World War II novelist, with the contemporary, as distinguished from those novelists who wrote mainly between the two world wars and who are often referred to—in articles and in college catalogue course lists—as modern. Sherwood Anderson, Sinclair Lewis, F. Scott Fitzgerald, Thomas Wolfe, Ernest Hemingway, and William Faulkner are now dead, and with their passing we have come to the end of a literary period. Those who wrote so powerfully between World War I and World War II have, of course, exerted a strong influence on those who came after; but with the emergence of novelists like Saul Bellow, Bernard Malamud, J. D. Salinger, Philip Roth, Joseph Heller, and John Knowles we have the beginning of a new period. Whereas Hemingway and his contemporaries tended to write of the struggle to maintain sanity and human dignity in a world that had gone to pieces, Bellow and his contemporaries tend to write of heroes who have not known the hopes of World

War I, the disillusionments of the twenties, or the depression of the thirties. Certain themes—shock, loss, isolation—occur in the literature of any culture, but the contemporary novelist places emphasis on the struggle to express love in a mass society, the effort to find meaning in a world in which bureaucracy and mechanization are accepted by people who have never known anything else.

Saul Bellow's work along these lines is remarkable both for quantity and for quality. *Dangling Man* (1944), *The Victim* (1947), *The Adventures of Augie March* (1953), *Seize the Day* (1956), *Henderson the Rain King* (1959), and *Herzog* (1961): all of these are good—perhaps excellent—novels.

A major theme in all six is the necessity of discovering brotherhood in an age which is uncomfortably close to the one predicted for us by Aldous Huxley and George Orwell. In some ways, Bellow's theme is the opposite of Thoreau's. In order to discover the values that are essential to man, wanting to distinguish the irrelevant from the real, Thoreau left society, temporarily, for the experiment at Walden Pond. Bellow's heroes, by contrast, come to see that—for their time, for their place—isolation is associated with arrogance and destruction. Their allegiance to essential values requires them to sense their place in society. Like Salinger's Glass family heroes who are enjoined to love the "fat lady," Bellow's heroes need to see the sacrality of the commonplace. There is no suggestion here that one should accept the hypocritical or the conformist values of society. The need, rather, is to accept the ethical burden of the 1960's, to admit that individual action is no longer tenable, to see that contemporary man must husband the old values on a concrete sidewalk, in a lonely crowd.

In *Dangling Man*, for example, the hero comes to feel that he is a consciousness residing in a temporary body. He recalls that as a child he had been attracted to a picture of his grandfather. Studying the picture, he feels that his grandfather's skull will one day overtake him, "curls, Buster Brown, and all." He is "upright" on his "grandfather's bones and the bones of those before him in a temporary loan." Leventhal, the protagonist of *The Victim*, remembers having seen men poor beyond hope, waiting without emotion for a mission-house cup of coffee. The remembered sensations are sharp, as "if it were *his* lips drinking that coffee, *his* back and thighs in that winter sun." And in *Herzog*, Bellow's latest, Moses Herzog contrasts the atmospheres of New York and Chicago, proclaiming that "in Chicago, the man in the street is me."

For many of our contemporary novelists, nothing is more fundamental (*necessary* is the word Bellow likes) than man's realization of his membership in an ironic brotherhood of human beings.

QUEST AND AFFIRMATION IN *HENDERSON THE RAIN KING**

by IHAB HASSAN

The hero of *Henderson the Rain King*, 1958, is very different from Bellow's earlier victims and favored sons of fate. In the fabulous story of Henderson, Bellow goes far-

* From Ihab Hassan, "Saul Bellow: The Quest and Affirmation of Reality," *Radical Innocence*, Princeton, N.J., Princeton University Press, 1961. Copyright 1961 by Princeton University Press. Reprinted by permission of the publisher and the author.

Passages from *Henderson the Rain King* by Saul Bellow, copyright © 1958, 1959 by Saul Bellow, reprinted by permission of The Viking Press, Inc.

ther than he ever did toward freeing the individual's spiritual quest from the enmeshing substance of society. To this end, the magic never-land of Africa is chosen for setting. The result, of course, is a work that reads like a romance and has, despite the author's warning to "those deep readers" forever engaged in a nervous quest of symbols, the universality only romance can bestow on action.[1] But the danger of romance is that, when it fails to awaken our sense of things permanent or large, it may appear no more than a happy use of fancy. This is a danger to which Bellow's novel is not entirely superior.

The hero of the book enjoys certain advantages of birth and power which the heroes of romance traditionally enjoyed. Henderson is not a Jew; he is the scion of an ancient American family distinguished for scholarship and public service. He is not poor, but many times a millionaire. And he is not defined by any particular urban role. Quite to the contrary, his roles and travels take him in the fifty-five years of his life over many strange grounds. Freed externally from necessity, he is thus forced to pursue the inner necessity of his being, to answer that unappeasable voice in him which constantly cries "I want, I want, I want," to burst his spirit's sleep and carry his life to a certain depth, to discover that service which, performed, may be the human retort to death. His travels are mental journeys, and the great turbulence of his spirit attests to the measure of his involvement with reality. A man of gigantic size and enormous strength, at once violent and tender, "an exceptional amalgam of vehement forces," he hauls his passionate bulk across the African wilderness like some buffoon or outlandish healer—his guiding image is that of men like Albert Schweitzer and Sir Wilfred Grenfell—seeking salvation and reflecting in

---

[1] See Saul Bellow, "Deep Readers of the World, Beware," *New York Times Book Review*, February 15, 1959.

his big suffering face, "like an unfinished church," all "the human passions at the point of doubt—I mean the humanity of them lying in doubt."[2] His search, first and foremost, is for reality, that same vibrant medley of fiction and fact which Eliot's celebrated bird pretended humankind could not bear too much of. But how much unreality can they bear, Henderson retorts? And though he claims to be on better terms with reality than most people—his second wife, Lily, for instance—it is in keeping with his spiritual progress, his humility and humiliation before life, that he discovers: "The physical is all there, and it belongs to science. But then there is the noumenal department, and there we create and create and create."[3]

Despite the archaic haze of fertility rituals, ceremonial hunts, and totemic cults through which the action of the novel flashes, the motive of Henderson's search and the stages of his spiritual progress remain clear. When Henderson leaves Lily behind, he leaves the only person with whom he has a struggling and irreplaceable relation. But in leaving her he also turns his back on the passive morality she represents, dampened by social pieties and noble hypocrisy. (Society is precisely what Henderson, like so many heroes of the American novel, cannot fathom; all his deeds, heroic or clownish, transcend their social reference.) The true starting point of his quest is a quotation he discovers in his father's library: "The forgiveness of sins is perpetual and righteousness first is not required."[4] Because his disorderly life is so full of errors and remissions—a father he cannot reach though he takes up playing the violin with great hairy paws to do so, his own son alienated from him, a first wife, remote and neurotic, who can only laugh at his quixotic idealism, a

---

[2] Saul Bellow, *Henderson the Rain King* (New York: Viking Press, 1959), p. 131.
[3] *Ibid.*, p. 167.
[4] *Ibid.*, p. 3.

career of false starts and frantic assertions—because of all this Henderson is compelled to seek redemption in a single act of charity, knowledge, and depth. The compulsion is as strong as death itself, the death of spirit and of matter too, that same death against which his hurtling soul is pitted and toward which it secretly moves. Bellow renders this fundamental antithesis of Henderson's character in a pattern of recurrent images: the octopus whose cold eyes and slow tentacles communicate to him a feeling of cosmic coldness, the dead man he has to carry on his back among the Wariri. In contrast to these intimations of death, the terrible fear of a traceless calm, there are the images of life to which Henderson responds with a singing soul: the wonder of a child in a world death has not yet touched, the rapture an African sunrise produces, "some powerful magnificence not human," pink light on a white wall with prickles and the whole physical universe wrinkling, heaving. Between life and death, turbulence and calm, reality beckons to Henderson, and the light of wisdom erratically gleams.

It is while Henderson is chopping wood at home—a log hits his face—that it first occurs to him truth must come in blows. Later, while he is wrestling with Prince Itelo, in a ritual gesture of acquaintance, he realizes once again that nothing but the *blows* of truth can burst the spirit's sleep. Yearning, he learns, is suffering, and suffering a kind of unhappy strength. But the latter is only a preamble to the wisdom which our experience already contains in fragments. With his unusual capacity to relate one fragment of experience to another—Bellow communicates this through a deft use of numerous flashbacks—Henderson, unlike Augie, gives the impression of creating the very destiny he seeks. Though he bungles the job of purifying the Arnewi cistern and lifting the "curse" on their cattle, he takes away, with his failure, the friendship of Itelo and the wisdom of Queen Willatale, who teaches him that a frenzied lust for living, "grun-tu-molani," not only affirms the basic value of human existence but further incarnates the desire to redeem its griefs. It is under the hypnotic influence of King Dahfu of the Wariris, however, that Henderson comes to realize that a rage for living is not enough. Man must also put an end to his *becoming* and enter the realm of *being*, the only realm in which love is possible. Between human beings, Henderson understands, there can be either brotherhood or crime, love or aggression. To attain the state of being man owes to his fellow man, humankind must turn to the beasts. This explains why the prophecy of Daniel—"They shall drive you from among men, and thy dwelling shall be with the beasts of the field"—is so constantly in Henderson's mind, and explains also why in the past Henderson raised pigs with such lavish care and performed with a bear in a roller coaster. The prophecy is actually consummated in a lion's den, under Dhafu's castle, where the king teaches Henderson in the dark, wordless presence of a lioness how to capture the emanations of a vital creature, how to be still and active, sufficient and attuned: how to *be* and how to *love*. It is not merely by journeying to Africa, with its strange kings and primitive rituals, nor is it merely by performing a serviceable act of extermination or rain-giving strength that Henderson begins to attain to wisdom. It is rather by learning how to absorb the pure moment which brings together the currents of life and death, ecstasy and numbness, absorb an animal presence, that he perceives the limits of human strife. The clamorous voice that used to cry, "I want, I want, I want," can now listen to other equally authentic voices: "He wants, she wants, they want."[5] Identity is found in communion and communion is reached not in the civilization to which we are born but out of it. Man must live with the rhythm of

---

[5] *Ibid.*, p. 286.

things, for he cannot *live* forever against it. In the last moving scene of the book, Henderson, on his way back to Lily, on his way to start medical studies at 55, clasps an orphan child to his chest and runs about the homebound plane with him, "leaping, leaping, pounding, and tingling over the pure white lining of the gray Arctic silence," knowing that though "for creatures there is nothing that ever runs unmingled," chaos does not run the whole human show, and ours is not "a sick and hasty ride, helpless, through a dream into oblivion."[6]

Precipitate, vigorous, candid as it is immensely colorful, the style of *Henderson the Rain King* leaps with the contortions of its hero's soul and sheds itself again on earth in a poetry of acceptance. Its exuberance is often controlled, and though it still rambles and digresses with the errant human spirit, it insinuates to us not the endless disponibility of Augie's life but a new idea of responsibility, namely, that man can never commit himself too late. The abstractness of a metaphysical romance is balanced everywhere by Bellow's awareness of the grotesque corporeality of spiritual experience—it is, for instance, while Henderson is wrestling with Itelo, and is tugged around prone on all fours, that he reveals to the prince the aim of his quest. But tragi-comedy, romance, and allegory sometimes add to a dubious mixture. We should be careful not to ascribe the uneasiness we feel about the novel to the conjured quality of the setting and action, for these remain within the realm of significant illusion. Our criticism, rather, must be that Bellow does not succeed in making us feel toward Henderson the detached and ironic sympathy which would have placed his clownery and shenanigans in the right dramatic perspective. Henderson's posturing and garrulous sincerity promise more than they finally reveal; his peculiar admixture of bravado and self-deprecation

---

[6] *Ibid.*, pp. 175, 341.

seems at times too easy a substitute for the range of human emotions lying between laughter and tears. The effect is sometimes like that of a pantomime co-authored by Rider Haggard and Dostoyevsky. Nor is Henderson's play-acting limited to the roles of braggart and breast-beater. He plays too often the part of an obsequious straight man in a Socratic dialogue with African sages, and frequently echoes, like a great blubbering reverbera-tor, thoughts which we would have liked to see developed rather than repeated—even so, the book could well stand some cutting. This is all to say that there is in Henderson a quality of emotional abundance or humility, Slavic or Hebraic perhaps but not entirely American, that puts a higher spiritual valuation on events than the events actu-ally warrant. The result is that Henderson's quest, lacking the reticence of struggle, seems a little faked; his final reconciliation to life appears self-induced. Fate, to be sure, makes buffoons of us all, yet some consent more easily than others to dance the crazy tune.

Henderson the Rain King remains, in a genuine way, the most affirmative of Bellow's works. Starting with the familiar figure of the solitary American hero, unattached to father, wife, or son, fleeing civilization and in search of love, prodigal in his services to all, Bellow leads Hender-son through reality's dark dream to a vision of light, and a commitment that can only bind man back again to life. Scapegoat, messiah, a king of plenty and of the spirit's drought—"He was despised and rejected, a man of sorrow and acquainted with grief," Henderson recites from Handel's *Messiah*—the American hero discovers at last that true innocence can be renewed only in the quixotic charity of pain.[7] And for once the American hero can go back home again.

---

[7] *Ibid.*, p. 84.

Study Questions

College instructors often begin their course in the modern American novel with a list of questions in practical criticism. There is nothing magic about such questions, of course, and if taken too seriously they can give rise to critical preconceptions. When used judiciously, however, study questions can be very helpful. The following is a typical list:

1. What are the values of the main characters? (Note that Babbitt tries two sets of values—both of which are wrong—before stumbling upon a third which leads to a belated insight into the world of Zenith.)

2. In what ways do the main characters keep or violate their values? (See the long paragraph near the end of chapter three, A Farewell to Arms, in which Frederic Henry berates himself for not living up to his own values.)

3. What values stand the test of experience? (Does experience confirm Holden Caulfield's belief that he should become a catcher in the rye?)

4. What kind of knowledge is possible? (Does the hero learn from reason, personal experience, intuition, authority? What different approaches to knowledge are illustrated by the main characters of The Sound and the Fury and Henderson the Rain King? In An American Tragedy is knowledge possible at all?)

5. What is the basic conflict, the basic problem of the novel? (This is one of the oldest and most fundamental of all critical questions. One version breaks the question into three parts: man versus society, nature, God. Another version looks for the grounds of the conflict: ethics, religion,

philosophy. More recent versions, because of the introspective nature of so many modern novels, are psychologically oriented. Note, for example, the use of psychological conflict in *Winesburg, Ohio*.)

6. Why was the novel written in this particular order? (The example of *The Sound and the Fury* is obvious, but the question applies generally.)

7. What (in terms of clothes, speech, education, religion, place, time, customs) is the context of the novel? (Note Fitzgerald's handling of Gatsby's early life, Nick's home in the West, East Egg as contrasted with West Egg. To a large extent, *The Great Gatsby* consists of the relationships among these contexts of meaning.)

8. Is the vehicle (setting, story, characters, language) appropriate to the meaning? (Is the story of an aged Cuban fisherman an adequate vehicle for the profound meaning obviously intended by *The Old Man and the Sea*?)

9. What is the historical context of the novel? (This question is stressed by the literary historian, who has made valuable studies of the twenties in relation to *The Great Gatsby*, of the depression in relation to *The Grapes of Wrath*, and so on. The question is associated with other background studies: politics and *All the King's Men*, and anthropology and *Henderson the Rain King*, for example.)

10. What are the major characteristics of the language? (Does the imagery come from science, nature, other literature? Does it appeal to our sense of sight, sound, smell, touch? Is it primarily symbolic or allegorical? Note the pattern of imagery Fitzgerald uses in his initial description of Jordan Baker and the ironic conversations that characterize *The Sun Also Rises*.)

11. Does the ending come out of the novel or does it seem to be tacked on? (Is the ending of *Henderson the Rain King* fortuitous? What does the closing comment on the American dream have to do with the story of Jay Gatsby?)

12. What is the viewpoint of the novel and is it an appropriate choice? (Is *All the King's Men* Jack Burden's story or Willie Stark's? Is Jack Burden an appropriate narrator? Does he participate in the novel?)

13. What is the author's attitude toward his characters? (Note that Sinclair Lewis does not hate the Babbitts of this world and that Thomas Wolfe, despite his autobiographical method, can be ironic about Eugene Gant.)

14. What is the relation between the internal self and the external force? (Does *An American Tragedy* end in defeat for the hero? for society? for all men? In what sense is *The Old Man and the Sea* affirmative?)

15. Is the novel, in the broad sense of the term, comic? (The comic often appears even in works of terror and violence. Note, for example, *As I Lay Dying*.)

16. To what genre does the novel belong? (Is it socioeconomic, psychological, philosophical, satiric, episodic, epic, realistic, romantic, naturalistic? *Genre*, it must be remembered, can be used as a term to include all other approaches. In no case is it meant to be a proscription. Even in a restricted sense of the term, *The Grapes of Wrath*, for example, is several types of novel in one.)

17. What is the chief relevance of other novels by the same author? (This is a necessary question, and it encourages the student to read as widely as he can within a given novelist. Thomas Wolfe, Ernest Hemingway, William Faulkner, and J. D. Salinger, for example, tell a continuing story.)

18. In general, what recurs? (This includes language, scene, event, line of reasoning, a type of experience.)

19. Is the novel unified? (This is perhaps the most central question of them all: do language, story, and meaning work together so that each seems to come out of the other?)

Selected Bibliography

There are numerous excellent bibliographies of the modern American novel in print, some of them in economical paperback editions. The purpose of the bibliography that follows, therefore, is to illustrate for the student and lay reader the kind of secondary material that is available.

General Bibliographies

The most useful guide to critical studies of the American novel is *The American Novel 1789–1959*, compiled by Donna Gerstenberger and George Hendrick, and published in paperback (Denver, 1961) by Alan Swallow. The principle of organization is by author, with critical studies of individual works listed separately from general studies of the author. This organization enables the user to find precisely what he needs. There is also a list of books and articles on the modern American novel in general.

Short Fiction Criticism (Denver, 1960), Alan Swallow's companion to *The American Novel 1789–1959*, is invaluable as a guide to criticism of short stories and novelettes. Compiled by Jarvis Thurston, O. B. Emerson, Carl Hartman, and Elizabeth V. Wright, the volume is subtitled "A checklist of interpretations since 1925 of stories and novelettes, American, British, Continental." Warren S. Walker's *Twentieth-Century Short Story Explication* (Hamden, Conn., 1961), published by the Shoe String Press, with a supplement bringing the work up to April, 1963, is a similar checklist.

The two standard journals for current bibliography are *PMLA* and *American Literature*. A new periodical, *Abstracts of English Studies*, is limited because of its recent beginning (1957), but it is especially useful for its inclusion of brief statements of the central idea of each article listed. The occasional Newsletters in *Modern Fiction Studies* deserve special mention for their coverage of new books on modern fiction and for a fairness and intelligence which is remarkably consistent.

Special Issues of Periodicals

The chief purpose of *Modern Fiction Studies* is the publication of critical articles on modern American, English, and continental fiction. There have been special issues on Hemingway (I, August, 1955), Faulkner (II, Autumn, 1956), Warren (VI, Spring, 1960), and Fitzgerald (VII, Spring, 1961). The special issues include general articles on the selected writer, articles on individual works, and a selected bibliography. Special issues on Steinbeck and Wolfe have been announced as forthcoming.

Among special issues of other magazines are *Shenandoah* (XIII, Spring, 1962), on Sherwood Anderson; and *Wisconsin Studies in Contemporary Literature* (IV, Winter, 1963), on J. D. Salinger.

Book Series

A surprising number of publishers are putting out series of books aimed at the student. Most ambitious, and thus far the best, is the Twayne United States Authors Series (Twayne Publishers, Inc., New York). Published first in hardback and then in paperback, Twayne books include a chronological chart, a biographical sketch, and a selected, annotated bibliography; but the emphasis is on critical interpretation. Of the volumes I have seen, a few have seemed weak, but a large majority vary from quite good to excellent. Volumes on modern American novelists currently available include the following: *Conrad Aiken*, Frederick J. Hoffman; *Sherwood Anderson*, Rex Burbank; *James Branch Cabell*, Joe Lee Davis; *John Dos Passos*, John H. Wren; *Theodore Dreiser*, Philip L. Gerber; *William Faulkner*, Frederick J. Hoffman; *F. Scott Fitzgerald*, Kenneth E. Eble; *Ellen Glasgow*, Blair Rouse; *Ernest Hemingway*, Earl H. Rovit; *Ring Lardner*, Walton R. Patrick; *Sinclair Lewis*, Sheldon N. Grebstein; *John P. Marquand*, John Gross; *Henry Miller*, Kingsley Widmer; *Wright Morris*, David Madden; *J. D. Salinger*, Warren French; *John Steinbeck*, Warren French; *James Thurber*, Robert E. Morsberger; *Robert Penn Warren*, Charles H. Bohner; *Eudora Welty*, Ruth M. Vande Kieft; *Thornton Wilder*, Rex Burbank; *Thomas Wolfe*, Bruce R. McElderry.

The American Authors and Critics Series (Barnes & Noble, Inc., New York), though keeping to the major figures and publishing in paperback only, is a similar project. Among volumes currently available are the following: *William Faulkner*, Lawrance Thompson; *Ernest Hemingway*, Sheridan Baker; *John Steinbeck*, Joseph Fontenrose; and *Thomas Wolfe*, Richard Walser.

Twentieth Century Views (Prentice-Hall, Inc., Englewood Cliffs, New Jersey) is a series of collections of essays (available in paperback and in cloth) on single authors of major importance from all fields. Readers who do not want to survey the criticism of a writer, but who want to read several of the best essays by twentieth century critics, will find this series especially useful. Under the general editorship of the distinguished Maynard Mack of Yale University, the series is noteworthy for the remarkably high level of scholarship and criticism which the names of the individual editors lead one to expect. Modern American novelists included thus far are *Faulkner*, edited by Robert Penn Warren; *F. Scott Fitzgerald*, edited by Arthur Mizener; *Hemingway*, edited by Robert P. Weeks; *Sinclair Lewis*, edited by Mark Schorer; and *Edith Wharton*, edited by Irving Howe.

Collections of Essays on Individual Authors

Distinct from the series is the individual publication which collects essays on a single author. Such collections are especially useful to the reader who has been able to read widely on a single novelist. Typically, they include a number of various critical approaches, often reprinting articles that are directly opposed to one another, and thus providing an excellent opportunity for the student to develop his critical abilities.

Among the dozens now available, the following are representative:

The Stature of Theodore Dreiser, edited by Alfred Kazin and Charles Shapiro (Bloomington, Ind.: University of Indiana Press, 1955).

William Faulkner: Three Decades of Criticism, edited by Frederick J. Hoffman and Olga Vickery (New York: Harcourt, Brace & World, Inc., 1960).

The Great Gatsby: A Study, edited by Frederick Hoffman (New York: Charles Scribner's Sons, 1962).

Ernest Hemingway: Critiques of Four Major Novels, edited by Carlos Baker (New York: Charles Scribner's Sons, 1962). The four novels are *The Sun Also Rises,* A *Farewell to Arms, For Whom the Bell Tolls,* and *The Old Man and the Sea.*

J. D. Salinger and the Critics, edited by William Belcher and James Lee (Belmont, Calif.: Wadsworth Publishing Company, 1962).

Critical Books on Individual Authors

The beginning student will profit most, in his critical studies, from reading articles which concentrate on a single novel. Those who continue their study of the modern American novel, however, will soon want to make a more detailed examination by reading critical and biographical works devoted to a single author. The following are examples of the kinds of studies that are available:

Sherwood Anderson, Irving Howe (New York: William Sloane Associates, Inc., 1951).

The World of Willa Cather, Mildred R. Bennett (New York: Dodd, Mead & Co., 1951).

The Novels of James Gould Cozzens, Frederick Bracher (New York: Harcourt, Brace & World, Inc., 1959).

Theodore Dreiser: Apostle of Nature, Robert H. Elias (New York: Alfred A. Knopf, Inc., 1949).

Theodore Dreiser, F. O. Matthiessen (New York: William Sloane Associates, Inc., 1951).

Dreiser, W. A. Swanberg (New York: Charles Scribner's Sons, 1965).

Faulkner in the University: Class Conferences at the University of Virginia 1957–58, edited by Frederick L. Gwynn and Joseph L. Blotner (Charlottesville: University of Virginia Press, 1959).

William Faulkner: A Critical Study, Irving Howe (New York: Random House, Inc., 1952).

Faulkner at Nagano, edited by Robert A. Jelliffe (Tokyo: Kenkyusha Ltd., 1956).

William Faulkner: An Interpretation, Irving Malin (Stanford, Calif.: Stanford University Press, 1957).

The Tangled Fire of William Faulkner, William Van

O'Connor (Minneapolis: University of Minnesota Press, 1954).

The Novels of William Faulkner: A Critical Interpretation, Olga Vickery (Baton Rouge: Louisiana State University Press, 1959).

William Faulkner: From Jefferson to the World, Hyatt H. Waggoner (Lexington, Kentucky: The University of Kentucky Press, 1959).

F. Scott Fitzgerald: The Man and His Work, Alfred Kazin (New York: The World Publishing Company, 1951).

The Far Side of Paradise: A Biography of F. Scott Fitzgerald, Arthur Mizener (Boston: Houghton Mifflin Company, 1951).

F. Scott Fitzgerald, Henry Dan Piper (New York: Holt, Rinehart & Winston, Inc., 1965).

Scott Fitzgerald: A Biography, Andrew Turnbull (New York: Charles Scribner's Sons, 1962).

Hemingway: The Writer as Artist, Carlos Baker (Princeton, N.J.: Princeton University Press, 1963).

The Apprenticeship of Ernest Hemingway: The Early Years, Charles A. Fenton (New York: The Viking Press, 1954).

Hemingway on Love, Robert W. Lewis, Jr. (Austin, Texas: The University of Texas Press, 1965).

Ernest Hemingway, Philip Young (New York: Holt, Rinehart & Winston, Inc., 1952).

Sinclair Lewis: An American Life, Mark Schorer (New York: McGraw-Hill Book Company, 1961).

Gertrude Stein: Her Life and Work, Elizabeth Sprigge (London: Hamish Hamilton, 1957).

The Wide World of John Steinbeck, Peter Lisca (New Brunswick: Rutgers University Press, 1958).

Robert Penn Warren: The Dark and Bloody Ground, Leonard Casper (Seattle: University of Washington Press, 1960).

Edith Wharton: Convention and Morality in The Work of a Novelist, Marilyn Jones Lyde (Norman, Okla.: University of Oklahoma Press, 1959).

Edith Wharton: A Study of Her Fiction, Blake Nevius (Berkeley: University of California Press, 1953).

Thomas Wolfe: A Biography, Elizabeth Nowell (New York: Doubleday & Company, Inc., 1960).

Thomas Wolfe: The Weather of His Youth, Louis D. Rubin, Jr. (Baton Rouge: Louisiana State University Press, 1955).

General Studies of Modern American Fiction

Many students, quite understandably, feel helpless when presented even a truncated bibliography of the criticism of the modern American novel. It is difficult to decide where to begin, and the prospect of reading it all gives one pause. It is also difficult for the professor or editor to know what to recommend to individual students whose backgrounds, too often, are unknown to those who would like to guide and suggest. Perhaps the best solution is for the student to read enough to be able to make his own decisions. Certainly any student who reads widely among the following books should soon find himself knowledgeable enough to make his own list.

John W. Aldridge, *After the Lost Generation: A Critical Study* (New York: McGraw-Hill Book Company, 1951).

Joseph Warren Beach, *American Fiction: 1920–1940* (New York: The Macmillan Company, 1942).

Wayne C. Booth, *The Rhetoric of Fiction* (Chicago: University of Chicago Press, 1961). More relevant in a bibliography of the theory of fiction or of English fiction, but included here because Booth's effort to correct a contemporary critical approach many have found too narrow is relevant to the work of any serious student of fiction.

Oscar Cargill, *Intellectual America: Ideas on the March* (New York: The Macmillan Company, 1948). An essay in the history of ideas, not limited to a period or genre, but certainly helpful—perhaps essential—in a study of modern American fiction.

Richard Chase, *The American Novel and Its Tradition* (Garden City, N.Y.: Doubleday & Company, Inc., 1957). Improves on an old and valuable distinction between the novel and the romance.

Alexander Cowie, *The Rise of the American Novel*

(New York: American Book Company, 1948).

Malcolm Cowley, *Exile's Return* (New York: The Viking Press, 1951). Standard background study of the Fitzgerald-Hemingway era.

Charles Feidelson, Jr., *Symbolism and American Literature* (Chicago: University of Chicago Press, 1953). A study which is both provocative and scholarly.

Leslie A. Fiedler, *An End to Innocence: Essays on Culture and Politics* (Boston: Beacon Press, n.d.).

Leslie A. Fiedler, *Love and Death in the American Novel* (New York: Criterion Books, 1960).

E. M. Forster, *Aspects of the Novel* (New York: Harcourt, Brace & World, Inc., 1927); available in paperback in Harvest Books, 1954, Harcourt, Brace & World. Often read in conjunction with Percy Lubbock's *The Craft of Fiction*. The two volumes present intelligent but quite different approaches to the novel.

W. M. Frohock, *The Novel of Violence in America: 1920–1950* (Dallas: Southern Methodist University Press, 1950).

Maxwell Geismar, *The Last of the Provincials: The American Novel 1915–1925* (New York: Hill & Wang, Inc., 1959).

Maxwell Geismar, *Writers in Crisis: The American Novel 1925–1940* (Boston: Houghton Mifflin Company, 1942). Geismar surveys from a critical rather than from a merely reportorial viewpoint.

Blanche Gelfant, *The American City Novel* (Norman, Okla.: University of Oklahoma Press, 1954).

Caroline Gordon and Allen Tate, editors, *The House of Fiction* (New York: Charles Scribner's Sons, 1954). One of the best of the many volumes aimed at the classroom.

Harry Hartwick, *The Foreground of American Fiction* (New York: American Book Company, 1934). Perhaps somewhat dated, but interesting, like Alexander Cowie's *The Rise of the American Novel*, as an example of an earlier approach to the study of American fiction.

Ihab Hassan, *Radical Innocence* (Princeton, N.J.: Princeton University Press, 1961). Considered the best critical study of the post World War II novel.

Frederick J. Hoffman, *Freudianism and the Literary Mind* (Baton Rouge: Louisiana State University Press,

1945). Psychology, Freud's in particular, has had a shaping influence on both the themes and techniques of modern fiction. Hoffman's study is still an excellent treatment of the subject.

Frederick J. Hoffman, *The Twenties* (New York, 1955), The Viking Press; new revised edition (New York, 1962), Collier Books. A detailed critical and scholarly study of the seminal decade in modern American fiction.

Robert Humphrey, *Stream of Consciousness in the Modern Novel* (Berkeley, 1954), University of California Press. One of the most important—and for many readers one of the most difficult—techniques associated with modern fiction has been called the stream of consciousness. Humphrey's study of the technique has won wide praise.

Alfred Kazin, *On Native Grounds* (New York: Reynal and Hitchcock, 1942); in paperback (Garden City, N.Y.: Doubleday and Company, 1956). Kazin is probably the best of those critics called, in a loose sense, socio-economic.

Harry Levin, *Symbolism and Fiction* (Charlottesville: University of Virginia Press, 1956).

R. W. B. Lewis, *The Picaresque Saint: Representative Figures in Contemporary Fiction* (New York: J. B. Lippincott, 1959).

Walton Litz, editor, *Modern American Fiction: Essays in Criticism* (New York: Oxford University Press, 1963). A collection generally similar to the one in hand, the chief difference being that Litz reprints essays which range over the works of the writer under examination. Includes essays on Dreiser, Stein, Anderson, Lewis, Fitzgerald, Dos Passos, Faulkner, Hemingway, Wolfe, Steinbeck, and Warren.

Percy Lubbock, *The Craft of Fiction* (London: J. Cape, 1954); paperback (New York: The Viking Press, 1957).

Edwin M. Moseley, *Pseudonyms of Christ in the Modern Novel: Motifs and Methods* (Pittsburgh: University of Pittsburgh, 1963). Studies a single motif, but the one selected is major, and the handling is intelligent. Includes essays on *The Great Gatsby*, *Light in August*, *The Grapes of Wrath*, and *The Old Man and the Sea*.

Walter B. Rideout, *The Radical Novel in the United States 1900–1954: Some Interrelations of Literature and Society* (Cambridge: Harvard University Press, 1956). Among the substantial number of critics concerned with the social implications of literature, Rideout is one of the finest.

Louis D. Rubin, Jr. and John Rees Moore, editors, *The Idea of an American Novel* (New York: Crowell-Collier Publishing Co., 1961). Selected pieces on the American novel in general, plus discussions of Dreiser, Lewis, Hemingway, Fitzgerald, Dos Passos, Farrell, Wolfe, Faulkner, and Warren.

Robert Scholes, *Approaches to the Novel* (San Francisco: Chandler Publishing Company, 1961). A superior book of critical instruction for the student.

Charles Shapiro, editor, *Twelve Original Essays on Great American Novels* (Detroit: Wayne State University Press, 1960). Includes excellent essays on *Winesburg, Ohio, The Great Gatsby, The Sun Also Rises,* and *Light in August.*

Edward Wagenknecht, *Cavalcade of the American Novel: From the Birth of the Nation to the Middle of the Twentieth Century* (New York, 1952), Henry Holt.

Joseph J. Waldmeir, editor, *Recent American Fiction: Some Critical Views* (Boston: Houghton Mifflin Company, 1963). Concerned with contemporary as opposed to modern fiction. Part I contains nine general essays. Part II contains essays on Bellow, Paul Bowles, Truman Capote, Ralph Ellison, Jack Kerouac, Norman Mailer, Bernard Malamud, Carson McCullers, Flannery O'Connor, James Purdy, J. D. Salinger, and William Styron.

M. D. Zabel, editor, *Literary Opinion in America* (New York: Harper and Brothers, 1951); paperback (New York: Harper & Row, Publishers, 1962). Contains a generous selection of major essays in both theoretical and practical criticism. Includes studies of poetry, drama, and fiction.